PRAISE FOR *EDUCATING IN DANGEROUS TIMES*

"Education is not only in danger but in need of direction—a direction that is bold, inclusive, and relentless in pursuit of justice. *Educating in Dangerous Times* is exactly that. Each chapter serves as a North Star. In times like these, books like this guide us toward the world that is possible. I am excited to use this book in my classes; I feel it is necessary."

—BETTINA L. LOVE, author of *Punished for Dreaming: How School Reform Harms Black Children and How We Heal*

"This is a powerful and timely collection that refuses to look away from the challenges facing public education while offering bold, humanizing visions for what schools can become. Drawing on the voices of leading scholars, it invites readers to reimagine schools as spaces of equity, dignity, and democratic possibility. Urgent, thoughtful, and deeply inspiring, this book is essential reading for anyone committed to the future of public education."

—DOUGLAS FISHER, coauthor of *The Illustrated Guide to Teacher Clarity*

"In a moment when public education is under coordinated attack—from censorship laws to privatization schemes—*Educating in Dangerous Times* is a powerful declaration that schools are not neutral spaces but sites of struggle over truth, dignity, and justice. These essays trace the fault lines of inequality running through our classrooms, from systemic racism to attacks on LGBTQ+ students to the silencing of Muslim voices, while also illuminating the possibilities that emerge when educators choose courage over neutrality. For anyone committed to teaching truth and transforming public schools into sites of democratic possibility, this book is a compelling invitation to organize for the future our students deserve. Read this book—and then join the resistance."

—JESSE HAGOPIAN, author of *Teach Truth: The Struggle for Antiracist Education*

"In this darkened shadow of the educational landscape, George Theoharis and John Rogers offer us textual flashlights, a compass, a mirror and extended hands to re-kindle a movement for educational reawakening. Indeed, *Educating in Dangerous Times* reminds us to attend to vibrant enactments of radical educational practice currently in our midst, to notice popular education rupturing on the streets, in labor union meetings; in the mutual aid gone wild in Minneapolis; in banned book clubs sprouting all over the country; in the radical refusals of complicity voiced by librarians, educators and students; in the pro-Palestine encampments and No Kings rallies that have dotted the nation. George Theoharis and John Rogers have served up a delicious collection of brilliant minds, gorgeous writers with big hearts and powerful imaginations, with scoops of resources and provocative questions, a book that warms the soul with hope and provokes our educational conscience with unapologetic mandates. The volume is luscious."

—MICHELLE FINE, Distinguished Professor,
CUNY Graduate Center

"This is the book we need right now. Part personal reflection, part dreaming, part prescriptions for policy and practice, this volume helps us think bigger and more ambitiously about the education systems that we need to prepare young people for the future. It both embraces and theorizes our education system as a core aspect of civic life, as a place where young people are supported in their developmental and identity needs, and a place where deep and consequential learning can occur. It is an invitation to keep our collective attention on what matters most and to redesign schools to do the important work of making society anew."

—NA'ILAH SUAD NASIR, president of
the Spencer Foundation

"These are difficult and challenging times—dangerous times for public education as the title of this book has it. The current assault on education—public schools, universities, libraries, cultural institutions, and museums—runs the gamut from drastic funding cuts to control over what can be taught and learned. This is not some random collateral damage from the intensifying counterrevolution but rather a necessary target for those who seek unchecked power. And it's important to remember that we were led down a bipartisan path toward this catastrophic precipice, that is, Democrats and Republicans agreed that high-stakes standardized tests were a good measure of school and teacher effectiveness, and both establishment parties favored schemes to privatize rather than extend the public space. John Rogers, George Theoharis, and their colleagues ask us to reject fighting a defensive struggle that would take us back to an imagined lesser evil; they inspire us to reenvision and reimagine what free people need our public schools to become, and then to commit to a battle to rebuild education with a robust vision of what's worth fighting for. The stakes are high, and *Educating in Dangerous Times* is an essential text for understanding both the dimensions of the crisis we face and a strategy to fight for the schools we deserve."

—BILL AYERS, author of *When Freedom Is the Question, Abolition Is the Answer: Reflections on Collective Liberation*

EDUCATING IN DANGEROUS TIMES

EDUCATING IN DANGEROUS TIMES

A CALL TO REENVISION PUBLIC SCHOOL IN AMERICA

EDITED BY
GEORGE THEOHARIS AND JOHN ROGERS

BEACON PRESS, BOSTON

BEACON PRESS
24 Farnsworth Street
Boston, Massachusetts 02210
www.beacon.org

Beacon Press books
are published under the auspices of
the Unitarian Universalist Association of Congregations.

Printed in the United States of America

29 28 27 26 8 7 6 5 4 3 2 1

This book is printed on acid-free paper that meets the uncoated paper ANSI/NISO specifications for permanence as revised in 1992.

Text design and composition by Kim Arney

Library of Congress Cataloguing-in-Publication Data is available for this title.
Paperback ISBN: 978-0-8070-2515-4
E-book ISBN: 978-0-8070-2516-1

The authorized representative in the EU for product safety and compliance is Easy Access System Europe 16879218, Mustamäe tee 50, 10621 Tallinn, Estonia: https://beacon.org/eu-contact.

FROM GT

To Ella, Sam, and Gabriela—for outbursts of joy and laughter, as well as inspiring me to keep taking up the words of Angela Davis, "I am no longer accepting the things I cannot change. I am changing the things I cannot accept."

To Gretchen—for your incredulous anger and unrelenting hope as we walk together through this dangerous time.

FROM JR

To Sharla, Jacob, Etai, and Miya—who bring forth whimsy and joy, and help me imagine a better world.

For my dad, Stanley Rogers (1934–2025), who taught me to be mindful of dangerous times and appreciate the power of education.

CONTENTS

EDUCATING IN DANGEROUS TIMES

CHAPTER 1

THE PURPOSE OF PUBLIC EDUCATION IN DANGEROUS TIMES

JOHN ROGERS AND GEORGE THEOHARIS

Let's begin by saying that we are living through a very dangerous time.

—JAMES BALDWIN, "A Talk to Teachers," 1963

Six decades ago, James Baldwin called upon teachers to recognize the expansive effects of racism and rethink the purpose of education. Racism, Baldwin reasoned, produces immiseration, social pain, and "reservoirs of bitterness."[1] It also prompts efforts to justify oppression and dehumanization—leading to lies about history and silences about the present.

Baldwin suggested that too often education is complicit in this ideological project. "What societies really, ideally, want" from education, he reasoned, "is a citizenry which will simply obey the rules of society." But Baldwin noted that such education faces a fundamental paradox: A society that succeeds in creating an obedient public "is about to perish." Looking out upon America in the early 1960s, James Baldwin saw a nation that not only was riven by inequality but also "menaced" by a lack of vision, an unwillingness to take up difficult issues, and an inability to think critically. If America was to change, Baldwin contended, education would need to foster the commitment and capacity to "look at the world," "ask questions of the universe," and take action "at no matter what risk."

Today, once again, young people are growing up in very dangerous times. There are a host of new challenges that threaten our health, our capacity to manage technological change, and our ability to nourish and protect the land that sustains us all. These perils are compounded by growing assaults on civil liberties and on the norms and institutions of democratic governance.

Baldwin's vision for education remains a powerful framework. Our critical moment calls for schools that encourage us to be curious, clear-eyed, caring, and courageous. But, even as the mission of public education is more important than ever, schools find themselves the target of attacks. They have been caught up in battles to reassert "order," reproduce long-standing power relationships, and reestablish racial, social, and gender hierarchies.

These dynamics are not entirely new. The struggle to create a public education system that serves the public good has always faced significant challenges. Public schooling arose in the United States with a rhetoric of equality, inclusion, and democracy alongside powerful forces that excluded, sorted, and controlled students in different ways.[2]

The Civil Rights Movement created something of a break from this past. While its effects were complex, between the 1960s and the mid-1980s, grassroots mobilization and legal advocacy combined to make many US public school systems more racially inclusive and somewhat more equitable. Changes were more evident in the South, where federal oversight was strongest.[3] A broad legal and policy emphasis on educational equity during this period also brought new attention and some additional protections and resources to students with disabilities, English-language learners, and girls and young women, who previously had been excluded from opportunities, in particular school athletics.

By the late 1980s, the legal and political climate began to shift from a focus on access and opportunity toward markets, competition, and high-stakes accountability.[4] In recent decades, equity advocates have continued to advance their cause. But, for the most part, educational systems have been driven by a loose policy consensus that has aimed to increase standardized test scores by ratcheting up pressures on educators.

The effects of these efforts today vary widely across schools, with some dramatic stories of improvement and numerous instances of heightened stress. Many schools remain sites of gross inequality. And too few schools take up Baldwin's call to foster questioning, far-ranging curiosity, and the impetus to act in the face of injustice.

The critically important and disappointingly imperfect project of public education has come under intense attack over the last few years. Against the backdrop of a rising tide of authoritarianism and white nationalism, a new and virulent strain of education politics has arisen.[5] Highly coordinated and well-funded initiatives—what we term "conflict campaigns"—have challenged efforts to create equitable and inclusive public schools that prepare young people for our not-yet-realized multiracial democracy.[6] These campaigns play on the politics of resentment, reaffirming racial and cultural hierarchies. They seek to tighten control over what is taught—challenging, for example, the ideal that schools should help young people understand the history and contemporary manifestations of racism. And these campaigns weaponize homophobia and transphobia to impose rules that undermine the sense of belonging and dignity of LGBTQ+ students.

The conflict campaigns have had wide-ranging impacts. Targets have included school board members, district and school leaders, teachers, and students. Compounding decades of questioning educators' professional expertise and the information sources that they draw upon, the renewed campaigns have had a chilling effect on individual educators and have undercut their collective power.[7] In many places, the campaigns have galvanized community members' anger against public education as an institution, leading to policies that usurp local decision-making, diminish public funding, and/or privilege privatized alternatives. Taken as a whole, such actions challenge public education as an institution, as well as the public's capacity to govern our schools and shape our collective future.

As if these conflict campaigns were not enough, the second administration of President Donald Trump has nationalized attacks on local public schools. Through executive orders, budgetary actions, and bellicose rhetoric, it has sought to limit, overturn, or outlaw diversity, equity, and inclusion initiatives; support for English-language learners; long-standing safeguards for immigrant students; efforts to address racially disparate discipline policies; civil rights data collection; protections for LGBTQ+ students; and funding and guidelines ensuring a free and appropriate public education for students with disabilities, among other actions. The Trump administration has empowered states to dramatically expand voucher initiatives, undercutting funding for traditional public schools. It has threatened to pull funds from cash-strapped districts that do not comply with their every whim. And the Trump administration has unleashed unfettered immigration enforcement efforts that have fomented fear and undermined learning in schools across the nation.[8]

We believe these forces pose a grave threat to the well-being of young people and families, the institution of public education, and the possibility of a multiracial democracy. But we also believe that there are many educators, students, parents, and community leaders who desire and engage in ongoing struggles to realize more equitable, inclusive, and democratic schools—schools that affirm the value of each student, foster feelings of safety and belonging, and encourage creativity, critical understanding, and commitment to social change.

CONSIDERING THE PURPOSE OF PUBLIC EDUCATION

Sixty years ago, in a very dangerous time, James Baldwin called upon teachers to rethink the purpose of education. The time has come for us to heed that call as well. To do so, we need help with naming and understanding the threats our public schools face. And we need to dream of schooling beyond those threats. This book aims to galvanize attention on the dangers facing our students and our schools and initiate public conversations around the question: *How should we reenvision public schools and collectively create the public schools we need?*

Reflecting collectively on the purpose of education is a civic and moral act. It encourages us to clarify our conception of power, our relationship with the past, and our assumptions about how to democratically effect change. This process is civic in the sense that it invites us to deliberate together about our beliefs and our dreams for the future. It is moral because the purpose of education touches on our deepest commitments. Considering the purpose of education entails grappling with our sense of what skills and understandings we value and what identities and ways of being we aim to foster. Such reflection prompts us to contemplate our beliefs about human potential and our obligations to one another and to the natural world.

Articulating a purpose of education pushes us to name and face threats that limit human flourishing, diminish social relations, undermine stewardship of the natural world, and restrict our ability to engage honestly and robustly with the past and bring about imagined futures.

And since reflecting on the purpose of education invites both dreams of a better future and a reckoning with the perils we face, it compels us to examine our own agency. Whenever we consider with full hearts and open eyes the purpose of education, we must ask: What can we do now? An initial response to this question begins with trying on and trying out different ideas—deepening our learning through study, dialogue, and inquiry.

At its best, such learning unleashes new and powerful ideas, propels novel practices and ways of being, and opens possibilities for innovative social relations. Of course, while educating ourselves is essential, it is rarely a sufficient condition for transformative change. Ultimately, learning must be paired with new forms of power to remake long-standing practices, shift institutional arrangements, and challenge prevailing beliefs and hierarchies. Ideally, as we learn, we forge bonds of understanding, consciousness of shared interests, and solidarities capable of collective action.

ACHIEVING THIS PURPOSE REQUIRES INSIGHT AND EXPERTISE

This book aims to catalyze broad-based dialogue and public engagement about the purpose of America's public schools and how we can advance this vision in dangerous times. A great many people across the country care deeply about the education of our young people—students, parents, and family members; teachers and school leaders; community advocates, artists, labor leaders, and state officials—the list can and should go on. All need to be part of this conversation and the movement for change.

The chapters in this book are written by education scholars from across the country who teach, study, and write about learning, school leadership, and the politics of education. The authors have taught in public schools, led school communities, parented school children, volunteered in local schools, and participated in efforts to improve their public school system. The education scholars who are part of this book are diverse in many ways, embodying an array of racial, language, ability/disability, gender, sexual, religious, and other social identities. Their varied backgrounds and wide expertise position them to springboard public dialogue in this very dangerous time.

Education scholars with deep experience working in schools and talking with the public are essential voices to ground conversations about the purpose of education. In this moment, when pundits and politicians pontificate widely on the problems in our public schools, the informed perspectives of education scholars are a helpful corrective. The authors in this book have spent many years observing classrooms, listening to young people make sense of the world, talking with teachers and leaders about their craft, and closely following education policy debates. Such attention has been enacted through deep relationships and in the spirit of curiosity. The time and desire to pay attention in this way affords critical insight, as well as deep empathy and appreciation for learners and educators. The authors balance a focus on the practicalities of schooling with a broad perspective informed by educational research and social theory. Because they have been engaged in this work over the arc of their careers, the scholars are not only able to locate current challenges within longer histories but are also able to help us all envision the possibilities that light the way ahead.

BREAKFAST, THE MOST IMPORTANT MEAL

The task of reimagining public schools is deeply personal. The authors come to this work with specific identities, experiences, perspectives, and readers will get to meet and understand the people who wrote the main twenty-one chapters of this book. However, this book was organized by two of us, George Theoharis (professor at Syracuse University) and John Rogers (professor at UCLA). We edited the book and wrote the first and last chapters together. We want you, the reader, to understand how and why we came to this work presently and over the past decades, why we find it urgent, and what aspects of ourselves ground our perspectives and commitments.

We live and teach three thousand miles apart from one another—John in Los Angeles, George in Syracuse. For more than two decades, the American Educational Research Association conference (an annual gathering for education scholars) has graced us with the opportunity to have breakfast together. It is always a precious time—an opportunity over eggs and waffles "to ask questions of the universe," talk about our work with educators, and check in on the well-being of our families.

> **JOHN**: Our breakfast dialogues build on a way of being I picked up in first grade. I was lost then during reading lessons, unable to discern many letters, and completely confused by the distinction between the *b*'s and the *d*'s. My undiagnosed dyslexia led me to be assigned to the "slow" reading group, where I floundered further until my mom began to work with me each night at the kitchen table. Being placed in a lower group was a gift for a young white boy with more than a little privilege. It afforded me critical distance from my own educational experience, the impetus to step back and consider why and how schools sort young people.
>
> In the decades since, I have been blessed to be part of many conversations—with young people, parent organizers, UCLA students, and George—asking searching questions about our public schools.

I have joined others in the delight of liberatory discovery as we name the underlying source of problems that previously had been cast as individual failures. I have experienced a sense of collective agency when we have happened upon a shared realization that seemingly permanent structures are not natural or necessary. And sometimes it has felt like freedom to imagine together what schools might become.

GEORGE: As a former long-haired public school kindergarten teacher and rebellious twenty-eight-year-old principal, I learned justice-oriented work requires community. I brought this with me when I moved into higher education. Breakfast time with John created space to wrestle policy issues facing school leaders, the struggles at our own universities, the inclusion of disabled students, and the rising attacks on queer kids. I looked through my own experiences of being the "slow" kid: slow to learn to read in elementary school, slow to enjoy reading (I did not feel the love of reading until I was twenty-eight and a principal); last to finish my schoolwork from second-grade math to eleventh-grade US history tests and even running laps on the soccer team; and I felt regular panic in college and again in graduate school knowing there were not enough hours in the week to complete the reading at my snail's pace. Alongside that slowness, I also learned, at a very young age, that I had a set of unearned advantages because of my race, gender, parental education, family religious traditions, etc. My mother instilled in me the deep belief that I was both "very special" and "not special at all"—"very special" because I had tremendous abilities and disposition to shape the world for good, "not special" because my privilege meant I would be given things not because I earned them, and thus had a greater responsibility to seek what she saw as "the common good." My call to education and specifically seeking a more just educational system is my life's work regarding the common good.

Breakfasts with John each year were full of sharing about bridging higher ed and local schools, the next research project, building equity-focused leadership communities, and preparing leaders for increasingly diverse schools. I shared about the ebullient joys of my life—my own kids. John heard about their thriving across arts, mathematics, politics, life—and challenges rooted in misogyny, disability,

> and personality from wondrous toddlers into queer adults. I learned about John's wondrous kids, and we saw connections between his and mine. Over decades, John listened as my partner, Gretchen, and I built a multiracial, middle-aged, non–Brady Bunch, *beautiful* post-divorce adult life. I learned about John's multiple generations in the LA area, his photography, running, and love of sports. John asked about my rock star sisters and listened as I tried to manage caring for my aging, disabled, neurodiverse, activist, politically minded, ice-cream- and cookie-loving, intellectual parents when they moved in with me and my kids.

We, John and George, share a similar "hair style" now: We are both bald. But, in the face of rising threats to public school, the decades-long breakfast club turned into a deeper connection—a shared desire to call out the dangers of this moment and reimagine with others the promise of schooling.

STRUCTURE OF THE BOOK

The book is organized to support the public to (a) identify the threats facing public schools and students; (b) reenvision what our public schools should be; and (c) take initial steps toward creating such schools. The heart of the book includes twenty-one short, personal, and engaging chapters. Each chapter is authored by a widely recognized education scholar or team of scholars.

Looking across the chapters, we see four overarching and interlocking principles for reenvisioned public schooling in this dangerous moment. These principles make up the four sections of the book.

1. *Asserting the brilliance of all students*
   Reenvisioning begins with recognizing the *brilliance of our students* individually and collectively and a steadfast commitment to unearth and cultivate the breadth of their interests and capabilities.
2. *Affirming diverse students and leveraging difference*
   Schools must communicate and enact support for, delight in, and love toward the diverse and complex identities of all students. Our students' multiplicity of backgrounds, experiences, and ways of being represent an extraordinary resource for advancing learning.

3. *Leaning into problems*
   Schools should be places that invite young people to be curious, wrestle with ideas, and listen to dissenting views and silenced voices. In such schools, students learn about and play a role in addressing thorny local, national, and global problems.

4. *Reasserting public and collective responsibility*
   Our public schools should foster mutual understanding and a sense of common purpose through the shared practice of democratic self-governance.

These design principles, or *core commitments*, are overlapping, so chapters raise issues that straddle ideas across sections. The principles were developed organically and come from the collective work of the authors and their chapters. We come back to these principles in the final chapter.

Within these four sections, the individual chapters speak to different threats and issues. Each focuses on an issue, a segment of the population, or a concern in public schools today. These are wide ranging and stretch from Black girls and women and queer youth to rethinking mathematics instruction and political education.

With that key focus, each chapter is organized in six parts:

- *Part 1* introduces the author's personal connection to the chapter's focus, explaining why it is important and how it is threatened currently.
- *Part 2* connects the author's personal story to the focus of the chapter.
- *Part 3* articulates an alternative vision regarding the focus of the chapter.
- *Part 4* proposes a set of ideas and strategies about *how* we can move collectively toward this alternative vision.
- *Part 5* advances reasons why this path forward matters and how it relates to our deepest values and social dreams.
- *Part 6* provides readers with ways to extend their learning and engagement with the issues in the chapter.

The six parts provide an intentional scaffold for readers. The personal connections invite a way into these complex issues. Extended engagement with the topic affords opportunities for deeper understanding. This grounding builds toward a central aim of the book: generating a new vision for public schools and ideas for how we might advance this vision. Resources and questions at the close of each chapter aim to spawn further inquiry, encouraging readers to continue their learning and move toward action.

The book concludes with a chapter pulling ideas together from across the chapters. In this conclusion, we (John and George) synthesize the threats, lift up principles for reenvisioning public schools, and set forth a call for readers to join in the shared democratic project of imagining and creating the schools we need.

CHANGING THE THINGS WE CANNOT ACCEPT

We come to the book with the belief that collectively we can and must help schools change. While there is value in the mindfulness and therapeutic understanding of acceptance (e.g., acceptance in regard to interpersonal relationships), in the case of schooling, we can accept neither the rampant inequality in our schools nor the current attack to dismantle public education. We believe this book supports the urgent and hard work of understanding the threats facing K–12 education and moving beyond them to a reenvisioned public schooling. We hope the ideas in this book will be taken up by educators, parents, community members, policymakers, leaders, future leaders, and current students. This book is not just for one of these groups but all of them. In this divisive and dangerous moment, we need broad and diverse engagement capable of challenging narrow thinking and recognizing our shared interest in building schools that serve us all.

We invite you to read the chapters across this book and deeply engage with the ideas, content, questions, bold paths forward, and continued learning. We hope you and your neighbors study and discuss the book in small and large groups—in school-district leadership teams and with school staffs; at your church, temple, mosque, and with your secular community groups (book clubs, pickleball leagues, trivia nights, and other social settings); with your municipal and regional leaders, and with your state and national organizations.

James Baldwin's insight—that we are now educating in a "very dangerous time"—offers a challenge for readers of this book. Baldwin calls it our "obligation" in such times to "examine society and try to change it." We hope that you join with friends, neighbors, and colleagues near and far and embrace this collective obligation. We ask that you take up the book and then share and discuss, share and discuss, share and discuss. Use the ideas you find across the book to bring people together to chart a path forward. Let's dive into the learning now. It's a beautiful day for reenvisioning our public schools.

SECTION 1

ASSERTING THE BRILLIANCE OF ALL STUDENTS

CHAPTER 2

DIGNITY AND BEAUTIFUL LEARNING ENVIRONMENTS

MANUEL ESPINOZA

MY CONNECTION TO EXPERIENCES THAT DULL MIND AND HEART

I think often—perhaps, obsessively—about how to design the kinds of educational environments that harmonize with human dignity and make possible the fulfillment of the universal right to education. Writing that opening sentence sparks a confession: *I feel myself an unlikely creature.* Throughout high school, I dreamt of rocketing out of Commerce City via Highway 2 in a 1967 Mustang with that Tracy Chapman song on repeat. (Where to? Home, fifteen minutes south to Denver.) Instead, I pushed an anemic 2.0 grade point average, unfortunately registered to my name, up the pockmarked road and across the tracks for four years. The Marine Corps would knock on my door—a suave, burly, and uniformed African American recruiter who spoke Spanish—but there was no patriotic fervor of that sort to awaken. I was then and am now an American in the key of *Cool Hand Luke*, *The Cisco Kid*, *Zoot Suit*, and *Gideon's Trumpet*.

Home life oozed distress that was stanched by genuine tenderness. I felt that I wanted a different life but could not foresee a day in which the majestic matters of human rights and education would pilgrimage the deserts of my mind. Rummaging, I find no road-to-Damascus moment, nor can I ascertain any earthly first cause. Rigorous retrospection yields but a humble suite of episodes that both sated an enigmatic hunger and stoked an appetite of indefinite origin.

Picture the scene: a young Chicano in a dim kitchenette, hunched over a musty paperback in the minutes before the rediscovery of light. I'm learning (I think) to scrutinize closely but am interrupted by images of the previous day: a teacher whose name I no longer recall talking to the rabble, a role we expertly improvised, about literature and film. He is not moralizing, but what he *is* doing I could not then categorize. A squat man with a push-broom moustache, pleated khakis, and burgundy sweater, planted at the head of a classroom, clutching a book across his chest and holding forth to a haphazard collection of poor white and Mexican teenagers. He speaks names that I intuit carry weight: Steinbeck, Hemingway, Truffaut, Faulkner, Bradbury. When he gets to Fitzgerald, tears freshen his face. Thinking back, how could I have missed it? He was crafting an offering, the kind you leave at the altar of a person's mind. For rose water, he gave art; for marigolds, he gave *The Winter of Our Discontent*.

I am circling words and scribbling notes—a dawning of serious annotation—when the man who chose to be my father shuffles into the weak saffron light.

You still with that book, son?

Yeah.

You like it, huh?

Yeah.

What's it about?

A lengthy pause as he boils water and unscrews the Sanka jar.

A talisman.

What's that?

I don't know yet.

At 8:11 that morning, I turned seventeen. My father slipped me a crisply ironed $10 bill—a sawbuck, son, wish I could give you more—but what I desperately needed was what Luther Vandross was singing about in 1988. Providentially, I would begin finding some of that in books. Today, when I think—without doubt, obsessively—about the design of learning environments, I imagine myself a chemist fusing an alloy out of unstable elements, which I superintend but tenuously: glinting past + ephemeral now + incandescent future. I meditate on the defining features of this "second-person" capability,[1] a unique form of creative social action that places the "Thou" before the "I" in order to cultivate the "essential We,"[2] and marvel at the role the pedagogical imagination plays in cultivating human potential. But I am also troubled because what dulled my mind and heart—dismal expectations, lessons that fail to enliven, faltering lines of communication, interpersonal relations lacking the quality of respect—continues to blunt the minds and hearts of youth today.

UNDERSTANDING WHAT IS POSSIBLE IN SCHOOLS

A global society that cultivates peace and respects human dignity is a hypothesis, and we are its living and interdependent variables. As the fresno of durable peace, education is the sine qua non of genuine comity within our republic and among nations. What Isocrates said to the Athenians about the "public safety" (*Areopagiticus*, ca. 355 BCE) applies with equal force to the American republic:

> [S]uccess does not visit and abide with those who have built around themselves the finest and strongest walls, nor with those who have collected the greatest population in one place, but rather with those who most nobly and wisely govern their state. For the soul of a state is nothing else than its polity.

Susceptible as we are to a legion of prejudices and vices, how are a mass of individuals to develop into the sociopolitical essence of a republic? Where is this transmutation to take place? Alongside the home and workplace, we turn to the public schools, which hold an almost auriferous value in American life. (Without doubt, schools are also convenient objects of scorn.) John Dewey asserted that education is the "laboratory in which philosophic distinctions become concrete and are tested."[3] Increasing the depth of field: Education is a process of human becoming mediated through a kaleidoscope of activities—e.g., inquiring, exchanging ideas, committing and correcting errors, making friendships, receiving and providing assistance, collaborating, participating meaningfully. Within the "miniature public space"[4] of the classroom, the possibilities for wise and noble governance find expression.

REENVISIONING THE UNION OF DIGNITY AND LEARNING

Written sixty-five years ago, C. Wright Mills's *The Sociological Imagination* offers a vibrant vision for the promise of learning:

> What [people] need, and what they feel they need, is a quality of mind that will help them to use information and to develop reason in order to achieve lucid summations of what is going on in the world and what may be happening within themselves.[5]

To those "lucid summations," we should add generative explanations of *how* dignity can be used to design learning environments that cultivate human potential. Hard-won and majestic, human rights instruments (e.g., declarations, covenants, protocols) require the toothy gears of energetic models of thinking and acting for their ongoing fulfillment.[6]

Human rights declarations, covenants, and protocols lift up the idea that institutions should recognize and cultivate the dignity of all persons. Clothed by nature in the raiments of dignity, irrespective of hereditary status or social rank, children and adolescents—i.e., human persons—enter the sanctuary of the public school as subjects of the rights and duties of international law.[7] We are inescapably and advantageously bound to help others and ourselves flourish. The *cursus honorum* of education is distinguished by its capacity to draw out (like salt) inherent gifts, generate (like a dynamo) novel capabilities, secure the continuous enjoyment of the expanding panoply of rights, and promote peace among the world's people.

Yet, a recent United Nations report states that "only one in six countries will achieve the universal secondary school completion target by 2030, an estimated 84 million children and young people will still be out of school, and approximately 300 million students will lack the basic numeracy and literacy skills necessary for success in life."[8] To be certain, the obstacles include, inter alia, war and its attendant social catastrophes, anemic political will, retrograde cultural mores, and underdeveloped or defective financing systems. Amidst these structural difficulties, what good can come from talking about educational design—i.e., the social action of conceiving, organizing, and sustaining learning environments—as a vital component in the realization of a universal right? Human beings thrive in learning environments where curiosity is spoon-fed, where the classroom action beckons you to peek in and nose around. We flourish in places where information freely circulates, where the art of slow disclosure is practiced in order to heighten the drama of discovery. We dream of schools where people can sip solitude yet not feel abandoned. Places where the experience of wonder is as abundant as the common squirrel. Places of order and the unanticipated, where your hands can touch tradition but also explore all that is uncatalogued. Places where the sky you have grown accustomed to, the one you amble under every day, is newly bestowed unto you.

A PATH FORWARD FOR DIGNITY IN EDUCATION

The history of our republic (with its glorification of sovereignty, its flickering promise of equality) and the global crusade for human rights (with its plodding movements, its banner of dignity and peace) are indivisible. (Remember at this perilous hour: The physical lighthouse of human rights, the United Nations headquarters, resides in our country.) We are justified in arguing that the end of public education, to which all other aims are subordinate, is the flourishing of the human person in the life of the community via meaningful participation. Education for humane growth strengthens both individual and community; it fosters agency rather than servitude and promotes solidarity rather than private advantage. Designers of environments for humane growth see the imprint of dignity upon the human person. Dignity is a value principle for the redesign of teaching and learning in the same way that mercy guides the design of a ministry and wonder the design of a scientific course of study. When young people enter the sanctuary of the public school, they do so as children of the republic, as subjects of domestic and international law with a right to learn and grow.

CONCLUDING THOUGHTS ABOUT DIGNITY IN EDUCATION

Human dignity is inherent, inalienable, and infinite.[9] Dignity differentiates human organisms, beings of immense complexity, worthy of admiration, from human persons, beings of exalted value, worthy of sanctuary. Experiences of dignity can exert an astonishing effect upon humans, causing people to reevaluate their relations with themselves, others, and the world. Dignity is a supreme and transmutable value with vast regulatory potential across realms of social life: law, education, health, family, and beyond.[10]

Our world is teeming with *quotidiennes violations*, everyday human rights violations scarcely perceived and never reported. It is also replete with *cumplimientos cotidianos*, everyday actions that fulfill the demands of human rights, faintly perceived and sporadically broadcast. We are justified in expecting wondrous things from the learning environments we design: revelation, fellowship, transformation. Educational experiences that harmonize with human dignity can engender flourishing, perhaps by igniting a sense of confidence where once there was self-doubt or by sparking curiosity where once there was apathy. The venerable education scholar Mike Rose argued:

> [The] many dimensions of learning affect our sense of who we are and what is possible for us. People change the way they think about themselves, how they comprehend their past and their abilities—and thus the way they see

their place in society and what the future holds for them. Engagement with a subject can affect not only what we learn about biology or literature or the culinary arts, but also more generally can affect our understanding of our dispositions and capabilities.[11]

Learning environments that recognize the dignity of the human person are marked by their capacity to cultivate humane growth via experiences of meaningful participation, which have tangible and intangible indicia. Among other things, these environments foster a recurrent feeling of awe regarding natural and social phenomena, a child-like wonder about one's potential, and an inquisitive sense of obligation and duty.[12] When advancement via learning is perceived as palpable possibility, when the thrill of creativity is felt, where vigorous participation is valued, where perpetual positive regard is experienced, therein hope blooms.

CONTINUING TO WORK ON THE COLLECTIVE DUTY OF FULFILLMENT

It is the right and responsibility of individuals and groups to promote and protect human rights and fundamental freedoms.[13] By right, we are empowered to act; by responsibility, we are obligated, jointly and separately, to creatively perform duties toward others. Thus, we ought to be informed of the organic documents that recognize these rights and responsibilities. Though far from an exhaustive list, the following instruments of the United Nations are essential reading for all people:

- The Universal Declaration of Human Rights (1948)
- The International Covenant on Civil and Political Rights (adopted in 1966, entry into force in 1976)
- The International Covenant on Economic, Social and Cultural Rights (adopted in 1966, entry into force in 1976)
- Convention on the Rights of the Child (adopted in 1989, entry into force in 1990)

As portions of the human heritage, the above documents ought to be read alongside others. To learn to sing and dream in freedom are prized educational opportunities, which require of us the alloy of courage and capability. To sing: to discover one's purpose in life and carry out its meaning. To dream socially: to envision change alongside others and use the panoply of creative and nonviolent means to shape the future. If not the dreams of prophets, then the dreams contained within the words of the Universal Declaration of Human Rights, which provide a shared understanding of where we must go, where we shall not. We dream socially to contribute to a global society that respects human dignity and usher in a time in which the social ills of poverty and social inequality are lifeless museum exhibits.

CHAPTER 3

LEVERAGING THE COLLECTIVE POWER OF YOUNG PEOPLE'S MATHEMATICAL IDEAS

MEGAN FRANKE

MY CONNECTION TO MATH EDUCATION

As a teacher, a mathematics educator, and a parent of two, I have spent years listening to and watching young people as they solve math problems. In classrooms, I find myself drawn to the young people, like my own, who do not seem to fit school and often are viewed as "behind" or "struggling." But I am continually struck by the power of their ideas.

I listened as preschoolers counted . . . 18, 19, 20, 20–11, 20–12, 20–13, 20–14.

I observed a classroom of first graders solve a word problem where they were figuring out how many cars they will need to transport a class of twenty-one students to their field trip if each car can hold four students. One student explained, "If we take our minivan we can fit five people in the last car, so we need five cars."

I heard a third grader solving 105 – 16 say: "Instead of lining all of those [numbers] up, the 5 and the 6 cancel out and leave one, so you can take away 11 from 100 and that is easy."

I assessed a fifth grader who was pulled out of math class for special support because he was struggling. When asked to solve algebraic thinking problems like $47 + 35 = \_\_ + 45$, he would say that 45 is 2 less than 47, so the answer has to be 2 more than 35.

Each of these students' solutions are mathematically insightful. However, in schools these ideas would often be identified as wrong, the student designated as needing more help and classified as not mathematically smart.

Devaluing these ways of thinking and sorting students as more or less capable results in limiting whose ideas become a part of the collective conversation and available to support the learning of others. Imagine how helpful it would be for students to collectively consider what happens if we change the sizes of the cars when taking students on a field trip, or wonder if the pattern 20–11, 20–12 also happens at 120, or compare different solutions to a problem.

As society grapples with increasingly complex issues, consider how critical it is to prepare students who can step back from a given problem and assess the constraints, look for patterns in what is happening, try another approach, and see themselves as creative thinkers who can solve problems in multiple ways. Mathematics education is failing to leverage the mathematical thinking of all of our students, and that failure is limiting our ability to collectively learn in ways that position us to productively take on the economic, social, and environmental challenges society faces.

UNDERSTANDING THE WHAT AND WHY OF MATHEMATICS EDUCATION'S FAILURE TO LEVERAGE THE DIVERSITY OF IDEAS

Unfortunately, rather than valuing the diversity of students' mathematical ideas, schools narrow what is considered mathematically smart and sort according to this narrow vision of mathematics. We sort students based on right and wrong answers, speed and accuracy, and level of conformity to certain behavioral standards. We sort in ways that limit learning no matter which group you are sorted into or the criteria used to make these determinations. Sorting students into ability groups has a long history in mathematics education, and decades of scholarship show that sorting leads to a racialized and gendered narrowing of who can participate in mathematics and who sees themselves as good at mathematics.[1]

Sorting begins as early as preschool. Preschools assess and then use these assessments to limit how much math a student can do, group students for more help, and decide who is "ready" for kindergarten. These forms of sorting continue throughout the grades, and once you have been designated as a "low" student it is very hard to get out of the "low group." Educators put forward many arguments to justify sorting: Teachers will be more effective if they can focus lessons toward students of similar math ability; grouping by ability allows us to target additional math support to those who need it most; or, simply, some students are naturally not as capable in math. While each of these reasons for sorting may on the surface sound plausible, rarely does the sorting leverage the range of mathematical strengths students possess, meet the students' mathematical needs individually or collectively, or even center on a student's mathematics knowledge.[2] Sorting may seem practical, expedient, and cost effective. But it has serious consequences for who is deemed knowledgeable and for what sort of learning happens in schools.

SORTING ELIMINATES THE BRILLIANCE AND DIVERSITY OF MATHEMATICAL IDEAS

When schools sort students in mathematics, the nuance and detail of their mathematical understanding is ignored. Decades of research demonstrate how much students know mathematically, how varied their ideas and approaches can be at a given moment, and how what they know can be communicated in quite different ways. Yet, in school, we expect, assess, and sort as if each student will think and explain in the same way. Consider a student who solves 13 – 6 by saying, "I know that 6 + 6 is 12. I need one more to get to 13, so it is 7." Or imagine the student who models the situation by putting out thirteen cubes, taking away six, and counting those that are left to get seven. These students are using strategies that are mathematically powerful, beyond memorizing the "fact" that 13 – 6 is 7. Their ideas are not only valuable for the moment but also valuable as they go on to solve more sophisticated problems. When students are allowed to solve problems in ways that make sense to them, they readily extend their own ideas, see themselves as capable of learning more math, and believe they are one of those students who is good at math.

And when they share those ideas and engage with the ideas of others, it fosters their learning and the learning of the classroom community.

SORTING LIMITS OUR COLLECTIVE MATHEMATICAL POWER

Whether in small groups in a kindergarten class or in "accelerated" and "regular" classes in middle school, sorting practices reinforce the idea that all students should be thinking and doing math in the same ways and limit opportunities for students to learn with and from those who think differently. The student who knows 13 – 6 is 7 does not get a chance to engage with their classmate who may not recall this math fact, but who is able to model the problem in a manner that highlights the nuances of the mathematical relationships in the problem. Engaging with each other's ideas creates new ways of thinking mathematically that may not otherwise have emerged. Elvis, a third grader, told me he liked engaging with other students' math ideas because "it adds texture to my idea." Elvis is not wanting someone to fix his idea; he wants to think more about and enhance his understanding as he engages with others. When we sort students, they are denied the opportunity to develop richer collective understandings, to learn to work with others who think differently than they do, to see the power of their ideas in relation to others' ideas.

SORTING IS NOT ABOUT MATHEMATICS

Schools regularly sort students in mathematics based on how students look or talk or behave. Often students are sorted into a particular math group because they are seen as "not focused" or "slow" or "don't have the language." By way of contrast, consider the language we use when we don't employ labels. Asked to describe how his second-grade student was doing in mathematics, a teacher, Mr. Richards, responded: "I do know he's good at showing 10. He's very comfortable, at least from what I've seen, with the number 10 in terms of building it either with bears using a 10 frame or cubes and assembling 7 plus 3 or 6 plus 4, making combinations."

This teacher is attuned to the details of what his student knows and can do and is well equipped to support this student to take up and extend his ideas in collaboration with others. A wide array of scholarship has found that the labels we use in school mathematics reflect the students' socioeconomic status, race, and gender and not the quality or substance of their mathematical ideas.[3] These labels ignore the mathematics that students can do and are not useful instructionally.

REENVISIONING MATHEMATICS EDUCATION

Schools do not need to sort. Herv Varenne and Ray McDermott remind us that stratifying systems that ignore the brilliance of young people limit collective learning in ways neither "natural nor inevitable."[4]

The potential for a new vision of mathematics education emerges from the young people themselves. Young people regularly report that school math is about memorizing and not relevant to their lives. Yet, when teachers open opportunities for students to think and solve problems in their own ways, students share mathematical ideas that are valid and valuable.

Students tell us how much it matters that they can engage with each other, ask questions, pause, and wonder about their ideas. Students want to take on issues like pollution, the lack of resources in their neighborhoods, and the cost of groceries or gas.

The possibilities are immense and exciting. Imagine students in Los Angeles working with community members to design for equitable rebuilding following the wildfires, or students in Texas taking on gerrymandering, or students in Arizona working on water policy. We have seen young people in schools collect data on CO2 levels or electricity use. Why not have young people work with the city and collect data together across schools in ways that inform district and community decisions? Imagine the counting tasks that young children could do! We count in almost everything we do. We count to purchase milk at school, to make parking decisions, to figure out how many containers we can ship, or to manage inventory in libraries and grocery stores. The mathematics in that counting can be quite sophisticated. Imagine what students would learn by partnering with others more knowledgeable, how their own intuitive and non-contaminated ideas can contribute to those of us who have been working on these issues for years. Imagine how much opportunity this would provide for students to share and see themselves as mathematically smart in ways that advanced broader civic goals.

A PATH FORWARD IN MATHEMATICS EDUCATION

The path forward requires a new set of relationships among people and mathematics education, and a new set of goals and practices. Supporting new goals and practices requires active engagement of both educators and the public.

In schools we can:

1. Listen to students. Expect brilliance. Challenge assumptions about what counts as mathematical thinking, participation, success, and therefore who can do math.
2. Create opportunities for authentic student- and community-driven problem-solving where mathematics is leveraged to solve real problems.
3. Stop allowing standardized tests to drive instruction and instead center student ideas.
4. Organize space and time differently. Find ways for teachers and students to collaborate across ages, expertise, and subject areas.

The path forward is possible. We have seen evidence of it developing. When provided the opportunity, teachers and school leaders eagerly and thoughtfully work together to create schools that support the collective mathematical ideas of students. What is needed is a systemic process that requires not the extraordinary effort of a few but the collective commitment of all to dismantle and rebuild.

In the public space, we can:

1. Engage together to reconsider what we want from school mathematics. Ask ourselves what kind of mathematics we hope for students.
2. Wonder together about whose mathematical ideas we value and why.
3. Examine why for one student to succeed others must fail and why it continues to be the same groups of students who fail (and succeed).
4. Invite young people into spaces where they can participate in the mathematics of their daily lives.

Everyone wants their child to succeed. I have wanted that, too, for my own children. But my children's success should not come at the expense of others. I want my children to benefit from the rich mathematical ideas of others, including the ideas not valued in school math. We all must be willing to see that our children will succeed best when we expand the very meaning of success.

The most successful problem solvers in our society are those who think outside the box, who question, who wonder if there are different ways. This is what we want for all students. We need a society where people can hear others' ideas, ask questions, and collaborate to construct new ideas. Public schools provide rich spaces for this to happen.

CONCLUDING THOUGHTS ON REENVISIONING MATHEMATICS EDUCATION

Throughout history, sorting in mathematics has limited who succeeds and has narrowed the voices and thinking available for students to collectively learn in ways that enable them to challenge the status quo and create new ways of solving problems. If, as a society, we are going to successfully tackle the imminent and profound challenges facing us, such as climate change, gerrymandering, or an aging population, we need mathematics. Bob Moses, civil rights activist, educator, and creator of the Algebra Project, taught us that math literacy is more than basic arithmetic; it is also a tool for liberation and necessary for participation in our democracy. He used the teaching of algebra as a vehicle for empowering young people and supporting them to develop the critical-thinking and problem-solving skills needed for taking collective action and challenging inequitable systems. Supporting the education that Moses envisioned requires an education that does not limit how we think mathematically but creates the conditions to think differently. We need public education that leverages the diversity of students' mathematical ideas and invites each and every student to participate.

CONTINUING TO WORK ON REENVISIONING MATHEMATICS EDUCATION

Schools can be designed to center the diversity of young people's mathematical ideas in ways that maximize the potential of each young person and the mathematical power of the collective. It will require the attention, questioning, and support of all of us.

Wonder and ask questions about who gets to do high-level math at your children's schools. How are students sorted, and what does that mean in terms of whose voices are in the conversation? When you attend back to school night at your child's middle school or high school, notice who is in your child's math class. Look for patterns around race, gender, and income. Ask why these patterns exist.

Investigate the ways in which young people get to share their mathematical ideas in your schools. Do all students' solutions sound exactly the same? Do students say they solved a mathematics problem the way they did because the teacher told them to do it that way or because this is how they like to do it? If you have a child who thinks about mathematics differently than other children doing school math, share that insight with their teachers.

Talk to others about what you think school math could accomplish. Where is it that we agree and disagree? Consider how the goals we have for school math are going to enable us to solve the problems of today and the future.

RESOURCES

The Algebra Project: https://algebra.org

DREME (Development and Research in Early Mathematics Education): https://dreme.stanford.edu (includes videos of the diversity of young people's mathematical thinking)

UCLA's Data for Democracy in LA: https://centerx.gseis.ucla.edu/data-for-democracy/

CHAPTER 4

ALL REALLY MEANS ALL

Recommitting to Inclusive Education During Dangerous Times

CHRISTINE ASHBY AND BETH MYERS

OUR CONNECTION TO INCLUSIVE EDUCATION

CHRISTY: When my daughter was four, she attended Jowonio, an inclusive preschool in Syracuse. For decades, Jowonio seamlessly educated students considered to have the most significant disabilities alongside typical peers. I was a graduate student pursuing a degree in inclusive special education at the time, and as any good researcher knows, we can't help but use the people we care about as data. To that end, I decided to do a little informal interviewing in the car one day with my daughter while we drove to Syracuse. I turned to Lauren and posed a question about a young boy in her classroom who I will call Tyler. "Lauren, Tyler doesn't walk and he doesn't talk. How do you play with him?" Her response was immediate. "He has a face he makes for yes and a face he makes for no. And when he wants something, he reaches out for it." Then she shrugged her shoulders, gave me a look I can only classify as "What's the big deal?" and went back to whatever she was doing. Both the parent and the researcher in me smiled that day as her simple statement revealed so much more than she perhaps realized.

BETH AND CHRISTY: Many of the children at that preschool went on to local inclusive elementary schools, including one known as a national model and one of the first inclusive public elementary schools in the nation. Both of us sent our children to this school, and two of Beth's children still attend it. Since the 1970s, this school has supported even the most complex learners, children who previously would have been housed in institutions, in supportive classrooms with their peers. Every grade has co-taught classrooms, where kids are taught both by a general education teacher and a special education teacher. In a documentary from 1987, we see children who are blind, medically fragile, and autistic all learning together in the same classrooms as their peers at this school.[1] But today we've taken steps backward. There are still co-taught classrooms, but in some of those classrooms, the students with disabilities outnumber those without. There are also several self-contained classrooms, where students with developmental disabilities or behavioral-support needs are taught separately from their peers, and most students with significant medical needs are sent to a separate school altogether. These are all moves away from inclusion and back into segregated education. Our neighboring districts reflect the same trends: kids who can't access communication in a regular classroom or have to choose between therapy time and math instruction. We know our schools can do better, but they aren't.

UNDERSTANDING THE IMPORTANCE OF INCLUSIVE EDUCATION FOR STUDENTS WITH AND WITHOUT DISABILITIES

Before the 1975 Education for All Handicapped Children Act (which later became the Individuals with Disabilities Education Act, or IDEA), students with disabilities did not have the right to go to school. Often, families were told that their child was too disabled to be served in their local school, or that the school or classrooms were not equipped to support them. Parents were told to keep their children at home, and many children, especially those with significant disabilities, were institutionalized. With this legislation, though, all students in the US, no matter how disabled, were finally guaranteed the right to go to school.

The EHA and IDEA established several major principles of special education. These included the mandate that all children are entitled to a free, appropriate public education (FAPE), for which families cannot be charged, and a multidisciplinary team, including parents and sometimes students, who have input into what is appropriate. Later legislation added to this, mandating that an appropriate education also required supports for more than minimal progress for a child's circumstances.[2] Other provisions required nondiscriminatory evaluations in a child's home language, that each child eligible for special education receive an individualized education program (IEP), and that procedural safeguards such as the right to mediation and due process are guaranteed.

One of the most important provisions of the law is also one of the most often disputed: the requirement that students with disabilities be educated in the Least Restricted Environment, or LRE. This provision states that students with disabilities must be educated with their nondisabled peers to the maximum extent appropriate. Unfortunately, the word "appropriate" leaves much room for interpretation and much space for argument. To use a term from Doug Biklen, this is "civil rights with escape clauses."[3]

During the 1970s and 1980s, the US experienced a steady movement toward the inclusion of students with disabilities in general education classrooms. What was called mainstreaming early on—placing kids in regular classes in regular schools—became later known as *inclusion*, truly supporting children with their peers in general education classrooms with access to the general education curriculum. Today, decades of research have demonstrated the benefits of inclusive educational opportunities for all students, including those considered to have the most significant support needs. Disabled students who were educated in inclusive classes showed significant gains in both reading and math over their counterparts in segregated classrooms,[4] and higher inclusion rates have been found to correlate with higher graduation rates.[5] Students with disabilities who were included in school are more likely to attend college, have higher levels of employment, and live independently.[6] They also show gains in communication, social skills, and adaptive skills.[7] But that's not all. Research also shows academic gains for nondisabled peers who are educated in inclusive settings.[8] As in Christy's opening story about Lauren, we also see social-emotional gains for all students.[9] There's a reason we both requested inclusive classrooms for our own kids every year: We know the research. Inclusion is good for all students.

Schools can, and should, be a microcosm of the world we wish to inhabit. That happens when all students have access to rich, meaningful academic and social opportunities, when students can learn from and with each other, and when diverse perspectives and experiences are seen as sources of strength, rather than obstacles to be addressed. Given the immense challenges we face as a nation, we need an educated and engaged citizenry that works toward a common good.

Despite the evidence, and its inclusion in federal law, the actual implementation of inclusion in our schools is at real risk right now. The current administration has made no secret of its desire to close the Department of Education and move toward state-level block funding. Currently, federal offices that oversee the provisions of IDEA are being gutted. We are witnessing the unraveling of decades of progress, however fragmented and incomplete. We are already seeing a slide toward resegregation for students with disabilities; this will only be exacerbated when there is no mechanism for oversight of the federal law requiring inclusion. Are we willing to let each state decide who gets included and who does not? Are we willing to let local areas choose how or if IDEA is implemented?

The current attacks on the educational system, the scientifically flawed and unsubstantiated claims regarding autism, and the continued scapegoating of disabled people only intensifies this crisis. Disabled bodies have long been cast as drains or even dangers to the success of "fitter" individuals. From institutions charged with relieving common people from the "burden of idiocy"[10] to zero tolerance behavioral policies that trap students with disabilities in the school to prison nexus,[11] disabled students have long been treated as expendable, their inclusion and access contingent on adhering to nondisabled and Eurocentric norms. These eugenic undercurrents have only been amplified under the current administration. Less than one month from the second inauguration of Donald Trump, disabled people were wrongly accused of bearing responsibility for a tragic airline crash.[12] While this meritless claim was refuted and debunked, the incident reflects an insidious tendency to deflect attention from systemic problems by blaming already marginalized individuals. Disabled FAA workers did not contribute to the airline disaster, and resources allocated to disabled students are not the cause of failing schools. On the contrary, schools have failed many disabled students.

REENVISIONING INCLUSIVE EDUCATION TO BE JUST "EDUCATION"

As we worked on revising this chapter, we received the news that the former director of the Jowonio school we referenced in the opening passed away. Given all the challenges of the moment, I (Christy) found myself yearning for the world that was created at Jowonio. I wanted to go back in time and stand outside the window of my children's classroom to observe inclusion in action, the sense of community and home and belonging that was fostered in that space. What would it take for all schools and classrooms to feel like that? What is the imagined future that all children deserve? How do we re-center the importance of inclusion and community during these divisive and confusing times?

We need strong, vibrant, inclusive community schools that are truly public: open to all and committed to educating every child, with all the backgrounds and identities they bring with them.[13] We want robust academic instruction alongside true community support: wraparound health services, access to mental health supports, family and caregiver engagement, and enriching extracurricular activities for all children. We want learning spaces that kids don't need to earn their way into or fear being removed from if their behavior challenges a normative standard of performance and participation.

We envision classrooms that are co-taught (that is, taught by a general education teacher and a special education teacher, or two inclusive education teachers who are trained in both). We want all teachers to be skilled in engaging all learners with high expectations. We want schools to be places where students, families, and educators all feel like they belong and have the resources they need to be successful, and where diversity of body and mind is celebrated. We dream of schools where disability is a valued resource and identity that deserves sustenance, not remediation and cure, where students have multiple entry points into content and differentiated ways of demonstrating what they have learned.[14]

We believe that every child can thrive with their peers with resources and support. Those need to be built into communities, and public education cannot be responsible alone. Dreaming of inclusion in individual schools is not enough. Current funding structures often incentivize segregation, with higher rates given to separate, and more expensive, school programs. Instead, states can incentivize inclusion and equipping districts with robust funding for staffing, professional development, and student support in the most inclusive school settings. Professional certification can be reenvisioned as fully focused on inclusive teaching practices. Integrated systems, from healthcare and early intervention to public housing assistance, could be refocused with an emphasis on school and community inclusion for people with disabilities. If we prioritize inclusion as a human right, then policy and practice must follow.

A PATH FORWARD FOR INCLUSIVE EDUCATION

So, how do we get there? How do we realize this vision in the face of such strong and federally supported headwinds? We need to start by planning with inclusive futures in mind. We need to stop asking if inclusion is a good idea or how much inclusion is appropriate or even tolerable and start asking, "What would it take to create schools that truly support all learners?" We need to ensure federal protections of disabled youth (e.g., IDEA and Section 504) and maintain rigorous compliance mechanisms through the Office of Civil Rights. Compliance with federal law isn't sufficient and should never be the ultimate goal, but we need to hold the line regarding rights that have already been earned as we work to increase access and opportunity.

We need to innovate and change with the times, but that doesn't mean abandoning community schools and public education. On the contrary, we need to increase research focused on best practices in educating all learners in inclusive settings. We need to equip teachers with the tools and resources to meet the needs of diverse learners and incentivize school districts that work to include more students with disabilities through financial support for professional development, planning time, and in-class resources. We need federal support for teacher education, teacher development, and teacher retention programs.

With the current attempts to dismantle the Department of Education and the elimination of staff in the Office of Special Education Programs, we need to both protect the gains we've made since 1975 and also seize on this moment to radically reimagine education and the role of law. While IDEA has critically important provisions, many aspects of the law, including FAPE (what counts as appropriate?) and LRE (can a segregated placement ever be least restrictive?), have been subject to much debate since its implementation. How can we reimagine a new system for today's current educational needs? What if students did not need to have a disability label to access differentiated supports and services within their community school? In this blueprint for the future, all students can access all educational spaces, fully included with their peers, supported by universally designed instruction. Services and supports are determined based on each student's need, not their educational label or fit for a preexisting program. Academics are taught with high expectations for all learners in co-taught classrooms. Support needs are met directly in the classroom, without the need for pull-out instruction or segregated learning spaces. Strong professional development, professional teacher salaries, collaborative practices, and high levels of support keep strong teachers in positions of direct instruction in the classroom with reduced burnout.

This blueprint also emphasizes inclusive school culture, where belonging is valued over perceived future contributions to a capitalist economy. Disability, like other differences, is seen as a normal part of diversity. Social, emotional, and communication supports are all built into the school environment and accessible to all members of the school community. Families and caregivers are fully involved and feel welcomed and empowered to participate in the educational process, no matter their own background or educational experience. Schools demonstrate transparent accountability through systems designed by educators, not legislators.

We need all families to insist on inclusive settings. Are there students with Down syndrome and cerebral palsy in your child's kindergarten class? What about their sixth-grade music class? What about their tenth-grade physics class? Are they included on the sports team, the chess club, the college visits? Do they have the supports they need to fully participate? Are they relegated to "special spaces" in the building, or are they utilizing the same classrooms and resources as their typical peers? Are the teachers in your building prepared to meet the needs of a diverse student body? Do they have opportunities to plan and learn from each other? Are parents and caregivers invited to the table as well? Do teachers, administrators, families, and schools have the supports they need to make this happen? We all need to ask these questions of our local schools and then take action to advance inclusive opportunities where they are absent or insufficient. We need to show up at board meetings and curriculum nights and work in solidarity and allyship with other parents and community members. We need to center inclusion in every conversation.

Teachers, school administrators, and teacher education programs need to stay at the forefront of this movement. Schools at all levels are under attack from all directions, but we can't sit on the sidelines and wait for new orders and proclamations. We can't hold our collective breaths and wait for the pendulum to swing back. Rather than distancing ourselves from commitments to equity and inclusion, we need to infuse *more* attention to teaching for diversity in our teacher preparation programs for all certification areas.

A dear colleague of ours is fond of saying, "We don't need mediocre teachers. We need outstanding teachers." We need teachers with unequivocal and unwavering commitments to the value of inclusive education equipped with the pedagogical and problem-solving tools that meet the needs of diverse classrooms. We need to radically reimagine teacher education and certification, eliminating different tracks and certification structures for general and special education, eschewing the notion that "special students need special teachers." All teachers should be able to teach all students.

CONCLUDING THOUGHTS ABOUT THE IMPORTANCE OF INCLUSIVE EDUCATION

These are truly dangerous and precarious times for disabled students and their families. The current administration thrives on pinning parties against each other, perpetuating false dichotomies and promoting a scarcity mindset that encourages people to cling to their own privilege and protect what is theirs. Disabled adults are cast as scapegoats or pushed to the margins, denied access to community living and opportunities for meaningful work. Disabled students are cast as drains on systems, rather than valuable members of our school communities. Families have to fight for their children with disabilities to gain access to the same education freely granted to other, nondisabled children. Students are expected to prove their readiness for an education that others simply get to receive. But the fight for quality inclusive education isn't won by arguing how it benefits disabled students. It is won by articulating the value to all children and all communities. It is won by rejecting the assumption that some lives, some bodies, some minds are more valuable than others. When we fail disabled students, we fail *all* students. When we relegate some bodies to the margins, we lose the opportunity to learn from each other; we deny the generative possibilities of difference and perpetuate a hierarchy that keeps disabled people on the bottom rungs. Inclusive education is about possibility. It is keeping the doors flung open as wide as possible so all young people can dream big dreams and have the opportunities and resources that make that possible. The work of inclusion is the work of all of us, and we have much work to do. Just like Lauren expressed of her preschool friend Tyler, "When he wants something, he reaches out for it."

CONTINUING TO WORK ON ADVANCING TRULY INCLUSIVE EDUCATION

DIALOGUE QUESTIONS

- What does special education look like in your space? How have you seen students with disabilities supported in schools, or how and where are students with disabilities supported in your school? What percentage of your students are fully included in general education curriculum and contexts?
- Consider doing a services and accessibility audit if you are a teacher or a school administrator.
- Are there reasons why you think a student might not be able to participate in an inclusive classroom right now? How could you imagine that differently? In a best-case scenario, with plenty of resources, what could it look like to fully include that student with their peers successfully? What are some other ways that could be successful?
- What do you think are the biggest barriers to school inclusion today? How could we imagine removing or reducing those barriers?
- How could you be more supported in inclusive education efforts? How could you be more supportive of inclusive education efforts?

TOOLS AND RESOURCES

J. Causton, K. MacLeod, K. Pretti-Frontczak, J. Rufo, and P. Gordon, *The Way to Inclusion: How Leaders Create Schools Where Every Student Belongs* (ASCD, 2023)

DiveIn: Diving into Special Education's Most Complex and Pressing Debates (podcast): https://divein.alitu.com/

Including Samuel (documentary film): https://includingsamuel.com/

Network for Public Education: https://networkforpubliceducation.org/

CHAPTER 5

SEEING THE GENIUS IN THOSE LABELED "SYSTEM IMPACTED"

JULISSA MUÑIZ AND TYRONE C. HOWARD

OUR CONNECTION TO THE EDUCATION OF SYSTEM-IMPACTED YOUTH

In this essay we give special attention to students who are among the most overlooked, over-surveilled, persistently punished, consistently reviled, and misunderstood in schools—those we refer to as the hidden geniuses. In particular, we focus on those hidden geniuses that are labeled as "system impacted." These are young people whose lives have been profoundly affected by various systems of state intervention, such as child welfare, juvenile incarceration spaces, or immigration enforcement.

We begin by sharing our own personal experiences observing, interacting with, and researching these systems. We then shed light on the often hidden geniuses in schools, as well as on the systems that reproduce harm rather than support young people. Finally, we provide a path forward for education researchers, practitioners, and policymakers to disrupt these harmful systems and unleash the genius within systems impacted youth. We come to this work as individuals who have witnessed both personally and professionally how these systems inflict harm on youth who are brimming with possibilities and potential. These issues are personal for both of us in many ways.

> **TYRONE:** Having spent time growing up in Compton, California, the reality of dangerous times was always real. Given the persistence of under-investment in an increasingly Black neighborhood, one of the saving graces was our schools. At a time when schools were majority-Black and comprised of teachers who lived in our communities, it was easy to see—up close and personal—educators who were willing

to "go for broke." These educators were warm demanders who had the highest of expectations for all of their students, insisted we perform at our personal best, firmly held us accountable for our actions, and did so with more than a modicum of love, care, and respect. And it was not uncommon for our teachers to be well connected with our parents and caregivers in ways that reflected the sort of home-school-community connections that historian Vanessa Siddle Walker has unearthed in her studies of the Jim Crow South of the twentieth century.[1]

Growing up in Los Angeles County in the mid-'80s, I found it was impossible not to see the prevalence of crack cocaine, police brutality, and persistent surveillance of the most vulnerable residents. Nonetheless, educators in those "dangerous times" did not allow themselves to buy into the super-predator label that was affixed to far too many Black and Brown young men. Many educators helped us develop a critical literacy to challenge why our communities were overpoliced, flooded with drugs, and lacking in mental health supports for substance abuse and addiction. They recognized our genius and supported it with intentionality and critically conscious teaching that encouraged us to become the change we wanted to see.

Also prevalent during the '80s and '90s was the tendency of public systems to divide families when some family members experienced incarceration or persistent substance abuse. I observed children being removed from their parents and being placed in a child welfare system that seemed less concerned with family reunification and more concerned with pathologizing parents who were being harmed by societal factors beyond their control. My own role as a relative caregiver and as someone who studies what Dorothy Roberts calls the "family policing system"[2] is rooted in painful memories, harsh realities, and enduring damage that still persists. This system vilifies Black and Brown families, criminalizes poverty, and embraces white supremacist values and patriarchal practices. What is often overlooked is the genius that youth, caught in the carceral entanglements of these systems, constantly demonstrate. For example, consider the uncanny problem-solving skills associated with keeping several siblings connected and together by simultaneously managing multiple living placements and attendance at different schools with different schedules.

JULISSA: As someone who studies teaching, learning, and identity development in carceral spaces, I have witnessed first-hand how dire the outcomes can be when we fail some of our most vulnerable students. For thirteen years, I have worked with incarcerated and formerly incarcerated community members in various capacities, including as an educator, a community organizer, a legal assistant, an advocate, a professor, and a researcher. I have learned that many youth experience schools as their earliest sites of violence, rejection, and educational abandonment.

Too often they felt that they did not belong, that they were "bad students," and that school was "not for them." Many were pushed into alternative schools and, in some cases, exposed to the juvenile legal system and the family policing system at early ages. I also have witnessed these dynamics within my own family, several of whom were forced into continuation schools and eventually pushed out of school altogether.

When I first started tutoring at San Quentin State Prison, I remember meeting an older Black gentleman who was likely in his sixties and had recently joined the high school preparation class to earn his GED. In order to determine his reading level, the teacher asked me to administer a word-recognition test. Yet, as soon as I sat next to him, he turned to me and said, "Miss, I don't want to waste your time. I don't know how to read. Can you instead show me the sounds each letter makes?" I was twenty-one years old at the time and unsure what to say or do next, but I knew at that moment that his inability to read was our collective responsibility, a failure of multiple public systems. When I asked him why he wanted to learn to read, his response was simple: He wanted to be able to read his grandchild a book over the phone. His response captures how and why learning can be dignity-affirming. It speaks to the importance of ensuring that all students—regardless of family income, geographic location, race, ethnicity, immigration and legal status—have equitable access to quality education.

I have seen and experienced just how transformative education can be when teachers, school leaders, and families work together to create the conditions for students to succeed. I was one of those students. I was fifteen years old and a sophomore in high school when I got pregnant.

Although I was young, scared, and uncertain about my future, I knew I wanted to continue my education for both myself and my daughter. I had the drive, but without my principal, counselor, coaches, teachers, and the right resources, I too would have been pushed out. For these reasons, I have always believed in the promise of education even as the conditions needed to meet that promise become harder.

UNDERSTANDING THE EDUCATION OF SYSTEM-IMPACTED YOUTH

System-impacted youth are young people who have interacted with, or been affected by, different societal systems such as child welfare, juvenile carceral spaces, or immigration systems. The term "dual system youth" specifically describes young people who are simultaneously involved in both the child welfare and juvenile justice systems. Within the educational context, these students often are treated and labeled as undesirable by many adults in these systems and considered unworthy of love, affirmation, and genuine teaching. The professional literature abounds with research aimed at fixing them to meet academic, social, emotional, and cultural needs.[3] They are frequently seen as troublemakers, but these perceptions stem from deficit thinking and what Carla Shalaby refers to as "pathological pedagogies."[4] In an effort to respond to the needs of system-impacted youth and other vulnerable populations, it is important to think critically about how to create more just, loving, and inclusive systems that can and do support them lovingly and holistically.

REENVISIONING THE EDUCATION OF SYSTEM-IMPACTED YOUTH

Given the sociopolitical moment and the ever-expanding reach of the carceral state, as witnessed with the ICE raids that have terrorized families in Los Angeles, Minneapolis, and a growing list of communities across the country, it is imperative that we recognize and center the needs of system-impacted youth, because as the reach of state systems extends so does the category of who constitutes the system-impacted. During dangerous times—such as those James Baldwin described in his seminal 1963 "A Talk to Teachers," where he emphasized that educators must "go for broke" in confronting societal injustices[5]—teaching takes on a profound responsibility to recognize, affirm, and protect the brilliance of these hidden geniuses. Baldwin insisted that in times of social turmoil and systemic violence, educators must help students understand the criminal conspiracies that seek to diminish their worth and must empower them to resist and transform these realities. The challenge is before us. We must have the moral conviction, political will, and unapologetic moral compass to do right by our most vulnerable students.

We call for a spotlight on the hidden geniuses—students many see as problems but who others recognize as brilliant beyond belief—across identities and circumstances, including BIPOC youth, those labeled aggressive, system-impacted, differently abled, multilingual, or impacted by poverty, white supremacy, or patriarchy. We highlight the harms schools inflict on these populations but also discuss possibilities for recognizing their promise and potential.[6] We lift up pedagogies, practices, principles, and policies essential for creating schools that truly serve and support them and for transforming classrooms into learning communities that affirm their genius.

A PATH FORWARD FOR SYSTEM-IMPACTED YOUTH

When thinking about the hidden geniuses who are caught in the web of systems that inflict harm, any path forward has to center an asset-based framework. It needs to see the uncanny strength, intellect, wisdom, and problem-solving skills that young people demonstrate in the midst of dehumanizing systems. A path forward for educating system-impacted youth involves a multipronged, holistic approach that addresses their complex academic, social, emotional, and life needs through coordinated efforts across schools, justice systems, families, and communities.

Key strategies include:

Providing rigorous, equivalent education in juvenile-incarceration or alternative-placement settings to ensure that youth receive quality instruction comparable to the best learning opportunities in traditional school settings, aiding their eventual reintegration. Recognizing hidden genius requires a commitment to making sure that alternative-placement settings are authentically redemptive and centered on assisting young people to recognize their various skills, knowledge, and talents. Such settings must also support transitions back into the wider society.

Engaging the voices of system-impacted youth allows them to name their needs, shape programs, and build self-efficacy and confidence as part of their education. When young people are empowered to share their perspectives, they become active agents in their own growth and community transformation. This process recognizes the often-hidden genius of many youth—strengths, creativity, and wisdom forged through navigating complex and challenging environments. Centering student voices not only amplifies these unique insights but also highlights systemic gaps and areas needing reform.

Supporting families and caregivers to participate actively in supporting hidden geniuses means advocating for and recognizing the important supportive roles that families and caregivers provide for youth. Many parents and caregivers are seen through a deficit lens and are blamed for their children being impacted by systems. Yet it is important to understand and address the intergenerational impact and the systemic forces families are up against. To play a vital role in the healing process, parents, caregivers, and family members should experience the same supportive interventions that are directed toward youth. They should also be encouraged to share their own ideas and insights about what their young people need to thrive and how public systems should be organized to support these needs. Local agencies might initiate and sustain partnerships with content experts, professional learning organizations, and colleges and universities around core competencies, skills, strategies, and resources needed for recognizing family strengths and providing family-strengthening supports to service providers.

Creating racially responsive and culturally caring systems led by professionals who understand the persistent harm that white supremacy, patriarchy, and cultural erasure inflict on hidden geniuses. Interventions to support system-impacted youth must attend to cultural and linguistic differences and cannot operate with a one-size fits all approach. They must be anchored in core knowledge, skills, and cultural considerations. Arguably, the boldest and most important step that can be taken to address the harm done to hidden geniuses is to address and dismantle the systemic racism that exists within public systems working with youth. Though controversial for many, and uneasy for some to digest, an acknowledgment of racism, and a serious and sustained commitment to eliminate racism in core practices, policies, ideas, and beliefs, is paramount in reimagining or eliminating harmful systems. The disproportionate number of Black and Brown children and youth in these systems reflects the persistence of systemic racism, deficit beliefs and attitudes toward poor Black and Brown families, and deep-seated pathologizing of racial and cultural differences.

CONCLUDING THOUGHTS ON SYSTEM-IMPACTED YOUTH

System-impacted youth are some of the most intellectually gifted young people. Unfortunately, they have to interact in systems that fail to recognize their genius. Hence, we need new approaches and levers to recognize the genius of system-impacted youth by confronting and dismantling harmful systems, practices, and policies, and replacing them with justice-centered, evidence-based, and youth-informed educational practices. Such practices must respond to young people's cultural and intellectual strengths amid historical oppression, ultimately creating schools and communities that support their transformation and success rather than punishment and marginalization.

CONTINUING TO WORK ON ISSUES RELATED TO THE EDUCATION OF SYSTEM-IMPACTED YOUTH

One of the threats that this current moment poses to public schools is the eradication of important fiscal resources that are dedicated to mental health, social emotional supports, high-dosage tutoring, and social workers whose tasks are dedicated to the most vulnerable students in schools. Among the questions we must consider are:

- How do we normalize culturally responsive wrap-around services in our most underserved schools?
- What steps can be taken to decriminalize Black and Brown youth whose families suffer from an accumulation of disadvantage and structural inequality?
- What role should public schools be playing during these dangerous times?
- What does community-centered resistance look like in the face of ICE detaining innocent people?

For future studying, learning, thinking, and action steps that can be taken to support system-impacted youth, the following resources are offered to support their pathways and possibilities.

ADVOCACY AND COMMUNITY ORGANIZATIONS

Adoptive Parents of Color Collaborative (APCC): Builds community and provides peer support, educational activities, and advocacy focused on the needs of adoptive and foster parents of color, including support groups and national research on BIPOC family experiences in the system.

Campaign for the Fair Sentencing of Youth (CFSY): Advocates to end extreme youth sentencing and support policy reform for justice-involved youth.

Citizens for Juvenile Justice (CfJJ): Advocates for statewide reform and equitable youth justice policies.

Hilton Foundation Foster Youth Initiative: Promotes equity and addresses disparities in education, well-being, and economic opportunities for transition-age foster youth, especially in BIPOC and marginalized communities.

Pact—An Adoption Alliance: Serves adopted children of color and their families, providing anti-racist programming, counseling, youth clubs, and community spaces for BIPOC adoptive and foster parents.

RESPOND (Foster & Adoptive Care Coalition): Culturally competent recruitment, education, and support for Black families interested in foster care in the St. Louis region, with a strong anti-racist and community-centered focus.

The EMBRACE Project (Kidsave): Advances equity for Black, Latino/a, and LGBTQ+ youth in foster care, offering mentoring, fostering, adoption support, and culturally specific resources for families and caregivers of color.

Vera Institute of Justice/W. Haywood Burns Institute/Youth Advocate Programs Inc.: Leads advocacy, restorative justice, mentorship, and culturally responsive care.

Youth First Justice Collaborative: National network focused on ending youth incarceration, organizing youth leadership, and redirecting resources to community-based programs.

CHAPTER 6

BEYOND CLASSROOM BORDERS AND UNDOCUMENTED SCHOOLING

ANTERO GARCIA, CHRISTIÁN PENA, AND ALIX DICK

OUR CONNECTION TO UNDOCUMENTED SCHOOLING

We write this chapter encroached by borders we didn't ask for. We live within the confines of being neither here nor there but, rather, fixed in the imagination of who schools expect us to become. Let us, then, begin by sharing an extended reflection from Christián that describes undocumented schooling within the bordered hallways of US schools:

> I entered kindergarten ravenous for an education that could teach me to read and push me to be in spaces my parents could only dream of for their families and themselves. I came to the US when I was two years old. Until the age of five, I existed in a primarily Spanish-speaking bubble. At six, with my newly formed tongue having just learned English from watching *Sesame Street* and VHS tapes of *Inglés sin Barreras* that my mother would blare through the TV while she cleaned and half-listened, the systemic borders that affected other immigrant children like my brother did not seem so apparent to me. While my brother was evaluated for learning disabilities and placed in additional reading classes and struggled to navigate school, I tore through every book in the Junie B. Jones and the Magic Tree House series. I joined band (I played the flute) and choir, participated in student council as treasurer, won a basketball championship with my team of friends, and remained on honor roll consistently from kindergarten through the fifth grade.
>
> I was the perfect immigrant student and the perfect immigrant daughter. My mother would call family back home and tell them that I had taught myself to read and write in Spanish and English and that I was an incredible

student. I translated at parent-teacher conferences when the school could not get a translator, and I told my parents how great a student my teachers believed I was.

The language of my childhood and my subsequent entrance into middle school changed the playing field drastically. The culture shifted; it felt foreign and terrifying to me. It was a language that my immigrant parents could not understand, and I could not begin to translate. This new system altered my love for education, and I remained in a fog until I finished the eighth grade. When I entered high school, I began to see the end of an era, the end of my childhood and the push for bigger things: college and a career. It was 2014, and when Barack Obama announced that DACA would be offered to students like me, my parents began the application process as soon as possible. After more than a decade of being a student in this country, I understood for the first time in my life what my Mexican citizenship meant, what being an immigrant in the United States meant. If I was not approved for DACA, I could not go to college or get a job, and the risk of being kicked out of the country I grew up in, the only country I have ever known, would be an ever-looming ghost.

The border closed in on me then. Its ghostly hands were palpable in every classroom. In history class, our teacher began discussing elections and passing around voting ballots to everyone who had turned eighteen. I placed it in my backpack and told her that I would fill it out at home while the class worked on theirs for the rest of sixth period. In English class, when we went to the computer lab for the period to fill out FAFSA applications and look for scholarships, the border seemed to grip its greedy fingers around my throat until I felt suffocated by the weight of a future that felt fleeting and unreal.

All of my labor, my hard work, suddenly did not matter. My GPA took a turn for the worst. My parents did not let me join sports, like tennis, badminton, or softball, because I did not have medical insurance and could not get the required physical to even try out. I spent a week preparing an application for a program that offered college courses and credits at a local community college. When I was called by the program and asked to come in and fill out additional paperwork, I had no way to get to the college because my father was at work and my mother could not drive. I wonder now if my lack of a Social Security number would have prevented my admission, even if I had found a way to get there.

We offer this extended description of Christián's schooling experience to highlight the many, often overlapping ways that the borders of schooling shaped her freedoms and the ways undocumented schooling threatens all members of our schooling communities.

UNDERSTANDING UNDOCUMENTED SCHOOLING

The personal details of undocumented schooling vary family by family in their vagaries. Christián's experience highlights key themes of exclusion, miseducation, and punishment created by US borders. Her narrative makes clear that schools writ large reinforce the US colonial project of the past two hundred and fifty years. Let us clarify. The *problem* isn't the dehumanizing experiences of undocumented students, parents, or even teachers. Awful as these experiences may be, they are the by-product of how borders orient the social, physical, and pedagogical geographies of schooling. Even more damning, these borders are ostensibly fictitious—though this chapter is rooted in the real consequences of their enforcement. The lines of delineation, making one land mass more American than another are not "real" in any god-ordained or physical way. As the late David Graeber neatly summarized, "There's all these imaginary lines drawn around the world with not so imaginary weapons protecting them."[1] And yet, the boundaries that arbitrarily deem one person more "legal" than another are tools for schooling and orienting whose identities count in schools.

The symbolic representation of borders, of US enclosure, creates the conditions that allow the US to justify its perverse treatment of an undocumented citizenry. This is not a unique phenomenon of historic mistreatment of a general group of people or of a particular period of US history. The story of undocumented schooling is as old as the intertwined systems that capture and dispose of the Black and Brown bodies dreaming in the US today. State-building, mass public education, and the prison industrial complex intersect on working-class communities. While these systems are not new, we are seeing new ways that borders are harming people of all ages today. It is this experience of undocumented schooling that we plan to reenvision in the second half of this chapter.

Borders assert the legitimacy of some, but not others, on one side of the demarcation line, and, in so doing, they powerfully shape the experiences of school-aged children and their families.

Though the border operating around the US is a constructed phenomenon, it is an idea that enacts very real power. The idea of the border influences the operation of school curriculum, legal and social services available within most cities, relationships to authorities and prison systems, and a cultural climate that conveys a consistent message that undocumented families serve at the behest of labor exploitation in this country. Family life and schooling, then, are bordered at every turn.

Today, through relationships with technology companies and billions of dollars funding nationwide deportation efforts, the identities of young people in bordered school settings are treated as illicit, illegitimate. Undocumented individuals experience a schooling that reinforces harmful borders through the pedagogical enforcement of colonial instruction; linguistic restriction in many "English only" learning contexts; carceral partnership that finds agencies like Immigration and Customs Enforcement (ICE) within and around schools; financial aid restrictions that often prohibit individuals from moving into higher education institutions; and broader cultural exclusion through the customs and practices that reinforce Eurocentric lessons for learning and celebration. In short, the stories like those Christián shares are not an anomaly or a by-product of US borders. They are the intended outcome.

Each day in schools reasserts a bordered definition of the United States in the consciousness of students and their families. Through the policies, curriculum, and structural conditions within and around schools, US public schools remake America, a civic enforcement of assimilation, restriction, and compliance. To be clear, our emphasis on the ways that borders configure schooling is not a claim about the permanence of this system, but of its potential malleability—a possibility for radical transformation—fomenting in classrooms, schools, and their surrounding communities.

REENVISIONING UNDOCUMENTED SCHOOLING TOWARD A SCHOOL SYSTEM BEYOND BORDERS

Because of the dizzying nature of what bordered schooling does for all transnational students, regardless of "legal" status in this country, it is not sufficient to identify singular policies to eradicate or adjust. Like other forms of systemic racism, the interlocking aspects of educational policy, cultural practices within schools, and curricular choices demand a reenvisioned school system that works toward alternate forms of academic progress and relationships within communities.

Knowing that the pragmatics of a school system divorced from state-sanctioned borders can feel impossible, let us start with and agitate around familiar language within the immigrant rights community: sanctuary. In the lead-up to anti-immigrant efforts during the first Trump administration, myriad cities, states, and municipalities including school districts labeled themselves as "sanctuary" locations, committing to not collaborating with federal immigration enforcement efforts or organizations like ICE. Sanctuary has played an important—even if often symbolic—role in recent efforts to maintain the rights of immigrant communities in the current contexts of federal legislation. A sanctuary, by definition, is a space of refuge; it speaks to retreat from everyday life to heal or restore to a healthier state of being. However, while this metaphor and the policies it enabled in recent years has been a useful counter-response to anti-immigrant policies, sanctuary is not a solution to bordered and undocumented schooling contexts.

Instead of seeking refuge from everyday life, unbordered schooling demands restructuring space and everyone's sense of freedom within it. Building on these possibilities, we raise the anarchist-articulated construction of "temporary autonomous zones" as a rudimentary blueprint for how schools might be configured.[2] A temporary autonomous zone recognizes that no space or governance is *always* enforced and in-place. David Graeber writes: "There are always temporary cracks and fissures, ephemeral spaces in which self-organized communities can and do continually emerge like eruptions, covert uprisings."[3] In recognizing that autonomy relies on mutual agreement rather than happenstance circumstances, Graeber's work has pushed toward "provisional autonomous zones" as a means of organizing, suggesting that spaces need only be as temporary as the needs and efforts of those who inhabit them. Indeed, in his own organizing efforts, Graeber's leadership with the Occupy movement in the 2010s illustrated how bodies of people can govern and organize beyond the articulated rules of the state.

If bordered schooling is about restriction and control—of one's body, mind, tongue, and navigational possibilities—an unbordered approach to schooling does not withdraw into a realm of sanctuary. Rather, parents, students, and educators, together, can maintain schools as sites of community-defined freedom and individual self-actualization. If we treat classrooms as opportunities for micro governance, what happens to student perceptions of dignity and self-worth? How might the "provisional" autonomies that educators can empower in their classrooms lead to a broader sense of civic imagination in the broader world?

Despite the initial scaffolding of anarchist theoretical terminology, our vision of unbordered schooling is not intended as a hypothetical future. Rather, there is a base principle that we are not simply seeking but demanding: Schools must operate as spaces that are safe for children and their families. Full stop.

The ongoing threats around immigration, anti-immigrant curriculum, and monolingual language that excludes and isolates do not merely create an unwelcome learning environment. They create harm.

A PATH FORWARD: SCHOOLING BEYOND BORDERS

We are under no illusions that the border policies of the US or of the modern world broadly will be reversed or toppled soon. Borders, though imaginary, remain convenient to the organizing logic of the United States. However, that does not leave us, as educators, parents, and civic participants, off the hook. We can create the provisional spaces for youth freedom and agentic personhood now, regardless of the policies presently harming communities.

While we'll zoom in on pragmatic moves in this present moment, we want to underscore that this reenvisioning does not fall solely on the shoulders of already overburdened teachers or parents. Particularly for the immigrant educators and community members already straddling multiple professional and personal borders, we recognize that the work of curating freedom-thriving spaces requires a shared capacity for holding imagination and ingenuity as sacrosanct.

The provisional spaces for autonomy require not an additional layer of work for individual actors within the educational system but, rather, a collective reimagination of how to act and treat all individuals with shared humility and humanity. This task, of seeding a space with an ethos of compassion, cannot be completed individually. *We*—everyone working and participating in an educational system—make our school spaces open, unbordered, and loving. Or we don't.

Let's look at one, singular aspect of autonomous, unbordered schooling: language. The role of English—as a source of power in school outreach and parental communication—often creates feelings of helplessness and inferiority for families. It is no secret that English has been weaponized to reduce the agency of immigrant families over time. How can translation salve the traumas of bordered schooling?

Small moves of broadening the repertoires of languages permissible across a school day will help erode the borders of what schooling feels and sounds like. Particularly now, a quarter of the way through our twenty-first century, we have passingly adequate tools for synchronous translation within nearly every classroom and school in the US. Further, if we were to create broader opportunities for families to participate in schools, digitally, asynchronously, and in person, we might also see classrooms that feel closer to home and home-learning environments that might reflect the learning goals of schools.

As you can imagine, tugging on the loose thread of language poses questions of who is allowed in schools, under what kinds of authority, in what kinds of time frames, and around what topics. While the interlocking nature of bordered schooling can feel insurmountable, every small move we make in chipping away at the borders of schools is one further small move toward a freer form of learning and being. To be clear, simply reflecting the various languages spoken outside of schools within classrooms will not halt the federal harm afflicting communities. However, it will begin the process of establishing the boundaries for a provisional autonomous space. More importantly, it will begin creating the ethos of a borderless *perhaps*: Perhaps, if every language is affirmed in this space, we might also affirm the cultures and histories tied to those languages. And perhaps if every young person has an elder who is welcomed in this space we might reimagine how classroom configurations and discipline are meted out. And perhaps. And perhaps. And perhaps. Language is not the solution to the harms of schooling while undocumented, but it might cast the spell that sustains provisional freedoms.

CONCLUDING THOUGHTS ABOUT UNDOCUMENTED SCHOOLING

When we imagine an unbordered form of schooling, we free ourselves of the binaries of being from here or from there. We open up new orientations of learning that have been cordoned off in traditional models of schooling. New disciplinary, linguistic, age-based, and communal forms of learning spring to life when the state apparatus of a border imaginary no longer dictates the structures of schooling.

The border extends its invisible and arbitrary lines beyond the southern border, beyond every colonized state harmed in the broader world, beyond the real and imagined. Every system has been infiltrated by the ghostly hands of the border. Even now, many of us struggle to imagine a way of living without border logics governing us. Even fleetingly, such a thought feels impossible. And yet, borders are neither fixed in place nor a permanent, phenomenological feature of our lives. We document these undocumented schooling permutations recognizing that alternatives can and always have existed.

CONTINUING TO WORK ON UNBORDERED LEARNING PARADIGMS

For the past several years we have been involved in community storytelling and journalism work that center the expertise and perspectives of community members labeled undocumented. *La Cuenta* (lacuenta.substack.com) and related publications emphasize the alternative digital spaces, research methodologies, and dispersed communities actively maintaining provisional autonomous zones.[4] We invite readers to join us with their narratives, questions, and pedagogical queries at *La Cuenta*.

As you continue to consider how schooling might resist the borders that have shaped undocumented schooling, we offer the following questions for your reflection:

- How have borders shaped your experiences in schools and in society?
- What are the ways that border logics intersect with other aspects of civic life? How do intersections between borders and, for example, law enforcement systems impact the experiences of *all* students in schools today?
- *La Cuenta* (which means "the bill" in Spanish) refers to the invisible costs incurred by individuals labeled undocumented. From your own reflections on the questions above, what kinds of costs can you name that the undocumented community experiences?

In addition to reading *La Cuenta*, we encourage you to explore additional narratives that are written by and center the experiences of individuals labeled undocumented:

Julissa Arce, *You Sound Like a White Girl: The Case for Rejecting Assimilation*

Alix Dick and Antero Garcia, *The Cost of Being Undocumented: One Woman's Reckoning with America's Inhumane Math*

Sara Saedi, *Americanized: Rebel Without a Green Card*

Jose Antonio Vargas, *Dear America: Notes of an Undocumented Citizen*

Quiann Julie Wang, *Beautiful Country: A Memoir of an Undocumented Childhood*

Javier Zamora, *Solito: A Memoir*

SECTION 2

AFFIRMING DIVERSE STUDENTS AND LEVERAGING DIFFERENCE

CHAPTER 7

SEARCHING FOR A SAFE SPACE IN AN UNSAFE SYSTEM

Black Queer Youth and Schooling in the Twenty-First Century and Beyond

JUDY A. ALSTON

MY CONNECTION TO QUEER YOUTH OF COLOR

These words still ring true: "I am one who stands outside of the circle of acceptable women because I hold these identities: Black, Lesbian, Soft Stud (masculine-of-center), Reverend. Yet I can sometimes stand inside of the circle because of other parts of my identity: upper middle class, degreed, Full Professor, author, sorority girl, former debutante."[1] As a young girl growing up in Charleston, South Carolina, I did not anticipate embodying all these identities. Nonetheless, I was acutely aware of my differences and recognized myself as intelligent, observant, a leader, and possessing a sense of humor. My awareness extended to being Black and lesbian, and I understood early on that societal structures were ill-equipped to comprehend or affirm the intersections of my identity. Born in 1965, I have experienced segregation and racism directly. My mother once recounted how, when I was very young and ill, a pediatrician refused to treat me due to my race. He actually said, "I don't see no [N-word] babies." Fortunately, she found another physician, Dr. Themy J. Chakiris, who provided my medical care well into my teenage years. He was a caring and amazing doctor.

My formative education took place in Diocese of Charleston Catholic schools from first through twelfth grades. During high school, I was actively involved in various activities and participated as a dedicated member of the marching and concert band. Although I dated boys, I was always cognizant of my attraction to girls (having known it since kindergarten). However, during the 1970s and 1980s in South Carolina, it was not possible to openly express this aspect of my identity. Certain realities went unspoken and unacknowledged in public discourse; for instance, while significant events such as the Jonestown tragedy on November 18, 1978, received extensive coverage, Harvey Milk's assassination on November 27, 1978, a notable event regarding LGBTQ+ rights, was scarcely mentioned in our news in Charleston. The educational environment addressed some topics but largely omitted those related to liberation. At the time, I primarily contended with issues concerning race rather than sex, sexuality, or gender. Despite these challenges, I persevered—not due to the school system but despite it. I found refuge in literature, which offered both a language and framework to understand my queerness, Blackness, and emotional responses.

Guided by my mother during my formative years, I cultivated an enduring appreciation for literature and the practice of reading. The main branch of the Charleston County Public Library and local new and used bookstores became important spaces for exploration and self-affirmation.

The works of Audre Lorde, Alice Walker, James Baldwin, and, later, bell hooks allowed me to articulate that the root of societal problems lay within the educational system rather than within myself. The words of Audre Lorde in *Zami: A New Spelling of My Name* (1982) and then Alice Walker's *The Color Purple* (also 1982) both arrested and freed me when I was a college freshman in 1983. For the first time, I saw me and my secret truth on the pages of books.

In Lorde's work, one striking passage that spoke directly to a young me was where she reflects that she learned early that the true terror was to pretend to be someone else in order to be accepted. That realization is what drove her to be open about her identity as a Black lesbian poet, even when the world offered little room for that authenticity. And like Lorde, I broke open my closed door to a part of my identity. Then I encountered in Walker's *The Color Purple* that Celie's experiences reveal how her identity as a poor, Black, queer woman is marginalized. Although formal schooling isn't shown in the book, Celie's limited education and stifled voice reflect broader exclusion. Her relationship with Shug Avery provides affirmation, highlighting the value of queer love amid social neglect—a theme that resonates with Black queer youth seeking acceptance today, as well as a young me then.

These formative years' experiences continue to inform my work as a scholar and advocate. I recognize aspects of my own journey in Black queer youth navigating educational systems that often fail to fully validate their identities. This chapter serves as an act of reclamation—a deliberate effort to name, resist, and reimagine prevailing narratives.

UNDERSTANDING MY STORY IN THE LARGER CONTEXT

Racism still exists within the queer community, mirroring wider societal patterns of exclusion and white supremacy. Despite an image of unity, internal discrimination—particularly against BIPOC individuals—persists and impacts Black queer students both personally and structurally in educational settings. My own experiences at these intersections reveal ongoing cultural and systemic shortcomings that prevent the creation of the inclusive community envisioned by Dr. Martin Luther King Jr., grounded in love, justice, and equality for all.

Black LGBTQ+ youth are uniquely vulnerable within American public schools, sitting at the intersection of multiple, compounding oppressions. Research continues to highlight how racism, heterosexism, and cisnormativity collude to deny these youth access to safety, representation, and dignity in educational spaces.[2] According to the Human Rights Campaign, Black LGBTQ+ youth report higher rates of harassment, marginalization, and mental health challenges than their white LGBTQ+ peers or Black cisheterosexual peers. In school, they are more likely to be disciplined, suspended, or expelled.[3] Disproportionate surveillance and punitive policies feed into the school-to-prison pipeline, particularly for queer youth of color whose gender expression or sexuality is read as defiant or disorderly.[4]

Schools often address queerness and Blackness as separate issues. Queer-inclusive policies may not account for racial differences, while racial equity initiatives may overlook considerations related to sexuality and gender identity. Crenshaw's concept of intersectionality highlights how overlapping identities—such as race, gender, and sexuality—create distinct experiences of marginalization and should be an important part of discussions about inclusive education.[5] Inclusive education aims to ensure all students are acknowledged within classrooms and schools, with teaching, leadership, and policy designed to provide equitable access and foster belonging for every learner. Without intersectionality, understanding the complexity of marginalizations is limited, as these factors interact in multidimensional ways rather than simply accumulating. The educational system does not always provide safe environments for everyone.

Research on LGBTQ+ youth of color in general has shown that schools nationwide are hostile environments for LGBTQ+ youth of color, where they experience victimization and discrimination based on race, sexual orientation, or gender identity, or all of the above simultaneously.[6] Although schools may display support for LGBTQ+ pride, these actions do not always address the particular circumstances or experiences of Black queer youth, who encounter both racism and queerphobia. Consequently, Black queer students may face challenges in spaces where considerations about race and queerness are not fully integrated.

According to Nhan L. Truong, Adrian D. Zongrone, and Joseph G. Kosciw, over half of Black LGBTQ+ students felt unsafe at school because of their sexual orientation, 40.2 percent because of their gender expression and 30.6 percent because of their race or ethnicity.[7] Furthermore, some Black queer students indicate feelings of isolation in Gay-Straight Alliances (GSAs) or LGBTQ+ support groups that prioritize white cultural norms.[8] The language, leadership, and references in these organizations can reflect primarily white queer perspectives, which might make Black students feel excluded or require them to adapt their behavior. Additionally, they may experience racial profiling, stricter disciplinary measures, or lack of cultural recognition in the broader school context, which can affect their educational outcomes.[9]

Gender expression is another topic of consideration. Some Black queer students, including trans and nonbinary individuals, may experience dress-code violations, bathroom restrictions, or comments about their hair and clothing. These policies are shaped by established standards regarding race and gender.[10] Consequently, schools that seek to support LGBTQ+ identities may also have practices that affect Black students differently.

Representation in curricula, staff, or school policy is also an issue for Black queer students. When Black queer history, literature, or figures are absent from educational materials, it can reinforce the perception that these identities are uncommon or unimportant. This lack of representation may contribute to students' disengagement from academics and challenges related to mental health.[11]

Even well-funded diversity, equity, and inclusion initiatives may fail Black queer students when these programs don't engage with intersectionality.[12] Inclusion is not a checklist item; it is a radical reimagining of who belongs and how we affirm them. Programs like GLSEN's Safe Schools Initiative have helped develop frameworks for LGBTQ+ inclusion. Some schools have embraced Gender and Sexuality Alliances (GSAs), but without robust anti-racist frameworks, these efforts fall short for Black youth.

REENVISIONING THE "SAFE" SPACE

To reenvision "safe educational spaces" for transformative education, today's teachers and leaders must believe and work to ensure that Black LGBTQ+ youth are not merely tolerated but loved, celebrated, empowered, and actually feel safe. Imagine a school where "safe space" is not a sticker but a standard. A space where Black queer youth walk through hallways without armor, where curriculum is truly inclusive of queer voices, where teachers and leaders are trained to see intersectionality as an ethical imperative. In this future, equity is not compliance—it is culture. Schools no longer erase difference for the sake of order but embrace difference as a site of innovation and joy. Students are taught to interrogate power, history, and systems through inclusive pedagogy. Black queer students can see themselves reflected in leadership, curriculum, and policy.

This vision reconceptualizes public education as a justice-centered environment, prioritizing democracy by affirming each student's right to complete inclusion. It seeks to create conditions in which Black LGBTQ+ youth are supported to thrive rather than merely survive.

Public education has the potential to function as a space oriented toward justice; however, for Black queer youth, this potential is frequently unrealized.

Schools often reinforce intersecting forms of oppression instead of practicing true inclusion. Disciplinary policies often disproportionately target Black and Brown students,[13] while curricula erase or marginalize queer voices, reinforcing systemic inequities.[14] For queer youth of color, these layered injustices illustrate Crenshaw's notion of intersectionality, as schools become sites where racism, sexism, and heterosexism converge to produce compounded harm. Schools need to be places of justice and love in action.

Educators who adopt a justice-oriented approach recognize that Black queer youth experience intersecting forms of marginalization. Instead of deficit-based views, such educators value these students' strengths and cultural assets.[15] Justice means creating learning environments that foster joy, safety, and opportunity, as described in abolitionist teaching that rejects punitive discipline and standardized tests.[16] Such classrooms affirm students' identities and support their potential.

Beyond academics, justice-focused educators engage families, celebrate community, and advocate for equity—ensuring that Black queer youth are supported holistically. Schools become spaces where these students can truly thrive.

A PATH FORWARD FOR SAFE SPACES

Transforming schools for Black LGBTQ+ youth requires genuine structural change, not just gestures. A path forward starts with educators, leaders, and community members considering:

1. Which voices are prioritized in lessons? Are Black queer figures included across subjects?
2. Do policies clearly protect against discrimination based on race, gender identity, and sexual orientation? Are discipline measures fair to queer youth of color?
3. Do queer students of color feel safe and valued? Is there a system for them to share their experiences?
4. Are educators well-trained in intersectionality and its impact? Is training ongoing rather than one-off?
5. Are families and Black LGBTQ+-led organizations involved in school decisions? Do partnerships support these students inside and outside school?

To move from exclusion to equity requires policy reform, curriculum transformation, school cultural shifts, capacity building, student power, and community partnerships. This path forward is possible—but only with courage, commitment, and collective will.

CONCLUDING THOUGHTS ABOUT SAFE SPACES

Public education is a significant institution for supporting the foundations of democracy. For Black LGBTQ+ youth, its effectiveness in fulfilling this role has varied. When schools perpetuate harm, silence, or erasure, they may not meet their intended objectives. Although education is sometimes called the great equalizer, its potential has not always been fully achieved. Realizing this potential requires more than neutrality—it involves intentional efforts toward justice, care, and transformation, especially for individuals who are marginalized within educational systems.

Progress toward a system that is democratic, inclusive, and equitable can begin with listening to those who have experienced marginalization. Their experiences and perspectives can provide valuable input for reimagining educational approaches. Ensuring all students' safety and well-being depends on schools being safe and supportive environments, particularly for those who are most vulnerable.

CONTINUING TO WORK AS JUSTICE EDUCATORS

Supporting Black LGBTQ+ youth in schools requires ongoing, collective commitment. The goal is to build just coalitions, challenge harmful narratives, and foster spaces where all youth are valued and included. For teachers, administrators, policymakers, professors, and education programs, this work begins with wrestling with the path-forward questions above and continues into what is outlined in this concise blueprint:

NEW KNOWLEDGE NEEDED

- Collect more disaggregated data on Black LGBTQ+ student experiences
- Publish scholarship on intersectional pedagogy and trauma-informed practices
- Provide case studies of successful inclusive school models

SPACES FOR DIALOGUE

- District-wide listening sessions with queer students of color
- Teacher learning communities centered on intersectionality
- Student-led forums to co-create policy recommendations

POWER-BUILDING ACTIVITIES

- Establishing student and family equity councils
- Strengthening Black-led GSAs and community partnerships
- Training youth as peer advocates and policy influencers

BEYOND SCHOOL WALLS

- Advocate for affirming foster care and housing policies
- Demand justice-based mental health supports in communities
- Hold religious institutions accountable for harm

POLICY IMPLICATIONS

- Federal: Enforce Title IX protections for LGBTQ+ students
- State: Require anti-bias training and inclusive curriculum
- Local: Audit discipline data by race, gender, and sexuality

PRACTICE IMPLICATIONS

- Require LGBTQ+-affirming practices in teacher evaluations
- Provide inclusive sex education and mental health services
- Ensure representation of queer Black leaders in school leadership

EDUCATOR PREPARATION

- Infuse intersectionality into teacher education and leadership preparation programs
- Offer courses focused on intersectional justice

SCHOOL FUNDING

- Allocate equity-based funding for culturally responsive resources
- Invest in student affinity spaces and affirming wellness centers

INTRAPERSONAL CHANGES

- Educators must examine their biases and unlearn harmful narratives
- Leaders must practice vulnerability and commit to lifelong learning

OTHER REMEDIES

- Engage parents and communities as co-educators
- Develop restorative practices tailored to queer students of color

RESOURCES TO EXTEND LEARNING

E. Brockenbrough, *Learning While Black and Queer: Understanding the Educational Experiences of Black LGBTQ+ Youth* (Harvard Education Press, 2024)

M. Dougherty, "Over the Rainbow: From Born This Way to Born Again," *The Melissa Dougherty Podcast*, November 15, 2021, https://podcasts.apple.com/us/podcast/over-the-rainbow-from-born-this-way-to-born-again/id1582245489?i=1000542233123

GLISTEN, National Climate Surveys, 2021, https://glisten.org/research/national-school-climate-surveys/

GLISTEN, Safe Space Kit, 2016, https://strongerconsulting.com/wp-content/uploads/2021/06/GLSEN-Safe-Space-Kit.pdf

E. P. Johnson, *Sweet Tea: Black Gay Men of the South* (University of North Carolina Press, 2011)

M. Sadowski, *Safe Is Not Enough: Better Schools for LGBTQ Students* (Harvard Education Press, 2016)

C. Siciliano, *Making Space: Three Decades of Fighting for Beds, Belonging, and a Safe Place for LGBTQ Youth* (Convergent, 2024)

M. I. Suárez and M. Mangin, eds., *Trans Studies in K–12 Education: Creating an Agenda for Research and Practice* (Harvard Education Press, 2022)

The Trevor Project, *Supporting Black LGBTQ+ Youth Mental Health*, June 1, 2020, https://www.thetrevorproject.org/resources/guide/supporting-black-lgbtq-youth-mental-health/

CHAPTER 8

WHAT SCHOOLS CANNOT HOLD

Muslim Students and the Promise of Learning Otherwise

ARSHAD IMTIAZ ALI

MY CONNECTION TO MUSLIM YOUTH AND THE DENIAL OF HUMANITY

I begin with Palestine because it is impossible not to. In 2023, I was co-teaching a supplemental class in a Muslim elementary school where children were grieving the unthinkable. Palestinian students told me of family members killed in Gaza, grandparents, cousins, entire households erased by the Israel Defense Force. On my college campus, in community spaces, and in virtual meetings, friends, students, and colleagues carried the weight of loved ones lost to bombardment. We could not name that grief publicly without being accused of anti-Semitism. To mourn Palestinians, to acknowledge genocide, was cast as beyond the bounds of public speech, especially in schools and on college campuses.

This silencing is not accidental. Schools teach young people that some lives are grievable, and others are not. Empathy stops where empire begins. The threat before us is not only Islamophobia but a global racial order that determines whose lives matter and whose suffering must remain unseen. It is the logic of empire that binds anti-Muslim violence to anti-Blackness, settler colonialism, and war. Within this logic, Muslim students are disciplined into silence, their pain rendered unspeakable to protect the national illusion of innocence. The denial of the right to grieve, to speak, and to be seen is beyond exclusion. It is the denial of humanity itself.

These experiences are not separate from the longer arc of my life as a South Asian Muslim man, nor from the history of Muslim life in the United States. I came of age during the first Gulf War, Operation Desert Storm, in

1991, when the United States waged a one-sided war that devastated Iraq. The bombardment crippled infrastructure, and the subsequent sanctions ensured it could not be rebuilt. The truth of empire was laid bare when Madeleine Albright, then US ambassador to the United Nations, was asked on *60 Minutes* in 1996 about estimates that hundreds of thousands of Iraqi children had died under US-led UN sanctions. She replied, "We think the price is worth it." That remark revealed the moral calculus of empire and taught me whose lives this nation renders disposable.

We do not need to imagine such a calculus in the abstract. After September 11, when three thousand people living in the US were killed, the country responded with wars that took the lives of hundreds of thousands of children and families abroad. To imagine half a million children here dying for the sake of geopolitical strategy makes plain how unthinkable such a statement would be. And we have witnessed, within our borders, how children's lives are weighed and discarded. From the thousands of migrant children held in punitive ICE detention facilities to those who have died in US custody at the border.[1] For the children, families, and communities who bore the weight of this unthinkable "price," we learned that their lives could be counted and forgotten, and that their grief would be illegible.

Later, in my twenties, after 9/11, the global War on Terror brought the invasions of Afghanistan and Iraq, justified in the language of freedom and practiced through occupation and the killing of four hundred thousand civilians.[2] For Muslim communities in the US, this era produced an everyday condition of suspicion, experienced by Muslim youth as dispossession, surveillance, and fear.[3] In the years that followed, the New York Police Department's secret surveillance program mapped Muslim neighborhoods, infiltrated mosques, and monitored student groups across college campuses, treating ordinary acts of community life like attending prayers, organizing charity drives, or gathering to discuss politics as potential threats.[4] Young people learned to lower their voices in public, to hide their Islam in school, and to assume they were being watched.[5] These are lessons in civics. They teach Muslim youth that their presence is conditional, that belonging must be earned through silence, and that their grief must never be made visible.

That weight is inseparable from a longer US history of suspicion and repression of Black Islam, from enslaved West African Muslims whose literacies and faith were criminalized to the twentieth-century surveillance of

Black Muslim movements and the ongoing policing of Black Muslim communities.[6] The empire under the skin was theirs first to endure, inscribed in captivity and resistance, and their struggles remind us that Muslim life in the United States has always been lived in relation to anti-Blackness, state violence, and the fragile hope of freedom carried in the body.

US public schools sit in the middle of this history. They are where the public meets its youth and where the nation's boundaries of sayable truth are enforced. Schools absorb the fears of empire and teach its habits. These are lessons in control. They teach the public to mistake silence for approval and obedience for learning. In these classrooms, Muslim youth become symbols of both danger and discipline, expected to prove that they belong while being marked as those who never fully can. The danger before us is clear. Schools that claim to cultivate democracy are also sites where empire teaches its own survival through silence, suspicion, and systematic dehumanization. I turn next to how this moment shapes US schooling, deciding what counts as knowledge, who may speak, and whose lives belong in the public.

UNDERSTANDING THE EXPERIENCES OF MUSLIM STUDENTS IN PUBLIC SCHOOLS

Moments of crisis have long been used to contain public life. After 9/11, crisis justified wars abroad and expanded surveillance across the US. In schools today, it performs the same work: to silence, to narrow, to police. In 2023–24, as Israel committed genocide in Gaza, US schools suspended educators for naming Palestinian humanity, disciplined students for wearing keffiyehs, and erased conversations about race, gender, and empire. The lesson was clear: Palestinian grief would not be mourned in public, Muslim youth would not be heard, and history would be taught only in ways aligned with views of those holding power. These are lessons in exclusion. They are taught through policy, punishment, and the quiet violence of omission. This is knowledge erasure. By forbidding certain histories and griefs, schools render communities illegible as knowers.[7] Muslim and Palestinian students learn that their loss and grief do not belong in the public sphere.

Public schools claim to teach democracy, yet for many Muslim students, schooling reveals the limits of liberalism. Teachers are suspended for acknowledging Palestinian humanity. Districts remove books centering Black, Indigenous, queer, or immigrant lives. Students wearing keffiyehs or speaking of justice are disciplined or told they are divisive.[8] These are lessons in obedience. The same institution that claims to cultivate possibility teaches submission to empire.

For Muslim youth, this contradiction is lived every day. My own research shows how students move through schools that mark them as suspect and make them responsible for the fears of others.[9] They describe police monitoring their student groups, administrators warning them to avoid politics, and classrooms where the word "Muslim" is spoken as a slur. In moments of global crisis, when their families grieve across oceans, students learn to hide their pain. Across the United States, we have seen Palestinian children's art memorializing relatives killed in Gaza removed from display for being "offensive," keffiyehs banned, and even requests for a small room for Friday prayer initially denied because of the anti-Muslim racism that casts Islamic practice as a threat.

These are lessons in belonging. They teach that acceptance and safety is granted through silence, that citizenship depends on compliance, and that public life has boundaries drawn by fear. Schools promise democracy yet enact its very opposite. They sort whose grief may be voiced and whose must remain unseen. To be Muslim in these classrooms is to live with democracy under the skin, to carry both its promise and its betrayal in the same breath. If education is to serve the public at all, it must begin by providing the right to speak, to mourn, and to remember.

REENVISIONING EDUCATION OTHERWISE

Through these cracks in the public order, we can glimpse what has always been true: young people, educators, and communities finding ways to continue the work that has never stopped. In these learning spaces, classrooms, and communities, memory is something to be voiced rather than buried. The stories of loss and survival are forms of knowledge, opening a different vision of what education might be.

Working with colleagues and community partners, we created a curriculum with Muslim children that places their ways of knowing at the heart of education. Grounded in Muslim storywork traditions, students study the twelfth-century Andalusian tale *Hayy ibn Yaqzan*, in which philosopher Ibn Tufayl tells of a child who comes to know the world through observation, contemplation, and wonder, in order to explore questions of care, responsibility, and relation.

The story imagines knowledge not as conquest but as attunement, where truth begins in relationship rather than domination. Unlike many Western tales that divide reason from faith and mind from body, *Hayy ibn Yaqzan* unites them as part of a single unfolding awareness.

In our classrooms, students read this story of solitary discovery and are asked what it means to learn from the world rather than to master it. They connect the story to their own lives: to growing a garden, to caring for younger siblings, to the rhythm of a prayer. Science and ethics cannot be separated. Inquiry becomes a form of attentiveness, to the earth, to one another, and to the ties that hold a community together. These are lessons in care. They teach that learning begins in wonder and in our relation to others and the world.

Children in our classrooms have asked whether plants feel grief, whether truly knowing the world requires care and connection to it, and how learning can help repair what has been broken. Through story, they have practiced recognition, the acknowledgment that their ways of making sense, the strength of their traditions, their memories, and their griefs belong in the public world of learning. These are lessons in diversity. It is a vision of education rooted in relation, where learning becomes an act of care and recognition.

What would it mean for a public school to foster such learning and protect the humanity of Muslim students? It would need to treat curiosity as sacred and care as a form of knowledge. Teachers would invite stories as archives of the present—stories from Black Islam to new diasporas, stories of migration, faith, and long struggle. Lessons might move between story and science, from reflections on water in cultural and spiritual traditions to experiments in ecology, from the poetry of resistance to the histories of liberation that shape our shared world. Every subject would ask not only what we know but how we live what we know.

To bring mourning into the classroom is to affirm that loss, too, is knowledge. When students speak of Gaza, of displacement, or of ancestors who carried tradition across oceans, through enslavement or exile, they keep alive a form of public memory that schooling has too often erased. Learning becomes an act of witnessing, an insistence that what is grieved is also what must be remembered. Public education cannot meet its promise by policing grief or erasing history. Public education must be rebuilt as a space where young people speak dangerous truths and keep memory alive, where knowledge is nurtured through relationships, sustained through care, and guided by the desire to make the world more whole.

To imagine education in this way is to refuse the comfort of easy victories and the false promise of neutrality. Knowledge is never neutral, and teaching cannot stand apart from the struggles that shape our world. It must align itself with those who tend to what has been broken, who hold close what continues to sustain life, and who carry forward the stories that systems of power have tried to erase. The task before us is to turn these commitments into practice, to build classrooms and communities where learning itself becomes an act of renewal.

To imagine education otherwise is to move beyond the limits of what schooling has been allowed to be. "Otherwise" does not mean alternative or supplemental; it means grounded in other ways of being, knowing, and relating that persist despite domination.[10] "Otherwise" names the knowledge practices that empire cannot fully contain: the living traditions of study, struggle, and care though which people sustain each other and keep open the possibility for a more just world.

A PATH FORWARD FOR BUILDING PUBLIC EDUCATION ANEW

If we are serious about reimagining education, we must admit that schools cannot carry this work alone. Any path forward must reach into the places where young people already live, learn, and imagine otherwise: mosques and churches, Indigenous ceremonial grounds, mutual aid networks, labor unions, refugee centers, diasporic art collectives, and the many other spaces where community life and learning endure. In these spaces, mourning and memory are honored. The violence of empire is brought into the light as the ground for collective survival.

Such spaces of learning are vital, not peripheral. Across the US, study circles and community gatherings in living rooms, mosques, and cultural centers preserve histories of migration, struggle, love, and faith. These practices echo older global traditions: madrasa networks that joined literacy with liberation, Palestinian refugee camp schools where teaching became an act of endurance and hope, and halaqas that weave poetry, story, and ethical reflection. These are lessons in collective wisdom. Knowledge in these places grows through relation and trust, sustained through conversation, memory, and a shared responsibility for one another.

Taken together, these practices form what I call *otherwise publics of learning*: educational formations that challenge the dominance of state schooling by grounding knowledge in community and memory.[11] They remind us that study is not an individual pursuit but a collective act of care bound to struggle. Schools should not be isolated and "perfected." Rather, they must be woven into a wider fabric of educational possibility. Only within that fabric can schools be reclaimed from the erasures demanded by empire.

To move toward this vision, educators can honor the knowledge that already circulates in families, faith communities, and movements for justice. Public institutions can build partnerships based on reciprocity, supporting community-led initiatives that nurture cultural and ethical learning. Curricula can be shaped through dialogue, transforming classrooms into spaces of shared inquiry rather than control. Funding and policy can shift from surveillance and standardization toward trust in the creative and moral capacities of communities themselves.

We do not begin from nothing in this imagining. Freedom Schools created spaces for Black youth to study liberation beyond the confines of segregation and racial violence. The Chicano student walkouts of 1968 demanded that history tell the truth of a people. Indigenous communities have long taught through land, story, and relation. Muslim communities across the world have sustained forms of study rooted in memory and collective responsibility. In Chiapas, Zapatista autonomous schools center Indigenous language and communal governance. In Senegal, Qur'anic schools preserve literacy and ethics against colonial rule. In Palestinian refugee camps, teaching remains an act of resistance and remembrance. Each of these practices refuses the machinery of power that seeks to monopolize knowledge and keeps alive the dream of education as freedom.

The way forward is not simply to reform what exists but to remember and practice what endures. To imagine otherwise publics of learning is to recognize that education already lives wherever people gather to tell stories, share knowledge, and sustain one another in the work of living in community. The future of education depends on learning from these spaces as models of what schooling might yet become: a renewed public grounded in care, relation, and collective life.

CONCLUDING THOUGHTS ABOUT EDUCATION AND THE WORK OF FREEDOM

The stakes of this reimagining are existential. To insist that Palestinian grief is knowledge, that Muslim memory and ways of knowing hold truth, and that Black, Indigenous, immigrant, and queer children's lives matter beyond metrics is to demand a different kind of public altogether. Such demands are treated as dangerous because they unsettle the foundations of US schooling and society that weaponize neutrality to silence dissent, sanctify nationalism as civic virtue, and render empire as the natural order.

Danger is not impossibility. Histories of refusal remind us otherwise: from Freedom Schools to Zapatista classrooms, from Palestinian refugee camps to the weekend schools and cultural circles of Muslim diasporas. None of these are utopic. They are grounded practices of survival and imagination, born of necessity and sustained by care. The future of education cannot rest on the goodwill of the state or on reforms that preserve its governing logics. The future of education will be built through solidarities that refuse silence,[12] through ways of knowing that cannot be enclosed,[13] and through practices of study that remain collective, relational, and fugitive in character.[14] The future of education is grounded in pedagogies that affirm life in the face of dispossession. The future of education asks us to take memory and survival as the very grounds of renewal.

Living otherwise requires teaching otherwise. To teach otherwise is to resist the erasures of empire but also to tend to what has been broken and to keep alive the meanings that power would have us forget.

CONTINUING TO WORK ON LEARNING AND BUILDING TOGETHER

The work of creating more just and humane forms of learning extends beyond the classroom, inviting us to reflect, listen, and act together in community.

WHAT WE CHOOSE TO KNOW

- What forms of knowledge are honored where you live and work, and whose ways of knowing are left unspoken?
- What would it take to create spaces where all children can speak their histories without fear?

WHAT WE CHOOSE TO REMEMBER

- How can communities make room for grief and remembrance as part of learning, rather than treating them as disruptions?

- How can public spaces such as schools, libraries, and cultural centers honor the losses that shape who we are and help us imagine what might yet be built?

WHAT WE CHOOSE TO BUILD

- What stories shape how you understand justice, care, and responsibility?
- What examples of community learning already exist around you, such as study circles, mutual aid efforts, art collectives, land-based education, or gatherings in faith and friendship?

RESOURCES FOR FURTHER LEARNING

Books

Thea Renda Abu El-Haj, *Unsettled Belonging: Educating Palestinian American Youth After 9/11* (University of Chicago Press, 2015)

Sohail Daulatzai, *Black Star, Crescent Moon: The Muslim International and Black Freedom Beyond America* (University of Minnesota Press, 2012)

Maryam Kashani, *Medina by the Bay: Scenes of Muslim Study and Survival* (Duke University Press, 2023)

Su'ad Abdul Khabeer, *Muslim Cool: Race, Religion, and Hip Hop in the United States* (New York University Press, 2016)

Junaid Rana, *Terrifying Muslims: Race and Labor in the South Asian Diaspora* (Duke University Press, 2011)

Podcasts and Websites

The Art of Knowing Project (www.artofknowingcurriculum.com)

Return of the Mecca (returnofthemecca.com)

Teaching While Muslim (www.teachingwhilemuslim.org)

CHAPTER 9

A MENACE TO SOCIETY

Anti-Trans, Anti-Democratic Education Policy

MOLLIE T. MCQUILLAN
AND KEVIN LAWRENCE HENRY JR.

OUR CONNECTION TO ANTI-TRANS, ANTI-DEMOCRATIC EDUCATION POLICY

We write this chapter as scholars who see the gender-based attacks on public education not just as an abstract policy debate, but as an issue we are deeply connected to as queer scholars specializing in gender, sexuality, race, and the politics of education. Though we came of age in different generations and regions of the United States of America, we are linked by a past that has simultaneously aimed to muzzle, contort, and erase our identities and gender expressions. We have been reminded by leaders, community members, and family that we are seen as less than, deviant, and unworthy of respect, protection, and care. That we should be "normal"—not to walk that way or talk this way or play that sport or love who we love; we've been told that our gender expression might be too conforming to be queer enough or trans enough.[1] We have been told we were abominations.

We are told that somehow we misunderstand the "basic science" of sex and gender, as if our degrees, research, and daily realities are somehow irrelevant. We are told that *silence* about who we are—and what we study—is golden. We share experiences of being rendered invisible in spaces we've helped build, disciplines we've shaped, and communities we've nurtured. These experiences are not isolated. They are part of a pattern that has emerged as politicians narrow the definition of who gets to learn, teach, be seen as fully human, and even exist as an American.

Queer scholars, activists, educators, and allies have always created community, resisted oppression, and demanded justice. We see ourselves as part of that lineage. We aim to not only describe conditions of inequity for LGBTQ+ youth and educators but also to create school conditions where youth and educators can bring their full humanity and where *all* students experience effective learning and healthy development. However, recent education policies have eroded that work by casting trans students as individually deviant and predatory, a symbol of societal moral decline, and a destabilizing threat to exclusionary educational ideals.

Manufacturing fear about trans students allows politicians to use children as a policy "problem" that can be solved through policy erasure.[2] This policy erasure takes the form of invasive government policies to control, surveil, silence, and ban teachers and students. For instance, policymakers have attempted to constrict or have constricted the teaching of inclusive curriculum, the collection of accurate data, the participation of motivated students in athletic activities, and the ability of young people to access their chosen public facilities (e.g., bathrooms).[3]

The focus on trans students is part of a right-wing political strategy aimed at challenging shared beliefs in the inherent humanity of trans people, commitments to equity and diversity, and the value of scientific expertise for educational decision-making. For example, when far-right politicians address issues of trans students, they often attack the science and empirical evidence on conditions supporting healthy development, principles for effective learning, and professional guidelines for inclusion of all students. These inherently anti-democratic attacks exacerbate the harms that trans students experience by situating them as the proverbial bogeymen.[4] Prohibiting trans students from accessing the bathroom of their choice or preventing the use of their preferred pronouns undermines the democratic mission and promise of public schools. Such actions leave students who are exploring different aspects of their identity—and especially transgender students—feeling uncared for and unwelcome.[5]

UNDERSTANDING ANTI-TRANS, ANTI-DEMOCRATIC EDUCATION

In this section, we discuss why democratic public education depends on interrupting threats to the humanity and rights of trans youth. Systems and practices of oppression hollow out and tarnish the meaning of democracy.

Schooling in the United States, of course, has long been shaped by interlocking oppressive systems such as enslavement, patriarchy, cis-heteronormativity, settler colonialism, white supremacy, and class exploitation. These systems of oppression create divisions, vulnerability, and violence. Current attacks on transgender and gender-expansive youth operate through historical practices of exclusion and othering, including legal, cultural, and discursive strategies that normalize and justify erasing the lived experiences of those pushing gender norms.[6]

Legislatures and school boards have passed laws, policies, and other administrative rules that remove protections, restrict supports, and outright criminalize common school practices that allow all children to explore different aspects of their identity, including gender identity and expression. These mandates include restricting access to restrooms of choice, censoring curriculum that addresses the experiences of trans people, and prohibiting teachers from using students' desired pronouns. Together, they contribute to the marking of trans and gender-expansive youth as different or lesser. Even further, they position trans youth as so threatening and predatory that discriminatory practices appear justified.[7] This framing contributes to higher rates of gender-based harassment, violence, and bullying in schools. Anti-trans political rhetoric amplifies fear and moral panic about practices intended to support youth through healthy identity exploration. In employing such rhetoric, policymakers not only create additional obstacles for academic success but also increase suicide risks.

Exclusionary and restrictive laws deepen institutional erasure and educators' fear about supporting students explicitly targeted for erasure. In the process, complex identities and developmental processes become reduced to marginalizing, unidimensional labels. Laws targeting school staff criminalize practices supporting students' ability to safely explore and celebrate multiple dimensions of their identities. Educational laws, policies, and procedures delegitimizing trans identities and other forms of gender nonconformity reframe basic supports that affirm all youth as radical, dangerous threats to parental control over their children and religious rights. Under this pressure, many educational leaders self-censor while community-wide moral panic about school activities intensifies.

Denying students' recognition and belonging has become part and parcel of a larger right-wing movement aimed at replacing diversity, equity, and inclusion with monotony, inequity, and exclusion. Erasing trans people from the curriculum, prohibiting name and gender procedures, restricting access to school activities, and preventing access to facilities of choice creates harm. It normalizes exclusion, delegitimizing identities, and positions trans children as scapegoats for broader societal issues. These are the hallmarks of political hierarchies, oppression, and disenfranchisement that seek to construct trans people as second-class citizens. Further still, the bans and political rhetoric dehumanize trans experiences and needs through these institutional and social "othering" processes. As such, anti-transgender policy initiatives—much like anti-DEI efforts generally—threaten public education's mission by redefining for whom and for what purpose public schools stand.

The framing of trans students follows similar rhetoric about lesbian and gay students in the 1980s[8] and emerges out of Christian nationalist fears about being culturally and demographically replaced.[9] As they do with replacement narratives concerning race and immigration, right-wing politicians use alarmist and anti-science language to frame the inclusion and affirmation of developing students' identities as "radical indoctrination" and a threat to Christian religious freedoms. For instance, at the 2022 Conservative Political Action Conference (CPAC), Donald Trump claimed:

> Across the country we need to implement strict prohibitions on teaching inappropriate racial, sexual, and political material to America's schoolchildren in any form whatsoever. And if federal bureaucrats are going to push this radicalism, we should abolish the Department of Education. We will keep men out of women's sports. . . . No teacher should ever be allowed to teach transgender to our children without parental consent. . . . You can't teach the Bible, but you can teach children that America is evil and that men are able to get pregnant.[10]

In this speech, Trump suggests he will protect conservatives from cultural (read: Eurocentric/white) and religious (read: Christian) displacement by framing inclusive programs and practices as "inappropriate" and "pushing radicalism." He erases trans identities by indicating that trans women who are student-athletes are actually men. He also creates a false, zero-sum narrative between Christian practices and inclusive sexual education, as well as between inclusive teaching practices and parents' rights. Inclusive programs and practices are framed as an attack on traditional values. Similarly, conservative leaders have sensationalized increasing rates of youth identifying as LGBTQ+, which follows the same line of reasoning as racial and immigration replacement theories. This replacement-theory rhetoric has been linked to increases in the number of anti-LGBTQ+ bills.[11]

Despite the extensive evidence about the effectiveness of creating inclusive schools that honor students' identities and cultures, restrictive educational policies reject diversity and inclusion as a legitimate element of public education's mission.[12] Instead, advocates seek to narrow racialized and gendered ideals in public and private educational institutions.[13] Anti-trans advocates frame schools as "battlegrounds" where traditional values have been attacked and intervention is needed to protect white (Christian) children and especially cisgender girls. Trans and other LGBTQ+ youth outside the model of the "ideal" student have been banned, disciplined, and excluded via harsh disciplinary actions.[14] Inclusive practices and ideals are then replaced, constricting access to educational opportunities and limiting what can be known, taught, and dreamed. This policy erasure, and the corresponding anti-trans rhetoric, not only hurts gender-diverse youth but results in the narrowing of all students' ideas about gender possibilities.[15] Furthermore, narrowing what counts as acceptable gender expression affects students and the adults who support them. These adults face increased scrutiny for helping students explore their own identities and for teaching about a diverse, complex world. For example, in Wisconsin, several educators have been fired for attempting to enact inclusive practices, and one teacher was even fired for her decision to have students sing the Miley Cyrus and Dolly Parton song "Rainbowland," which is about broad inclusion and doesn't mention LGBTQ+ identities.[16] When schools can't teach critical thinking, perspective-taking, and respect for diversity, then democratic education itself is undermined.

The dehumanization and erasure of trans identities are now embedded throughout related education-policy initiatives. For instance, the Heritage Foundation, a leading conservative think tank that was a major contributor to Project 2025, urges the adoption and expansion of school-choice policies such as vouchers, charter schools, and homeschooling to fight against "wokeism" and "gender ideology." These subtle forms of anti-trans policy erasure allow caregivers to opt out of the shared responsibility of public education, to build exclusionary communities and reject LGBTQ+ families and students. This process limits robust, democratic curriculum and practices honoring diversity, historical and scientific facts, and difference within our communities.[17]

Conservative reforms thereby undermine the public's responsibility for democratic education by turning access to quality education into a commodity, not a public good. Schools and educational policy become sites for "opting out" of educational justice and expanding markets of exclusion, dispossession, and discrimination. They politicize not just people but the science, curriculum, and empirical scholarly evidence supporting inclusive education. These times are dangerous not only because of harmful laws and policies but also because democracy itself is being distorted and unraveled in troubling ways. These ways include the use of ideology to control teaching and learning, the erasure of trans experiences and communities, and the construction of sameness and exclusion as moral virtues.

REENVISIONING THE PROMISE OF GENDER-INCLUSIVE SCHOOLS

Even in the face of dehumanizing, anti-democratic efforts, schools can be sites of inquiry, belonging, empowerment, and democracy. A strong democratic education requires ensuring that every student has the freedom to learn and thrive by resisting the educational projects attempting to obliterate the Civil Rights Movement's legacy and the ideals embedded in the US Declaration of Independence. Gender-inclusive leaders embed such civil rights and related affirming practices into proposed policies, professional development, administrative procedures, and school routines.[18] These steps include nondiscrimination and bullying policy protections for gender identity and gender expression, clear complaint procedures, and remediation steps so that equal treatment is not just an ideal but a predictable set of practices that keep all students safe and all community members accountable. Gender-inclusive policies and other interventions to reduce bullying and nondiscrimination improve academics, a sense of belonging, social relationships, and health for all students.[19]

In addition to protective policies, gender-inclusive leaders support normalizing multiple aspects of identity development, including gender identity and expression exploration. Building inclusion and respect for diversity into school culture and ethos includes respecting students' pronouns and affirmed names, inclusive facilities and routines, and modeling adult acceptance. Everyday practices can transform learning environments where students celebrate the humanity of all community members regardless of gender identity, which also promotes learning without exclusion and judgment.

Additionally, curriculum is a core part of our reenvisioning. An inclusive curriculum is a pathway to collective possibility and navigating the real complexity of human identities.

A historically accurate, scientifically grounded curriculum can explore the multifaceted, interconnected nature of thought, society, the biological and physical world, and students' lived experiences. An inclusive curriculum centers diverse voices across subject areas and teaches students how to critically evaluate evidence. Our vision includes not only what educators teach (and their professional autonomy to do so) but also critically provokes us to imagine our pluralistic, democratic communities anew. Educators have expressed the need for additional training, time, and protections to implement and make inclusive practices a routine rather than the exception. An inclusive curriculum not only affirms students' experiences and identities; it also prepares students to civically engage in a diverse, complex society. Rather than a niche program, gender-inclusive education is a practical test of whether schools fulfill the democratic promise to value equality in a pluralistic society.

A PATH FORWARD FOR TRANS*FORMING EDUCATION

The scholar and author bell hooks framed public education as a site for both social reproduction and radical possibility. In *Teaching to Transgress*, hooks writes that "[t]he classroom remains the most radical space of possibility in the academy."[20] How can parents, educational leaders, school staff, school board members, and students sustain this "radical space of possibility" while public education faces sustained efforts to control, diminish, segregate, and undermine its democratic mission? In this section, we propose a practical blueprint for how to move the nation and public education forward to realize the reimagining set out above. It is important to acknowledge that community members will need different resources and scaffolding depending upon where they are "starting" in their learning journey about gender diversity.[21] Additionally, central to our blueprint are collective questions that local communities will continue to wrestle with, including who should take up leadership responsibilities and where these conversations should occur.

Democracy rests upon valuing shared civic understandings and also multiple ways of knowing, identifying, and living. Still, educational leaders can collaborate with families and students to give voice to diverse experiences even in small communities. When conditions are safe, students and families can be powerful advocates who can challenge assumptions and motivate action.

Students and community members can be powerful storytellers, social media leaders, and media literacy experts who shape the narratives that support inclusive policies and counter exclusionary proposals at school board meetings. Tools like coalition mapping identify allies across sectors, such as those with mental health organizations, public libraries, racial justice and LGBTQ+ community organizations, public museums, libraries, and social services organizations. Building alliances and coordinated responses can be essential, as other public institutions also face a dangerous rollback of democratic and civil rights.

District and school administrators can also provide sustained, comprehensive, inclusive professional development and procedures for all staff, from bus drivers and librarians to athletic coaches and classroom teachers.[22] Administrators can allocate resources for inclusive facilities, resources, and hiring (and sustaining) gender-expansive staff. Regular school equity audits[23] and community audits[24] can also reveal needs and gaps, though advocates should also recognize that institutions often don't collect data on gender identity. It is important to defend identity data collection as an essential tool for meeting students' learning needs and documenting harms. In the classroom, educators can embed inclusive language, practices, and curriculums across subject areas so affirmation becomes a routine.

Education advocates can also champion nondiscrimination and antibullying protections explicitly including gender identity and expression. Legal and policy efforts should be paired with local organizing, media training, and evidence translation so that courts, legislators, and school boards hear clear, accessible research about the harms and benefits of laws and policies concerning gender. While change may not be immediate, education advocates can strive for a social contract prioritizing a public investment in schools that foster critical thinking, belonging, civic engagement, and a platform for diverse voices. These collective strategies can form the foundation for making gender-inclusive, democratic schools a reality.

CONCLUDING THOUGHTS ABOUT GENDER-INCLUSIVE, DEMOCRATIC EDUCATION

"Democracy," John Dewey remarked, "has to be born anew every generation, and education is its midwife."[25] Educational policy and practice have increasingly restricted the very possibility of public education for trans and gender-expansive students. A growing false, all-or-nothing narrative frames transgender and gender-expansive students as dangerous, as disposable, as disruptive, as "unnatural." It then proposes institutional and social exclusion as a strategy to protect "traditional family values." This political strategy weaponizes public education as an exclusion and erasure mechanism. If education is democracy's midwife, our obligation is not merely to resist these harms but to reimagine what public education can be. Equitable, inclusive, and democratic education insists that every student—not despite their differences but through them—has the right to belong, flourish, and shape our collective future.

CONTINUING THE WORK OF EDUCATIONAL JUSTICE FOR TRANS AND GENDER-EXPANSIVE STUDENTS

EXTENSION QUESTIONS

- What does "parental rights" mean in your local context? Which parents are vocal and have their beliefs about their rights heard? Who is left out? How could that concept be reframed as a shared commitment to every family's well-being?
- How do local school policies, procedures, and practices around pronouns, restrooms, locker rooms, athletics, curriculum, library materials, mental health resources, sexual health, student organizations, and other gendered spaces reflect or erase trans and gender-diverse students' existence? How about cisgender students who do not conform to traditional gender norms?
- Which community voices have been historically excluded from school governance in your local community? How might public education advocates invite and engage with these community members to ensure that their perspectives are embedded into decision-making? Who are the allies, networks, or local organizations you

can partner with to build solidarity across identities and ensure that inclusive practices endure?

- How can social media, local news, and community events be used to amplify the mission of democratic schools? How about positive stories of trans and gender-diverse students thriving in public schools?

EXTENSION ACTIVITIES

- **Coalition-Building Action Plan**

  Map local organizations—LGBTQ+ centers, disability rights advocates, faith groups, youth clubs—and identify joint initiatives (petitions, workshops, public panels) to advance the shared inclusive mission across organizations, including targeting possible policy reforms, practical changes in processes, material resources, community outreach, and education efforts.

- **Mapping Policy "Gray Zones" and School Spaces**

  In small groups, pick one ambiguous policy from your state laws and local district school board policy manual or handbook. These could include multiple directives mentioning gender initiatives. Brainstorm two interpretations of each policy: one restrictive and one expansive when considering the pluralistic US society. Then, conduct a physical school audit looking for gender-inclusive or exclusionary symbols, signs, spaces, and resources. Discuss how each policy interpretation and the physical space shapes staff and students' daily experiences.

CHAPTER 10

THE COMPASS AND THE ALGORITHM

Navigating Uncertainty in the AI Age

VINCENT CHO AND KATIE DAVIS

OUR CONNECTION TO ARTIFICIAL INTELLIGENCE (AI) IN EDUCATION

Writing these lines is not easy. This page has stood mostly blank for weeks. Should we have AI write these words instead? Is AI writing them right now? Or has AI played a more liminal role, dancing on the edges as an editor, a research assistant, or a critical friend? We wonder what you would do if placed in our shoes. Perhaps you are the type to invest days searching for *le mot juste*, believing that the productive toil of finding the right words offers a human, resonant bloom to something precious. Or maybe you have deadlines, plus dishes, plus tennis practice to drive to. In this cost-benefit analysis, toiling at the keyboard without AI seems grim.

But when it comes to AI in education, the issue is not just about writing. It is about big questions, like what makes us human and what about schooling serves those aims. Already, many of the everyday tasks that we ask of students and teachers can be done by AI, with little prompting. Yes, many know that a middling essay can be generated within a few seconds. But fewer know that clicking "deep research" will instead generate an insightful, graduate-level paper (including citations) in five to thirty minutes. Yet fewer educators realize that agentic AI (e.g., Perplexity's Comet, ChatGPT's Operator) can tackle complex, multistep workflows autonomously. At a recent gathering of university faculty from throughout the US, we demonstrated how easily such systems can plug away at all the activities in a master's level course. A sidebar even shares the system's "metacognition" as it assesses situations, backtracks, and decides next steps. Jaws dropped; professors cringed.

For K–12 audiences, imagine a browser window with Google Classroom. A human prompts the agent to "complete the civic action project," then sits back or kills time elsewhere. The AI mouses around, reading the project's instructions, digesting assigned readings and videos. It launches a separate tab, searching the internet for local community issues. It weighs whether to beautify the town's lake or expand access to bike lanes. Deciding upon one, it tackles next steps (e.g., gathering outside research, identifying and emailing local officials) before going back to double-check assignment rubrics, submit a progress report, and so on—all without additional prompting.

From an educator's perspective, this sort of AI use might save a student toil yet also cost them in growth (e.g., academic and nonacademic skills, interpersonal relationships, sense of service and accomplishment). Even the best students, however, might not see that value. What's more, it is hard to tell teachers that the grinds of grading, creating rubrics, and cooling down an angry email are worth doing on one's own. Today, people turn toward AI for everything from health questions to deciding what to wear. With easy answers everywhere, what do we—as individuals and as a society—stand to lose or gain? This problem of convenience versus consequence, human agency versus its abdication, are at the heart of AI's emerging role in education.

UNDERSTANDING AI AND EDUCATION

Technological developments, ranging from the printing press to social media, have altered how people approach learning, friendship, authority, and even self-worth.[1] Even so, the changes wrought by AI today feel faster, less predictable, and more foreboding. This unease has real foundations, and understanding them requires grappling with AI's role in education at multiple levels.

Most immediately for school and district leaders, AI intensifies practical challenges like data privacy and security. Beyond the risk of users divulging sensitive or personal information to AI chatbots, schools already face serious cyberthreats. Districts (e.g., the Los Angeles Unified School District) and educational technology companies (e.g., PowerSchool) have been held ransom by cyberattacks or had their data sold on the dark web,[2] and 82 percent of K–12 schools have experienced some kind of cyberthreat.[3] AI amplifies these risks. It can be weaponized to pose as humans, exploit technological vulnerabilities, and operate at scales and speeds impossible for human attackers.[4]

Already, hacking attacks on Amazon (whose cloud services are often used by districts) have now surged to one billion per day.[5]

Further, there are debates about the future direction of AI and whether it will serve or undermine education's core purposes. Silicon Valley elites advance a utopian vision in which AI systems equal or surpass human-level intelligence (i.e., artificial general intelligence, or AGI) by 2030–2040.[6] Imagine teams of thousands of AI bots working in concert—"machines of loving grace"[7] serving as stewards for the planet and humanity—to solve intractable problems like disease, poverty, and climate change.[8]

Indeed, some have already begun advancing a vision of schools without teachers. Students enrolled in Alpha Schools spend only two hours a day on academics, engaging independently in AI-driven personalized learning.[9] Adult "guides" provide motivation and social support but not instruction.

Yet critics warn that the tech elites' vision masks self-interest, a "techno-chauvinism" that privileges computerization over humans and communities and ignores deeply embedded flaws in AI's ethical reasoning.[10]

At a deeper level, AI poses threats to schools as public institutions essential to democracy. Schools are vital for preparing citizens to engage with ideas, evaluate information, and participate thoughtfully in public life. As AI becomes a conduit for everything from curriculums and lesson planning to tutoring, it is important to question which values and worldviews AI might reinforce or even silence. The leading AI models encode Western epistemologies and are largely trained on data produced in English and shaped by Western, white, and male-dominated institutions.[11] These systems can marginalize Indigenous or other non-Western ways of knowing, while perpetuating racism, sexism, and other patterns of exclusion. For example, AI writing feedback might overlook racist stereotypes underpinning one student's essay while discouraging another student's uses of African American English or critiques of white privilege.

More unsettling, some AI designers may openly encourage biases or misinformation in order to skew or misdirect users' thinking.[12] For example, internal documents at Meta reveal intentionally broad leeway for demeaning people based upon race, as well as for generating false medical information,[13] and Elon Musk has been regularly accused of steering Grok toward racist and antisemitic views.[14] Meanwhile, President Trump recently issued an order to combat "woke AI" and other attempts to make AI more equitable and inclusive.[15] Beyond simply reinforcing ideologies, AI can be used to intentionally fragment or disrupt democracy. AI-generated deepfakes have already begun to pollute elections in the US and around the world.[16] Equally troubling, AI has been found effective at skewing and flipping entrenched political beliefs, both via explicit conversations about politics[17] and through masked biases hidden within systems.[18] Thus, as AI and AI-generated content become more widespread in schools and society, the foundations of informed citizenship come under unprecedented threat.

Most fundamentally, uncertainties abound about AI's future impact on schooling and its purpose. Some industries are already turning to AI for basic tasks (e.g., drafting computer code, customer service), making it harder for college graduates to find entry-level employment.[19]

Predicting impending and large-scale job displacement, AI industry leaders have advocated for universal basic income policies.[20] What becomes of education if it can no longer promise economic gain? Even beyond the economic upheaval, there are unresolved questions about what becomes of schools and students that rely heavily on AI. For example, the ease of AI can dull students' willingness and capacity to engage deeply in learning.[21] If classroom activities serve a role parallel to what physical therapists describe as "time under tension," helping strengthen cognitive muscle, then the convenience of AI may tempt all of us away from those productive toils.[22]

REENVISIONING AI IN EDUCATION

The preceding passages have described only a few of the pressing challenges that AI can present to education and democratic society. We cannot predict what technological advancements lie ahead, only that the AI we have now is the least advanced we will ever have.[23] This makes it important to set our compass, if not with clear destinations, then with some guiding principles.

1. **Remember what's human.** Many traditions emphasize valuing the uniqueness, value, and dignity of others and ourselves. As Zen master Thich Nhat Hanh was known to say, "Be beautiful. Be yourself." As we navigate the AI age, it is important to honor the roles that schools can play in helping young people discover themselves and their world through various disciplines and experiences. When AI adoption prioritizes the convenience of a final product, it risks diminishing authentic expression, exploration, and what makes us most human.

2. **Learning is the fruit of relationship.** In schools, teachers and students alike get to share the amazements of a science lab or the collective grief when the dog at the end of a novel dies. In contrast, when schools replace teachers with AI-driven, "personalized" learning, they confuse individualized efficiency for something far more valuable: a shared love of learning that continually benefits individuals and communities alike.
3. **Preserve human agency.** Early AI conversations emphasized keeping "humans in the loop," with the idea being that people should supervise and evaluate the quality of outputs. Unfortunately, this principle is ill-suited for educational settings. Students often lack the expertise to make quality judgments, and more fundamentally, the final product is only part of the point. The goal is to develop academic and non-academic skills that are important for later success. Moreover, agentic AI systems (the kind that can plow through an online course or civic action project) are explicitly designed to minimize human decision-making and supervision. While useful for many tasks, agentic AI may be inappropriate for educational contexts, where the learning process itself matters most. Similarly, while AI may provide useful feedback to students, its role in such practices should be transparent and not interfere with students genuinely with their own learning.
4. **Enhance, don't replace.** Despite these cautions, there is also room for AI to enhance schooling. For example, AI can improve accessibility, such as by tailoring a textbook and multimedia to accommodate individual students' reading levels and interests.[24] AI could also enhance inclusivity, such as via assistive technologies (e.g., speech recognition, robotics)[25] or real-time language translation for multilingual families.[26] Further, AI can serve as a thought partner, such as when refining lesson plans, managing "bureaucratic nonsense," or smoothing the tone of an email.[27] Parent advocacy might also benefit from AI, such as when attempting to navigate terminology, practices, and rights relating to special education.

A PATH FORWARD FOR AI IN EDUCATION

Before articulating a path forward, let us first look at the example of a different technology: social media. In many ways, social media began as an unfettered experiment, with few guardrails and little debate about foreseeable harms or impact. Rather than protect human well-being and shared truth, the attention economy brought forth by social media was founded on grabbing users' attention and time, such as by exploiting social insecurities, provoking outrage, or intensifying political division.[28] AI may replicate or even intensify these harms, with some users engaging compulsively with chatbots, developing delusions (e.g., "AI psychosis"), and even committing suicide.[29] In this light, the path toward a more balanced relationship with AI requires not only regulations and guardrails but also increased general knowledge and sensemaking about AI.

Unfortunately, the current political climate dims the likelihood of policy-level interventions. Immediately upon taking office in January 2025, the Trump administration revoked Biden-era orders on safety, oversight, and bias prevention, instead making regular moves toward deregulation and industry expansion. This does not mean, however, that targeted regulation is not possible. For example, many states have enacted laws regarding intimate deepfakes, and the US Congress passed similar legislation with bipartisan support in April 2025.[30] One could imagine education policymakers prohibiting harmful practices (e.g., allowing agentic AI to complete student coursework) or establishing transparency requirements regarding teachers' uses of AI. Moreover, there is growing interest in using existing laws to hold AI companies accountable for liability and negligence. This approach is complicated, however, by how courts might interpret the specific technologies and harms in particular cases, as well as whether AI-generated content might qualify as speech under the First Amendment.[31] In education, liability could be easier to establish in cases involving data privacy or discrimination than in cases involving misinformation. Although it's not impossible, AI companies are unlikely to proactively implement guardrails without regulatory pressures.

Setting aside regulatory concerns, there is a more urgent issue: AI is broadly used by educators, students, and parents, but few understand its inherent nature and risks.[32] In this way, ignorance, ambiguity, and overwhelm feed one another. In complex, rapidly evolving contexts, building capacity for distributed sensemaking is not a substitute for action but rather a launchpad for advocacy and adaptive responses to AI as it continues to evolve. In other words, step one is developing individual baseline knowledge, including, but not limited to, current applications of AI (e.g., agentic systems, AI-powered information discovery and decision support tools, generative text and multimedia); the limitations of AI and risks of AI (e.g., "cloning" one's voice or likeness, AI's unethical decision-making); contrasts between AI and other technologies (e.g., traditional search engines); and the underlying biases and environmental concerns associated with AI. This can be done by experimenting directly with AI tools and following the news or podcasts, such as those listed at the end of this chapter. The point is not for individuals to know everything about AI but rather to get used to thinking about what it means to be human and how AI could encroach on experiences or productive toils beneficial to human flourishing.

Step two involves getting together, sharing, and organizing. Individuals need not know everything; that is what the collective is for. A prime example is cultivating communities of practice around AI.[33] In other words, create opportunities for people facing similar challenges to share ideas and troubleshoot together. With AI presenting educators with a tinkerer's bin of dubious parts, pulleys, and promises, teachers need structures in which to puzzle out AI together (e.g., critical friends groups, instructional rounds, team-based cycles of inquiry).[34] Such collective thinking isn't a nicety; it is the heart of adaptation, innovation, and making the collective smarter than the sum of its parts. If, as some reports suggest, teachers are already saving six hours of work per week due to AI, then even modest reinvestments of that time could yield outsized returns.[35]

Indeed, if the advent of AI brings upheaval and uncertainty to education, then connecting multiple people and stakeholder groups with varying experiences, interests, and vantage points reduces that uncertainty. It is the difference between staring in one direction into the fog versus standing on a hill with various eyes looking in many directions. In this way, pooling insights across educators, families, developers, and policymakers makes it possible to envision needs and possibilities when it comes to ethical design and implementation. For example, the National Academy of AI Instruction, a partnership among the American Federation of Teachers (AFT) and major AI companies, promises to give AFT members both training and opportunities to co-develop new teaching practices.[36] For AI companies, this also means both feedback for product development (e.g., use cases, market relevance, ethical priorities and guardrails) and broader market adoption. More locally, district-community AI forums, policy task forces, and community-based design or research partnerships may similarly offer opportunities to pool diverse perspectives and steer AI's future in education.

CONCLUDING THOUGHTS ABOUT AI IN EDUCATION

Sometimes it can feel as if, rather than taking tentative steps, the world has leapt into the AI age at a disorienting pace. In a troubling report, Elizabeth Laird et al. found that students who attended AI-friendly school environments were more likely to also engage in romantic relationships with AI—and that parents often knew little about this potential.[37] The AI world can feel like a runaway train, one focused on profit and dominance over the common good. But just as education itself has never been a lone endeavor, negotiating AI's place in education is also a shared social challenge. It is through community that we can create norms, policies, and AI systems in alignment with deeper needs like authenticity, justice, and connectedness. The guideposts we've offered can help orient us toward conditions that build collective power and agency around AI's evolving role in education and human development.

CONTINUING TO WORK ON AI'S ROLE IN EDUCATION

We are all on different pages when it comes to our understandings and attitudes about AI. Talk to five or more parents, students, or others in your workplace and community—or get them all together. Discuss:

- Where and how is AI showing up in our daily work or lives, both officially and unofficially (e.g., grading, assistive technologies, plagiarism, translation)?
- What unsettles us about AI right now? What excites us?
- What about school or work feels especially human and important to maintain that way?

ADDITIONAL RESOURCES

The AI Con: How to Fight Big Tech's Hype and Create the Future We Want—Exposing Surveillance Capitalism and Artificial Intelligence Myths in Information Technology Today (book) by Emily M. Bender and Alex Hanna. Sharp critique of AI hype and the marketing of AI as destiny. Explains how claims about "intelligent" systems often obscure social harms and corporate interests and suggests ways to challenge dominant assumptions and narratives.

Hard Fork (podcast) by *The New York Times*. Accessible and entertaining coverage about technology and the future, including frequent discussions of AI. Available as an audio podcast or via YouTube.

Your Undivided Attention (podcast) by the Center for Humane Technology. Podcast aiming to deepen conversations about ensuring that technologies serve, rather than harm, society, democracy, and human relationships.

CHAPTER 11

WE'VE BEEN HERE BEFORE

Reflections on Being a Black Woman Leader in Education Today

MARCELLE M. HADDIX

MY CONNECTION TO THE THREATS ON BLACK WOMEN IN LEADERSHIP

Each morning, I begin my day with reflection and journaling. This daily ritual is in many ways my morning prayer time—a way that I center and ground myself before I meet the day that awaits. I am leading a school of education during challenging times, but I am not alone. Truly, anyone in a leadership role during this moment is facing challenges that can at times feel unprecedented and even insurmountable, but *we've been here before.*

I learned the importance of daily ritual from the women in my family and in my community. My mother is on the prayer line every morning before the sun rises, praying with other women from her church community. I remember a particular Monday morning over a year ago now when she joined the prayer line, and this time, she was the focus of the prayers of her sister circle because her mother, my grandmother, was transitioning. Later that morning, she would get the call that Grandma had passed, and she immediately began the preparations to lay her to rest.

That same week, I had my campus interview for the dean of the school of education at the University of Wisconsin–Madison. I knew, as I gave my talk to the school community that I would soon lead, that my grandma was with me. That I was standing in her legacy, that of an early childhood education leader and pioneer in the Milwaukee community. That I was a reflection of her commitment to serve, to advocate, and to lead in crucial times. Knowing this has informed the way I lead as the first Black woman dean of this school of education in times that are fraught and where bold and intentional leadership is required.

What I know well—what my mother and grandmothers have taught me—is that Black women understand the importance of community, service, and activism. Black women know that there is power in collectivity. We know that there is power in the prayer circle. Even in times that feel hopeless and full of despair, we can and will overcome. We will and must continue to do the work, in service and commitment to the past, the present, and for the future. *We've been here before.* This is our legacy.

Now more than ever we need leaders with this understanding and commitment. We need Black women leaders—yet, Black women are consistently challenged, attacked, and forced out of educational spaces. Our legacy is under threat. We face targeted erosion—not just from burnout or bureaucracy but from a coordinated political climate that weaponizes race, gender, and authority against us. Whether it is the erasure of our histories, stories, and identities from curriculums, the surveillance of our teaching, or the targeting of our bodies as "radical" and "dangerous," Black women leaders are consistently framed as too much—too loud, too political, too assertive.

My essay is about the persistent threats to Black women leaders in education. Black women leaders have been singled out, pushed out, and actively targeted—in higher education, in the corporate world, in the media, and in government and public office. There are constant examples of Black women "stepping down" from office or being forced out of positions. The forced silence and absence of Black women leadership is of grave consequence to equity and justice. Though we've been here before, the current moment presents a heightened awareness of the realities Black women have faced and challenged for decades. In this chapter, I emphasize the critical importance and need for Black women's knowledge and experience in addressing the critical issues in education today and for the future. Whether teachers in the K–12 classrooms or presidents of major universities, Black women are painted as both the problem and the solution and, in the end, expendable either way. This essay is about the long line of Black women leaders—before and beside me—who continue to do this work in a system that sees us as threats rather than stewards of progress and change.

UNDERSTANDING THE THREATS FACING BLACK WOMEN LEADERS

"We are the 92 percent."

The phrase "we are the 92 percent" is a nod to the long-standing civic engagement and voting patterns of Black women, especially in recent presidential elections. It has become shorthand for the political reliability and power of Black women voters, especially in contrast to other demographic groups whose voting patterns are more divided. The phrase is used as a statement of pride and solidarity, emphasizing that Black women show up to vote for progress, often without seeing proportional returns in political recognition or policy benefits. It ties into larger conversations about how Black women are the backbone of democracy, though often underrepresented in leadership and decision-making roles within the political system. Yet Black women continue to show up. At the ballot box, we lead with clarity and courage. In the 2024 election, Black women voted for a future that included healthcare, reproductive justice, racial equity, and education reform. We are the moral compass of this democracy—and still we are doubted, questioned, and even blamed.

This disregard and dismissal of Black women's social, political, and economic contributions are evident in recent impacts on Black women in the workforce and in leadership in higher education. In the first six months of 2025, over three hundred thousand Black women left or were forced out of the US workforce.[1] In April alone, more than one hundred thousand Black women lost jobs, the highest decline among any demographic group.[2] This surge in job losses happened during policy rollbacks in diversity, equity, and inclusion across federal and corporate sectors, as well as sweeping federal workforce reductions. These swift changes disproportionately impact Black women. The impact erodes economic stability for Black women, affects households and communities, and weakens the nation's economy.

Black women in high-level executive positions, from CEOs to college presidents, are facing great pressure. Many are being forced out or are making the decision to resign to preserve their sense of self, their health, and their well-being. The removal of Black women presidents at colleges and universities across the nation highlights persistent challenges related to systemic racism, sexism, and institutional resistance to transformative leadership.[3] Despite their qualifications and dedication, Black women in these roles face heightened scrutiny, lack of support, and undue pressure to navigate environments steeped in traditional power structures. Their departures—often abrupt and surrounded by controversy—reflect deeper issues within academia's governance, where efforts to promote equity and inclusion are frequently met with pushback. The pattern of their departures, whether framed as resignations or administrative shifts, reveals the persistent challenges of navigating leadership in environments resistant to systemic change. The dwindling presence of Black women in these roles represents a broader institutional failure to protect and sustain diverse leadership, ultimately stalling efforts toward a more inclusive and just academic landscape.[4]

Historically, Black women have long been seen as dangerous in educational spaces. After *Brown v. Board of Education* (1954), thousands of Black educators were pushed out of their positions as schools desegregated, while white teachers kept their jobs. Black educators—often more credentialed and more connected to their communities—were let go en masse. Still today, the national teacher force reflects mostly white women teachers, despite significant efforts and strides in recruiting, preparing, and retaining teachers of color, and, in particular, Black teachers. Widespread teacher shortages across the nation persist, while the mainstream narrative on the role and work of teachers is discouraging and even depressing, significantly impacting our work to encourage the next generation to enter the profession. Many, including myself, have written about the absence and pushing out of teachers of color in K–12 schools—this is not a new phenomenon. Yet the current attacks on education signal renewed energy to dismantle efforts toward diverse representation in the teaching force that will have long-standing effects on the educational experiences and outcomes for generations.

REENVISIONING THE FUTURE FOR BLACK WOMEN LEADERS

All that you touch, you change.

—OCTAVIA BUTLER[5]

What is dangerous about the current moment is that Black women are devalued and positioned as threats to democracy. In fact, Black women have consistently advocated and fought for this democracy and for a world that is equitable and inclusive for all. Black women's leadership threatens efforts designed to maintain the status quo and even create autocratic power structures and systems.

To imagine a future world where Black women's leadership is valued and lifted up, I turn to speculative writer and author Octavia Butler. Butler was a visionary who crafted futures where Black women not only survive but lead, shape, and reimagine entire worlds. Her work was revolutionary and even prophetic in that she envisioned a future where Black women were not marginalized by society's dominant narratives of who and what they should and could be. For Butler, Black women were central to society's survival and transformation.

An analysis of Black women characters in Butler's fiction reveals a vision for Black women leaders that looks beyond traditional forms of leadership. Rather than prioritizing control, hierarchy, and individualism, her model is rooted in adaptability, empathy, historical memory, and spiritual imagination. In a world increasingly marked by uncertainty, Butler's characterization of Black womanhood reminds us that the most revolutionary act may be to imagine otherwise—to insist on futures where care is more powerful than defeat, where survival is not just individual but communal, and where leadership emerges not from dominance, but from the courage to change and be changed.

In the worlds constructed in Butler's fiction, Black women are not merely surviving—they are redefining what it means to thrive. Inspired by Butler's vision, I imagine a future where Black women's leadership is sought after, valued, and sustained. I see a future where Black women's leadership is recognized as the exemplary model for transformative and equitable outcomes in education, and this recognition is reflected in policy, research, and practice.

This vision is realized in the recruitment, hiring, and retention of Black women in teaching, in educational administration, and in leadership. This requires a reenvisioning of our collective understandings of what it means to teach and to lead and of our visual understandings of who can teach and lead. The rapid surge of job losses for Black women is dangerous, and the impacts are far-reaching. I imagine a future state where there would be collective outrage and activism that challenges the possibility of such erasure and disposal of Black women's contributions.

Social movements that mobilize us to support, uplift, and amplify Black women with hashtags like #BlackWomenLead, #CiteBlackWomen, and #ProtectBlackWomen will be catalysts for real change and material investment in Black girls' and women's futures. Black women's leadership will not be narrowly defined or understood as "diversity work" but recognized as equitable and just leadership that affects positive change and outcomes for everyone.

A PATH FORWARD FOR BLACK WOMEN'S LEADERSHIP

"Black women will save us."

I titled this chapter "we've been here before" because this experience for Black women is not new. Black women continue to lead for equity and justice and to protect this democracy yet are repeatedly undermined and under supported in the work. Black women consistently are the 92 percent. Yet, in moments of crisis, we look to Black women to save us. We depend on the labor, dedication, and service of Black women leaders to guide us through challenging times—though we are reluctant to credit or even acknowledge them.

In addressing the threats to Black women's leadership, I offer a few ideas for paths forward. First, we must reframe how we think about Black women's leadership. Black women's leadership is strategic, decisive, forward thinking, innovative, and transformative. Can we imagine a table where every seat is determined and occupied by a Black women leader? Where Black women's voices and perspectives are not merely at the table but critical and integral to decision-making and solution-generating in research, policy, and practice? Black women are not merely servant leaders—their leadership should not only be viewed as "in addition to" or as secondary to others. Yes, Black women are committed to service and to "giving back," but this is more pointedly in service to and in the best interest of those in our communities. Black women's knowledge is valuable, and their experiences frame the ways we think about education, freedom, and liberation. Black women's knowledge is knowledge in and of itself—it does not need the validation or approval of others. Black women's leadership *is* leadership.

The second idea is that we name Black women, read and listen to Black women, and cite Black women. Black women's work remains systematically overlooked, undercited, and underappreciated in scholarly and professional contexts. To cite Black women is not just an act of acknowledgment; it is a critical practice of justice, accuracy, and intellectual integrity. A path forward advocates the necessity of citing Black women scholars and researchers—not as a token gesture but as a foundational practice that challenges dominant epistemologies, disrupts historical erasure, and enriches our collective understanding of the world. Citing Black women is an ethical responsibility and underscores that Black women's contributions and leadership are central and not peripheral to the work necessary to affecting equitable and just change. This practice also redefines our understanding of who can be a knowledge producer, who can be considered an "expert," and who we value as leaders. In school curricula, a path forward integrates Black women's scholarship and literature as foundational and not supplementary.

Black women leaders should not be alone in this work. We cannot expect Black women to save us in this moment. As a third idea, a path forward must include a radical shift in how we think about allyship and accountability. This shift can only happen with dialogue and a willingness to talk about hard truths—and, in particular, the social and political relationships between Black and white women. Allyship between Black women and white women is often complicated by historical truths that are frequently overlooked—one of which is the fact that many white women were also enslavers.[6] While feminist movements have long called for solidarity among women, this call often fails to account for the deep racial hierarchies that shaped early American society, where white women not only benefited from but also actively participated in the institution of slavery. This legacy complicates efforts toward allyship, demanding that white women confront their historical roles in systems of racial oppression rather than positioning themselves solely as victims of patriarchy. True solidarity requires not just shared gender identity but also an honest reckoning with this past and a commitment to dismantling the intersecting forces of racism and sexism that continue to shape women's experiences differently.

CONCLUDING THOUGHTS ABOUT THE THREATS TO BLACK WOMEN LEADERS

The threats to Black women's leadership in education are not new—*we've been here before*. And in these times, Black women's leadership has remained unmoved and unshaken. Our response to dangerous times in leadership is not to panic but to provide steady leadership that is decisive and transparent.

To truly understand the threat facing Black women leaders, we must reckon with the fact that their erasure is not incidental—it is systemic. It is the result of a political and cultural refusal to see Black women as worthy of authority, protection, or power.

We are not the threat. We are, in fact, the compass for democracy. Protecting Black women's leadership is protecting democracy. Elevating and believing in Black women's leadership is supporting democracy and education for everyone.

I conclude this chapter by returning to what I learned from my mother and my grandmothers—my exemplars of Black women's leadership. Their leadership was and is imbued with love and care for and with community. It is anchored in commitment and persistence toward change and transformation. It takes risks and is strategic. It is connected to the past, inspired by the present, and shaping the future. We've been here before. And we will be here after.

CONTINUING THE WORK ON SUPPORTING BLACK WOMEN LEADERSHIP

I offer the following questions for reflection and to encourage critical dialogue:

- Are we ready to embrace a future shaped by Black women's vision and leadership?
- What will it take for us to honor and listen to Black women's voices on educational freedom and liberation?
- What are specific steps we can take to protect and serve Black women's vision and leadership?

In addition to engaging with the questions above, here are three immediate actions we can all take toward honoring Black women's leadership in these times:

- **Uplift Black women.** Take stock of who is sitting at your leadership tables. Engage in an honest assessment of your hiring and retention practices.
- **Read more Black women.** To understand this current moment and to imagine different futures, I lean into speculative and science fiction by Black women writers like Octavia Butler, Toni Morrison,

N. K. Jemisin, and Jesmyn Ward. Some additional books to begin further exploration on Black women's leadership in higher education:

Crystal E. Chambers, ed., *Black Women's Pathways to Executive Academic Leadership: Lessons from Lived Experiences* (Universal Write Publications, 2023)

Stephanie Y. Evans, Stephanie Shonekan, and Stephanie G. Adams, eds., *Dear Department Chair: Letters from Black Women Leaders to the Next Generation* (Wayne State University Press, 2023)

Mary Dana Hinton, *Leading from the Margins: College Leadership from Unexpected Places* (Johns Hopkins University Press, 2024)

Menah Pratt-Clarke and Johanna B. Maes, eds., *Journeys of Social Justice: Women of Color Presidents in the Academy* (Peter Lang, 2017)

Beverly Daniel Tatum, *Peril and Promise: College Leadership in Turbulent Times* (Basic Books, 2025)

- **Listen to Black women.** Black women's voices and perspectives are well represented on social media, podcasts, and other media forms. Follow and engage in conversations and dialogues led by Black women.

SECTION 3

LEANING INTO PROBLEMS

CHAPTER 12

LEARNING FOR A NEW WORLD

Reimagining Education for a More Just and Sustainable Future

PEDRO A. NOGUERA

MY CONNECTION TO LEARNING IN A TIME OF THREAT AND UNCERTAINTY

We are living in dangerous and uncertain times. Indicators that our existence on this planet is precarious and endangered are everywhere and increasingly undeniable. However, often, those currently privileged with safety and wealth (myself included), fool ourselves into believing that the status quo will hold, that everything will be alright, and if not, the experts will save us. I increasingly believe that this is the height of delusional thinking.

The uncertainty of our times compels me to ask: How do I/we prepare for an uncertain future? For me, as the father of five and grandfather of five, this is not an abstract or a hypothetical question. I contemplate the answer with utmost seriousness and sobriety. As has been true throughout my life, I am drawn to the power of education for answers.

The uncertain and precarious nature of our times became vividly clear to me most recently when fire struck Los Angeles in January 2025. As I watched the images of fires burning out of control in the Pacific Palisades and Altadena on the television, just a few miles from our home, and then heard that evacuations had been ordered nearby, I was faced with these questions: What are your priorities? What really matters most at a moment of impending catastrophe? While my family avoided the destruction that thousands of others experienced, as we prepared for a possible evacuation and loaded our car with little more than a few suitcases and our most important documents, I experienced a moment of profound clarity: The status quo is not sustainable.

Even though the environmental threats around me have subsided for the moment, I am keenly aware that other threats that are just as catastrophic are present if we choose to acknowledge them. A few months after the fire, ICE (Immigration and Customs Enforcement) descended on LA, rounding up workers at Home Depot and car washes, separating families, and sparking a resistance from those who refused to passively accept the mass deportations. Once again, I was reminded that at any moment calamity can strike. Unlike the fires, this threat was man-made and political but no less devastating to those impacted.

Every day the news is filled with reports of natural disasters, violence from war, mass shootings and crime, and relentless human suffering in various corners of the world. As I drive through the streets of LA on a beautiful sunny day, I am constantly reminded that suffering is all around me if I choose to bear witness. I see individuals, some of whom are plagued with severe mental illness or suffering from substance abuse, finding a way to survive on the sidewalks. The lucky ones have tents; others lay or sit in a hapless and helpless stupor in public spaces, serving as a constant and blatant reminder that all is not well. Rather than reacting with outrage to the suffering and neglect, I drive by. Like so many others, I have *learned* to accept the unacceptable.

UNDERSTANDING THE PURPOSE OF EDUCATION AMIDST THREAT AND UNCERTAINTY

But what if we *learned* to respond differently to suffering, to threats or impending danger? What if rather than tuning out by distracting ourselves, or looking to the tech titans or our political leaders for solutions, we looked to each other for answers? What if we tried to harness the *power of learning* to find solutions to the problems we face? What if we could unleash the ingenuity of millions of ordinary people by engaging them to devise solutions and creative responses to the challenges we face, and thereby revive a sense of hope about our future?

I know that throughout human history all societies have relied upon education to address two essential needs: (1) to ensure that each generation is equipped with the knowledge and skills needed to participate in society as it is, as workers and citizen members; and (2) to address the challenges confronting society that have stymied and plagued previous generations but demand answers and new approaches.

After working in the field of education for over forty years, I have concluded that we spend too much time on the first purpose of education and too little on the second. Of course, I am not the only one who has come to this conclusion. My friend and colleague, the late Sir Ken Robinson, and his wife, Kate, offered these thoughts on the purpose of education: When students "leave school to engage in the economic, cultural, social, and personal challenges they will inevitably face in their lives," they will need competencies such as "curiosity, creativity, criticism, communication, collaboration, compassion, composure, and citizenship."[1]

Throughout much of my career I have worked with schools and policymakers to ensure that all students receive an adequate education. As I near retirement, I am compelled to acknowledge that this objective remains largely unattained. In part, our shortcomings can be explained by the complexity and difficulty involved with ensuring that *all students* have access to an education that allows them to acquire the skills needed to function and, hopefully, thrive in society. Extreme inequality and growing political hostility toward immigrants and the poor have allowed social barriers and a lack of resources to limit opportunity and the development of human potential. I have learned from my own experience that our difficulty in ensuring that all students have access to basic educational opportunities stems not from a lack of knowledge about how to prepare all students but rather a lack of commitment and will. The situation has worsened under the current administration.

Having worked at several elite universities, I know from experience that the US has little difficulty ensuring that a small percentage of students receive a "good" education and advanced training, making it possible for them to earn high salaries in professional and managerial roles. In our highly stratified, capitalist society, many forces—affluent parents, politicians, universities, and corporations—work to ensure that inequality in outcomes is maintained and privilege is reproduced across generations.

Historically, pursuit of the second goal of education has been left to a small number of experts and scholars, most of whom work at a small number of research universities and laboratories. These institutions have been generously funded to make it possible for the most highly trained scholars, many of whom are from other nations, to engage in research aimed at finding solutions to the problems facing society. This approach has produced advances in scientific knowledge and technological innovation, but because it is often influenced by the relentless pursuit of profit, it has done little to reduce the threats posed by the looming problems and challenges facing humanity.

As a child, I came of age at a time when the threat of nuclear or chemical war seemed imminent. While today children are no longer asked to hide under their desks (as we were) in case of a nuclear attack, they now perform even more draconian drills when they are instructed to run, hide, or fight to prepare for the possibility of a mass shooter.[2] Today's children grow up with an awareness that environmental disasters and the collapse of ecosystems caused by climate change are likely; that pervasive hunger, violence, and disease will continue to afflict large segments of the world's population; and that global migrations of people from poor to rich nations are inevitable, and many are learning that those who cross our borders in pursuit of a better life should be feared and treated with hostility and force.

Given the state of this nation and the world, we cannot afford to leave the search for solutions to "experts." Often, the work of such experts is guided and funded by powerful elites who are primarily concerned with innovations that lead to more power and profit. In fact, several signs suggest that technological innovations like artificial intelligence may hasten rather than delay the pace of calamity.

Albert Einstein warned about the dilemma he saw coming as other scientists drew upon his theories and ideas to construct weapons of mass destruction that they soon realized would be difficult to control. He warned: "You cannot solve problems with the same thinking that created them."[3] Einstein's suspicion of expert knowledge is echoed by Yuval Noah Harari, the author of the highly acclaimed book *Sapiens* (2015). In his latest book, *Nexus*, he writes:

> Instead of a march of progress, the history of human information networks is a tightrope walk trying to balance truth with order. [. . .] Contrary to what the mission statements of corporations like Google and Facebook imply, simply increasing the speed and efficiency of our information technology doesn't necessarily make the world a better place. It only makes the need to balance truth and order more urgent.[4]

How do we find a balance between truth and order in a world where facts and information are deliberately distorted and frequently undermined by various sources of misinformation? It is increasingly clear that powerful tech companies are more concerned with using algorithms to generate viewers than to disseminate accurate information. Furthermore, the election of Donald Trump appears to have significantly undermined our ability to rely upon "experts." Elite research universities and scientists that study global problems like climate change and vaccines now find themselves threatened with significant reductions in funding by an administration that regards them and their work as an ideological enemy. International students and scholars, who have made up a disproportionately large portion of the researchers in STEM fields, are now threatened with the prospect that their studies will no longer be funded, and they may not even be allowed to enter the country.

Under the guise of ending "woke" education, the Trump administration has banned books it deems insufficiently patriotic and begun dismantling the US Department of Education. It has not offered a new plan for K–12 education. Instead, it has reduced federal spending on programs that serve children in poverty, recent immigrants, and those with learning disabilities, and it has all but eliminated the Institute of Education Sciences, which historically monitored the academic performance of students in the US.[5]

REENVISIONING LEARNING AS PROBLEM-POSING EDUCATION

Despite the actions of the Trump administration, I remain hopeful about the potential of using education to advance equity and justice. My hope rests on my awareness that there are millions of educators and even a larger number of students and parents who refuse to give up on the dream that education can be used to transform lives. For that reason, I am unwilling to give in to pessimism and despair, or to foist responsibility for fixing the mess we are in onto the next generation.

Instead, the question I ponder is: What can I do to help? I am a pragmatist, no longer easily swayed by idealistic rhetoric about the possibilities for change. I know enough about the state of the world to know that the problems we face are complex and won't be fixed by simple solutions. I also know that disaster can strike at any time, in any part of the world. Finding a balance between pragmatism and optimism has led me to seek out wisdom and guidance from a variety of sources. Most recently, I discovered the work of philosopher Bayo Akomolafe. He warns us about the seduction of wishful thinking that leads us to believe that experts and technology will save us from calamity. He writes: "The easier thing to say about the goings-on today would be to gently insist that everything is going to be alright, eventually. The difficult thing to say (though still as convenient, perhaps) might be to insist that everything is going to get a lot worse now—but by 'doing your part' we can slowly resist the convergence of forces making our planet even more dangerous, lining the skies with the fonts of war."[6]

What is "our part" in resisting the forces that make our world more dangerous? As an educator, my search for a course of action has led me to ask: What if we encouraged schools to make space in the curriculum for students to learn to grapple with the challenges facing the world? What if schools deliberately cultivated the creativity, critical thinking, and imagination of students so that they generated new ways of thinking about the problems we face? These questions are even more pertinent given the rapid pace of technological change. Social media has already radically transformed the lives of many children, adding to the anxiety and depression that many experience regularly, and artificial intelligence will soon make several types of jobs obsolete.[7] Philosopher Eckhart Tolle warns us that AI is being designed to weaken our ability to be creative because it robs us of our ability to focus and concentrate.[8] Education must contend with these threats if it is to serve as a resource we can turn to for solutions. Beyond providing students with the skills needed to find jobs and adapt to change, it must also provide opportunities for students to become actively engaged in grappling with the challenges facing the world they will inherit.

What should this form of learning entail and how should the challenges facing the world today be engaged? The good news is that there are already schools where the type of learning I will describe is already occurring. Before describing some of these, I will start by briefly describing the theory behind this kind of educational practice.

In his first major book, *The Pedagogy of the Oppressed*, Brazilian educator Paulo Freire made the case for what he called "problem-posing education," a form of learning premised on dialogue that he envisioned as an alternative to "banking education."[9] Freire suggested that whereas traditional education is premised on the notion that the teacher possesses the knowledge and must *deposit* it into the brains of students, problem-posing education is rooted in dialogue with a goal of activating critical agency. According to Freire, "Education either functions as an instrument which is used to facilitate the integration of the younger generation into the logic of the present system and therefore bring about conformity to it, or it becomes the practice of freedom, the means by which men and women deal critically and creatively with reality and discover how to participate in the transformation of their world."[10]

To engage students in addressing the problems facing the world, dialogue is essential.

While teachers have responsibility for guiding their students in analyzing and addressing challenges that concern and affect them, they don't have the answers to these problems. Finding ways to act locally on issues like climate change, poverty, or violence is particularly important for the actions proposed to have a tangible impact. To maximize impact, teachers and students must cooperate in analyzing, strategizing, and acting on a plan they create together. They must tap into their critical-thinking, problem-solving skills, and creativity to devise a course of action. Critical agency, and by that I mean collective action taken to address a problem that is based upon critical thinking and analysis (Freire called this *praxis*), is essential because it makes it possible for what is learned to be applied in ways that have an impact on a particular problem in concrete ways.

A PATH FORWARD

In various parts of the world there are projects that exemplify the ways learning can be used to address societal problems. A few examples include a school in Los Angeles that utilizes meditation to address trauma and improve the mental health of teenage mothers; a community program in Oakland that engages young men in efforts to counter violence and promote community development; an initiative in the Central Valley of California that engages parents, teachers, and students in harvesting surplus food to counter hunger among farmworkers. The good news is that there are many, many more.

CONCLUDING THOUGHTS ON AN URGENT CALL TO SLOW DOWN

The challenge is to spread the word about the importance of this type of learning now. Given the scale of the threats facing the world, projects such as the ones described here need to be launched on a massive scale. Unleashing the power of learning by proliferating projects like these may seem insufficient considering the immense, complex, and intractable problems facing the world today. But I take heed of the words of Bayo Akomolafe, who advises us: "The time is urgent, so we must slow down." We must slow down to think, plan, and act together, wherever we are, on whatever issue we feel compelled to confront.

As we come to terms with the toll that plundering resources without regard to the environmental and human costs, and as we acknowledge that the current path of development is unsustainable, the question we must then each ask of ourselves is this: What can we do to alter the direction and help in transforming conditions? How each of us answers that question may well determine what kind of future the youth will inherit.

CONTINUING THE WORK

Here are three examples of the type of engaged, problem-posing learning that I believe holds the potential to transform our collective helplessness into activities that can generate hope. Read about these examples, discuss them with neighbors, then plan and act together.

- **The Center for Cities + Schools at UC Berkeley:** CC+S engages youth in urban planning to address the challenges facing marginalized urban communities. A look at the CC+S website (https://citiesandschools.berkeley.edu/) shows some of the projects that schools have taken on using the Y-PLAN model in various parts of the world.
- **The Center for the Community School, Nelson Mandela University, South Africa:** https://ccs.mandela.ac.za/.
- **Kia Aroha Campus, Auckland, New Zealand:** Founded by educator Ann Milne in 2002, the school centers the language and culture of Maori and Pasifika (a term used to describe people from the islands of the South Pacific) students it serves. See https://www.kiaaroha.school.nz/the-learning-model.

DISCUSSION QUESTIONS

For teachers: How will your role in the classroom need to change to facilitate the type of learning described in this essay?

For students and teachers: What steps are necessary to address a big problem like poverty or climate change in your community? How will you know if you are having an impact on the problem? What background information will you need to address the problem you would like to focus upon? What skills might be necessary?

For community: What support will schools need to focus on big problems and the type of learning described here? How will schools need to change to facilitate this type of learning?

CHAPTER 13

REENVISIONING POWERFUL LITERACY EDUCATION

NICOLE MIRRA

MY CONNECTION TO LITERACY EDUCATION

As a first-year English language arts teacher at a small high school in Brooklyn, New York, I was assigned all ninth-grade classes. My colleagues shook their heads apologetically—the veterans tended to opt for the upper grades, eager to avoid that squirmy, wild-eyed freshman energy.

But I saw some poetry in the parallel journeys that my students and I were embarking upon—just as they were figuring out high school, I was figuring out teaching. After a bumpy start, I came to the crucial realization that finally allowed us to bond. Rather than fretting so incessantly about every little move *I* was making, I shifted my focus to learning who *my students* were. And I found, of course, that they were hilarious. Curious. Brilliant in forms both evident and subtle.

I kicked myself for not being able to reclaim the precious months that it took to reach that magical point where we came to truly *know* each other—as readers, as writers, and as individuals.

And then, improbably, we were granted more time.

Because of various structural factors, like teacher departures and the consolidation of classrooms (but what I now see as good fortune), I was assigned to teach many of my students again for their sophomore year. As it turned out, I ended up looping with them for almost the entirety of their high school careers. I witnessed them growing up through the prism of our English class—an incredible gift.

In their senior year, when they crowded around me with demands to sign their yearbooks, I had the opportunity to pause and consider what I truly wanted them to remember about our time together. What was it about English class in particular that I hoped could serve them in their lives to come? I ended up telling them that it did not matter to me if, twenty years down the line, they could recall in detail the plot of *Hamlet* or if they remembered not to split infinitives.

Rather, I wanted them to continue to see the power of literacy as a conduit for understanding and bettering themselves, others, and the changing world around them. I wanted them to leverage their reading, writing, listening, and speaking skills to advocate for their communities in the face of injustice and to build more compassionate futures.

Ever since that moment, my career has been animated by the desire to understand how youth, educators, and members of the public think about the purposes of literacy teaching and learning. And increasingly, as I check in with my family members and friends, and as I research literacy instruction throughout the US, I am troubled by what I see as a rejection—sometimes explicit, sometimes implicit—of the powerful, civically engaged vision that energized my students. Literacy education is under threat of being severed from its role as the voice of democratic life because of the rise of a narrowly functional and stubbornly antisocial approach that privileges the mechanics of language and suppresses the civic purpose of it. I frame civics here not as a collection of facts about governmental structures but rather as the practice of learning to live together in a social and political community.

Of course, the purposes of English have always been multiple and contested—there has never been consensus. My teaching days were influenced by the pressures of standardized testing that have been steadily increasing since the 1980s. But today the pressures have multiplied. My niece and nephew tell me that they spend the majority of the time in their middle school English class completing reading comprehension and grammar exercises on their Chromebooks. A friend who teaches in a Pennsylvania suburb shares about the raucous school board meetings in her district during which novels are removed from the approved reading list. Another colleague explains that he is afraid of potential backlash if he allows discussion of any current events in his classes.

Simmering beneath these tensions are these fundamental questions: What is literacy in schools for? Who decides? What could it be?

UNDERSTANDING THE CURRENT STATE OF LITERACY EDUCATION

The education of a society's children reflects its ideological priorities; as a result, those who seek to chart the nation's course seek to influence the practices of its schools.[1] The subject of English language arts has reflected these power plays ever since the founding of public education in the US. In an 1894 meditation on the purpose of English in secondary school, scholar and politician Samuel Thurber declared that its aim should be to "bring the individual mind into closest possible touch and sympathy with the national mind."[2]

Thurber and other nineteenth-century educational theorists believed that literacy's civic purpose could be activated through a program of study in "great books" and instruction in formal oratory.[3] The discipline was seen as an assimilationist tool for forging a shared cultural heritage around certain Western European authors (think Shakespeare) and establishing a standard for what a "good" reader and writer could do at a time when immigration was diversifying the country. The impacts of this approach to literacy persist today—the most commonly taught novels in today's English classrooms remain nearly identical to those taught decades prior, and recent attempts to broaden the curriculum to better reflect the multifaceted nature of US society have sparked backlash.[4]

The power play over literacy is at work again now as conservative politicians decry what they describe as a "radical left-wing agenda" occurring in K–12 schools and universities.[5] Novels, short stories, and other texts that seek to expose students to diverse characters and experiences are being banned from classrooms and libraries at an unprecedented rate, and the American Library Association has found that the great majority of these censorship campaigns are being driven by a coordinated network of conservative advocacy organizations.[6] A 2023 PEN America report pinpointed the impetus for these attacks, declaring that "overwhelmingly, book bans target books on race or racism or featuring characters of color, as well as books with LGBTQ+ characters."[7] The "agenda" being attacked involves the celebration of diversity and the opportunity for members of historically marginalized communities to tell their American stories.

Under the guise of concerns about the age-appropriateness of complex topics, these efforts represent an increasingly blatant attempt to restrict whose stories—and by extension, which people—matter in this country.[8] Stories are the target of censorship precisely because of their documented impacts on the development of empathy and civic consciousness.[9] Generations of literacy scholars, including myself, have documented how the study of literary texts—both those that reflect our specific identities and experiences, and those that illuminate the lives of others—help students cultivate empathetic connections with neighbors far and wide, as well as commitments to public engagement.[10] Philosopher and educator Maxine Greene saw literature and art as catalysts of "social imagination," allowing us to dream of more creative and compassionate solutions to our thorniest challenges.[11] Banning such texts from the English classroom robs the discipline of its civic purpose.

Indeed, this is in fact the aim of a substantial sector of the educational establishment, even those opposed to book bans: to decouple subjects like English from any connection to social issues at all and concentrate instead on the "basics" of narrow skill-building. A growing number of educators report that their students are not reading novels much, if at all, in class, a trend connected in part to the pressures of preparing for high-stakes standardized tests that privilege the comprehension of informational passages over creative interpretation.[12]

While the utilitarian purposes of literacy are of course critical to the functioning of society, does that represent the entirety of what we want youth to experience in the literacy classroom? In survey after survey, young people are indicating their desire for something more; many report feeling disengaged and adrift in class.[13] They share that what they are learning in their classes does not map on to the complexities and urgent needs of a world on fire beyond the school walls. We owe them—a generation who will bear the consequences of our fractured democracy—a more robust vision of what literacy can offer.

REENVISIONING POWERFUL LITERACY EDUCATION

You think your pain and your heartbreak are unprecedented in the history of the world, but then you read. It was books that taught me that the things that tormented me most were the very things that connected me with all the people who were alive, who had ever been alive.

—JAMES BALDWIN, "The Doom and Glory of Knowing Who You Are," *Life*, May 24, 1963

As I think again of the messages I wrote in my students' yearbooks all those years ago, I can see reflected the age-old purpose of English: to bring the individual mind into sympathy with the national mind. But I urge us to consider that such a joining together should not be done in the vein of Thurber's focus on a shared cultural appreciation of the canon or on today's related crusade to reestablish a mythical, singular (white, male) American identity. Rather, I suggest that such joining should be done in the spirit of James Baldwin: literacy as a project of radical empathy, of connecting not to flatten and assimilate experiences into one American identity but rather to celebrate the strength and ingenuity arising from our diversity in order to build a shared civic future.

English class can be the place to wrestle with the paradoxes that arise from the stark differences amid our common humanity. The emotional bonds that are created when we read and write creative texts can be applied not only to the development of interpersonal empathy but also, when combined with analyses of power and privilege and history, to the development of what I call *critical civic empathy*. Critical civic empathy involves seeking to view the world from alternative perspectives for the purpose of figuring out how people can live together according to values of equity, dignity, and common cause.

This project of instilling civic commitments in youth is often thought to be the domain of social studies classes alone. But I find it important to recognize that English classes are crucial sites of civic education as well. While understanding the arc of history and the architecture of our democratic institutions is key to sustaining public life, so too is the ability to interpret this information through a wider humanistic perspective. This is what English class can do. It can remind us that we should not put our faith in any particular structures but rather in our commitments to each other.

To be clear, enacting such a civically engaged vision of English is not accomplished solely through the study of literature. It involves thinking about the practices of reading, writing, listening, and speaking expansively and creatively—what the affordances of each are in public life and how young people can play with them as they are developing their own understandings of themselves as civic actors. The beauty of English is that literacy skills can be taken up in so many ways. We need not prescribe particular texts for all students to read or particular essays for all students to read. Instead, we could develop common values or thorny social tensions to explore and then let the teachers and students in various communities tackle those in a way that builds upon but also pushes on their own contexts. Digital texts, action projects, community dialogues, all in service of supporting our children to develop agency and compassion in public life—this is what English class can be.

A PATH FORWARD FOR THE LITERACY CLASSROOM

Before tackling the practicalities of how to enact this vision on an everyday basis in the English classroom, we must first consider how to build public will for the paradigm shifts that will be necessary to undergird such changes. As mentioned earlier, support for schools (let alone English classes) as sites of civic learning in any capacity is shaky amid the pressures of college and career readiness. Furthermore, we have witnessed how even when a civic purpose is acknowledged, it often manifests as either bland exhortations for civility or rancorous battles for control over the American story.

The first (and in some ways most difficult) step toward more empathetic civic literacy learning involves vulnerable conversations between families, communities, educators, and the broader public about how we want to live together both in the world as it currently is and in the world as it could be. Do we want democracy to continue to devolve into a winner-take-all competition over scarce resources, or can we find a path toward a more cooperative mindset? Do we want to view our neighbors as strangers or friends? Schools cannot face a rising tide of division alone—we must commit to a more compassionate path in every area of public life.

These conversations can start at the local level—at libraries, at community centers, at places of worship, at our elementary schools. We must take a brave step out of the silos we often find ourselves in and dialogue with each other, reaching outward further and further until we find common ground with people utterly unlike ourselves. Educators and leaders of community organizing groups often have the training to facilitate these conversations. And, crucially, shared texts can serve as a touchstone for these dialogues. Novels, memoirs, short stories, or informational texts can all help provide language, scenarios, and a shared frame of reference to facilitate vulnerable conversation.

As ties of solidarity form, communities can break down the boundaries that are often erected between schools and their surroundings. The doors must be thrown open so that educators can share how school policies and curricula are developed and communities can enter into partnerships with teachers to foster opportunities for meaningful civic literacy projects with students. When educators and community members communicate, they can not only avoid battles over books at school board meetings but also organize together against structural forces standing in the way of authentic civic literacy learning such as onerous standardized testing mandates and inadequate funding. They can put pressure on their elected officials to act in support of the shared commitments they develop with and for their young people.

Just as these efforts will take patience, commitment, and time, so will the process of changing instruction and curriculum inside of individual English classrooms. Moving beyond the same canonical texts is already a struggle; helping teachers approach their subject as one in which young people learn how to use their literacy skills to practice democracy will require wholesale shifts in how we prepare and support teachers across their careers. But again, teachers and teacher educators need not do this work alone; when we take collective responsibility for the education of our youth, we can create opportunities for the expertise of many to contribute.

CONCLUDING THOUGHTS ABOUT THE POWER OF LITERACY

Lately, whenever I gather together with people I care about—family, friends, colleagues—I take advantage of a break in the conversation to pose a specific question. I say, "Think about a young person in your life that you love. Imagine they are graduating from high school and are about to embark on whatever their next step might be. What are the most important things you hope they have learned through their K–12 education?" I have asked this question dozens of times, and no matter who I am speaking with, I invariably receive in return some variation of the same response. People tell me that they want the young people they love to be able to think critically and adapt to a world that is constantly changing. They want them to love themselves and love learning. And they want them to be able to get along with and respect all different kinds of people.

This makes me think about my yearbook message again. And it makes me think about democracy. School is where we place our greatest hopes for our children and our society.

Language is how we express those hopes into being. Literacy classes are uniquely positioned to support young people in figuring out what we might build together, acting as a base camp from which they can set out to imagine new civic futures.

CONTINUING TO WORK ON REENVISIONING POWERFUL LITERACY EDUCATION

QUESTIONS TO SPARK DIALOGUE

- Consider the question from this chapter that I shared with my family and friends: Think about a young person in your life that you love. Imagine they are graduating from high school and are about to embark on whatever their next step might be. What are the most important things you hope they have learned through their K–12 education?
- What do you remember about your experiences in English class? What was most meaningful to you? How do you use your reading, writing, listening, and speaking skills today to engage in public life?
- Imagine that all the class sets of books in your local high school disappeared. What sorts of activities, assignments, or projects—beyond reading classic literature—do you think would be meaningful and useful for students?
- Think about the range of individuals, groups, and organizations in your community who do powerful literacy work outside of schools. What kinds of partnerships could you imagine between these folks and educators? What sorts of opportunities might be made available for young people?

RESOURCES

The Better Arguments Project, Aspen Institute, https://www.aspeninstitute.org/the-better-arguments-project/

Carol D. Lee, Na'ilah Suad Nasir, and Mary Helen Immordino-Yang, *Civic Reasoning and Discourse Across the Curriculum: Disciplinary Practitioner*

Reports, National Academy of Education, 2024, https://naeducation.org/wp-content/uploads/2025/03/NAEd-CivicReasoningDiscourse-Intro.pdf

National Council of Teachers of English, *Reading, Writing, and Raising Voices: The Centrality of Literacy to Civic Education*, 2022, https://ncte.org. CIVICS-GUIDE-11.2.pdf

Writing Our Future, National Writing Project, https://writingourfuture.nwp.org/

CHAPTER 14

POLITICAL EDUCATION, REPRESSION, AND THE PURPOSES OF LEARNING

SHIRIN VOSSOUGHI

MY CONNECTION TO POLITICAL EDUCATION AND THE THREAT OF REPRESSION

Do the pilots who bomb children have children? This was a question asked by a child in Gaza and shared with the world by the UK Palestine Trauma Centre in the summer of 2025. I have been thinking about this child since I first read the question. Maybe they thought the answer must be no. How could someone who has felt the tender depth of parental love do to others' children what they cannot fathom done to their own? Perhaps they also grappled with the meaning of a world where some pilots tuck their children to bed at night with silly stories and drop bombs on other families by day. Maybe they wondered, as many of my students do, about how these pilots (and soldiers, state officials, CEOs, journalists, university administrators . . .) became capable of such unfathomable harm. What did they learn to extinguish in order to see the children of Gaza as non-children?

I sense a kinship with this child when I remember first learning about a thing called bombs. My home country, Iran, was at war with Iraq for the first eight years of my life. We were living in the United States, yet our frequent calls with family brought the language of *bomb shelters* and *missiles* and *teenagers given keys to heaven as they were sent to the front* into our home. I must have been a teenager myself when I learned that while the US and its allies were supporting Iraq, several countries—including the one where we now lived—were financing both sides. Maybe my father decided I was old enough to wrestle with that truth as the US went to war with Iraq when I was eleven. I imagine he grappled, as many caregivers and educators do, with when and how to discuss the extent of such cruelty with children.

I was teaching high school in New York when the US initiated another war on Iraq in 2003 and the military came to recruit our predominantly Black and Brown students. The officer arrived at our classroom with two screens—one for the slides he used for his presentation and another that replayed the image of the Twin Towers falling over and over again. The best I knew how to do as a baby educator was sit in a circle on the carpet with my students afterwards and debrief. This was the time of Abu Ghraib and "shock and awe," images I carried with me to and from work each day, holding back tears on the train when a few moments of calm allowed the reality of what was being done to our people to rush into my mind. I was called into the principal's office later that day after two of my students asked the recruiters visiting another of their classes how they felt about bombing innocent people. This would be the first of many times I would encounter students' honest questions and reasoned dissent blamed on educators willing to discuss the world's truths with young people.

Today I work on a campus where student protests against a genocide funded in our names have been met with intense repression, and where our capacity to teach with integrity is increasingly threatened.

UNDERSTANDING POLITICAL EDUCATION THROUGH THREE QUESTIONS

These stories reflect several questions I see as essential to resisting the intensified authoritarianism of our times, understanding how we got here, and building alternative educational systems rooted in collective well-being. First, are our visions of educational equity and racial justice national or global? I remember processing my experience of the recruiters that day with older (mostly White) teachers at our school, some of whom reminded me that the military was a primary avenue of opportunity for our kids. These tensions around narrow educational pathways flattening the space for global analysis and ethical meaning making have replayed in different versions over time: through discussions of equity in STEM education that do or do not address the ethical and epistemic complexities and harms of STEM knowledge production;[1] through equity efforts that emphasize upward mobility (for some) and deemphasize the ways students navigate the demands for cultural and political assimilation entangled with success in schooling and professional life;[2] and through the 2024 presidential election, when the Democratic Party sold a largely unsubstantive vision of representational politics alongside overt financial and political support for the genocide of Palestinians. The repression of radically internationalist visions among Black, Brown, and Native movements in the 1960s and 1970s in service of a more reformist national agenda find their apex in Kamala Harris's speech at the 2024 Democratic National Convention, where she promised that the US would maintain "the strongest, most lethal fighting force in the world." The crowd in the convention center cheered in response.

The question of nationalism can be framed another way: *Which children are ours? Who counts as children?* And *What of their mothers and fathers, their elders and neighbors?* Maya Mikdashi argues that the emphasis on the death toll among "womenandchildren"[3] in Gaza feeds the racialized presumption of danger and guilt among Palestinian men and boys while painting women and children as passive victims.[4] In *Perfect Victims and the Politics of Appeal*, Mohammed El-Kurd rejects such narrativized victimhood and the need for Palestinians to prove their humanity to deserve to live.[5] These attunements to language and power take shape across racialized and gendered bodies and forge solidarities that our young people are eager to grapple with. And the extent of today's repression can be seen in part as a reaction to the ongoing sustenance of the internationalist, anti-imperialist traditions we have inherited.[6]

Second, how do we define the purposes of education? Students are often given the narrowest reason for learning in school: Education is important for getting a job. This "why" is reflected in the routine reinforcement of compliance, docility, and putting your head down and doing your work. Critical thinking and dissent are often punished, from students being disciplined for asking their real questions to the kid who does worse on a bubble test because they can see how multiple answers could be true depending on the perspective.

And, yet, there are other educational purposes and lifeways, many of which live in the classrooms of educators working to build another way, and in families and communities who dream beyond survival. I often think about how my father, a lifelong anti-imperialist, navigated the stories I was receiving in public school in the 1980s under President Reagan.

When my own daughter went to school, and I felt the tension between refuting some of the messages they were receiving and not wanting them to distrust everything they were learning, I realized that I couldn't remember a single time when my father countered my textbooks. Instead, he chose to tell me a different set of stories.

This leads to a third question: If we understand the need for global visions of educational justice, and for wider and deeper purposes of learning, what are the forms of political education we need in these times? While all education is already political in that power and ideology routinely shapes the content, processes, and goals of learning (whether we are aware of it or not), this question asks us to reenvision learning as intentionally engaging with these histories and relations of power and with what it means to live ethically in and with the world. As the Trump administration (and the bipartisan leaders acquiescing to his policies) rapidly police critical discourse, there is a risk that our political struggles will be limited to fighting for the space to critique, or to recover what is being lost, rather than continuing to imagine and grow the possible.

REENVISIONING POLITICAL EDUCATION

Changing education changes the world. This truth is continuously revealed through the fears of the powerful and their repressive tactics (book bans, anti-trans and anti–critical race theory laws, the suspension and expulsion of student protesters), and through the ways children enveloped in life-giving education go on to move and shape society. A public education responsible for a global vision of collective well-being must be truth-seeking, supporting students to work out their real questions and ideas and wrestle with complexity.[7] A truth-seeking education means that *we don't hit one another to solve our problems* while *our country bombs other countries* won't fly. It means that the histories and continuities of the United States as a settler-colonial and imperialist society, the weight of these systems for various communities, and for the values embedded in the subjects we study, will be a central focus of inquiry and reimagination.[8]

Such a vision of political education understands family knowledges, languages, stories, and connections to place as powerful resources for learning. Schools will be re-rooted in the purposes of learning developed with families and community members through iterative processes of co-design that have been shown to strengthen educational self-determination.[9] Families will be able to spend substantive time in schools, and educators recruited from the communities they serve will spend substantive time with families. Multilingual education will be routine, supporting children to learn in their home languages and deepen relationships with the multiple ways of knowing they carry.[10] Such a change is itself a radical act of reconnecting with the world and raising children rooted in their full humanity.

Given the imperative for human communities to learn to engage in ethical deliberation and decision-making with the natural world, learning will also be reimagined as a routinely outdoor activity that is deeply connected with place.[11] A powerful example of such reimagination can be seen in the Learning in Places Project, a collaborative network of educators, families, and community partners working to cultivate equitable, culturally thriving, socio-ecological systems learning and ethical decision-making through transdisciplinary field-based science education. Carefully designed outdoor learning reconnects students and educators with the histories and futures of our places, with our responsibilities to Indigenous communities and their sovereignty both locally and globally, with our sense of wonder and awe, and with family knowledges and communal practices of sustainable living and changemaking.[12] Such learning weaves together science, civics, literacy, math, and the arts to engage in transdisciplinary investigations driven by fundamental questions of ethical life. The books students read and the writers, scientists, social scientists, and artists they learn from are drawn from a wide range of local and global perspectives, including regions bearing the greatest weight of climate change with important leadership and knowledge to share about what it means to adapt and live well with the natural world and with one another.[13]

Ethical and developmentally attuned practices of political education also require supporting educators to avoid "pedagogies of despair" (a phrase I first learned from high school teacher Tiffany Childress Price) and guide students to attune to the brutal and beautiful aspects of the world in ways that nourish possibility and well-being. This includes confronting the lived realities of oppression in ways that push beyond singular adult heroes toward everyday and intergenerational efforts to make change and sustain life. Nourishing forms of political education also model an ethic of revision and loving critique around texts and ideas. Such ways of knowing can reimagine the tendencies toward binaristic reasoning (agree or disagree) common in schools and the conditions they create for cancel culture and other forms of lateral violence common within many activist spaces.[14] An ethic of revision also invites students to consider the ongoing decisions we make as readers and writers as consequential to the stories we are inheriting and creating. The role of the arts will be central to a political education that sustains children's relationships with play, beauty, and imagination; provides resources for healing; and nurtures the spirit.[15] Imagine the world generations raised up through these forms of learning would embody and help to create.

A PATH FORWARD FOR POLITICAL EDUCATION

Enacting such a vision requires a radical transformation of educational values and new structures of learning for educators, administrators, leaders, and policymakers.[16] The learning environments through which these decision-makers are currently trained often belie the knowledges and ways of seeing children and families that are necessary for building another way. Critical histories of schooling, its deep entanglements with coloniality and assimilation, and communal efforts to enact educational self-determination would provide foundational knowledge both for those making decisions that impact the majority of children of color who attend America's public schools and for those serving children from dominant backgrounds who need support to grow beyond stories of supremacy.[17] Such knowledge would necessarily include an expansive view of human learning that rejects carceral ideologies and recognizes the brilliance of young people and the conditions that support its blooming.[18]

Such a vision requires resourcing schools and districts to develop structures for deep reflection, family engagement, and ongoing learning as a routine part of educators' work. Educators would also have opportunities to continue learning about the edges of their disciplinary fields in ways that shape both what they teach and how they attune to the details of students' sensemaking as tied to these edges.[19] Teachers invested in liberatory possibilities often find ourselves reaching for pedagogies we may never have experienced in school. Learning environments that support educators to experience such possibility and wrestle with the layered paradigm shifts, identity work, and forms of ethical development involved in educational transformation are therefore key.[20]

The question of resources must also address what we will divest from in order to invest in life. Calls for divesting from the state of Israel raise broader questions around how we can redirect ethical divestments from genocide, militarism, environmental degradation, policing, and incarceration. A key lesson of the COVID-19 pandemic involved the radical shifts in policy that became possible when necessary—the ways the state stepped in to provide basic income for working families, or the ways educational institutions suspended standardized tests as gatekeeping mechanisms. Today many of these shifts have been reversed, and the budgets for ICE and the military have multiplied. Educational decision-making that is responsible to the world would consider how the United States is a global outlier across multiple indicators: our military budgets and incarceration rates, our school shootings and gun violence, the costs of higher education and healthcare, our physical and mental isolation and unhealth. The energy dedicated to repression and to spinning the narratives that uphold such a status quo is a direct reflection of the power of social movements and principled leaders to demand that we re-channel our resources toward collective healing and thriving.

CONCLUDING THOUGHTS ON THE ETHICS AND PURPOSES OF LEARNING

In the summer of 2025, Yazan Danis, a Palestinian graduate of Aston University in Birmingham, England, dedicated his degree to Hind Rajab, a five-year-old girl who was executed by the Israeli military in the Gaza Strip alongside the paramedics who arrived to rescue her following the killing of six members of her family. In his graduation speech, Danis shared:

> Education can be just as destructive as ignorance. . . . Our education only holds meaning if we apply it with conscience, passion, and responsibility. You see, the creative designer who used their imagination to build a weapon, a skilled engineer who used their precision to bring it to life, a well-dressed politician who vetoed every resolution that could have ended the killing, a respected editor who used their headlines to hide the reality of children under the rubble, you will find many of them holding degrees and even honorary doctorates. Education gives them the power, but it never gave them the most basic and the most important thing, which is the humanity we owe to one another.[21]

While the event's livestream was cut as Danis began to speak about Palestine, a video of his speech was shared on social media. "Whatever path you take from here remember this," Danis concluded, "you will make a difference whether you mean it to or not. . . . We don't have to drop the bomb to be part of the destruction; we just have to stay silent. So use your education, use your voice, and never accept normal when normal is built on injustice."

Danis confirms what I have learned from years of working with young people: Many are willing to speak as he does, and fewer are willing to become the person who cuts the livestream, the editor who hides the story, the ICE agent who separates families, the pilot who bombs children and their loved ones. What kinds of learning environments would build societies where no one would be willing to engage in such acts? Where gentleness felt more natural than cruelty? Where questions like *Do the pilots who bomb children have children* would become a "distant memory and cautionary tale"?[22]

CONTINUING THE WORK ON POLITICAL EDUCATION

- What memories do you hold about the people and places that taught you how to think about the world?
- What do you and the people you work closely with see/dream as the purposes of education?
- How do your everyday practices of teaching and learning reflect these purposes?
- Where does nationalism show up in your context? How can the frameworks of equity and justice enacted in your setting reflect global solidarities and visions?
- How do you navigate pedagogies of despair and reach for nourishing forms of political education? How can we support students' real questions and ideas in ways that nurture collective well-being?
- What relationships do you see between your work and the futures you are helping shape?

RESOURCES FOR FURTHER STUDY

J. Anderson et al., "Agency and Resilience in the Face of Challenge as Civic Action: Lessons Learned from Across Ethnic Communities," *Educating for Civic Reasoning and Discourse* (2021): 157–243

Mohammed El-Kurd, *Perfect Victims and the Politics of Appeal* (Haymarket Books, 2025)

Adom Getachew, "The New Black Internationalism," *Dissent* (Fall 2021)

Ann M. Ishimaru, *Just Schools: Building Equitable Collaborations with Families and Communities* (Teachers College Press, 2019)

Learning in Places website: learninginplaces.org

Shirin Vossoughi, Ananda Marin, and Megan Bang, "Toward Just and Sustainable Futures: Human Learning and Relationality Within Socio-Ecological Systems," *Review of Research in Education* 47, no. 1 (2023): 218–73

CHAPTER 15

LEARNING ALONGSIDE CREATIVE ARTISTS

Improvised Music as a Process of Storying Relations

ANANDA MARIN, LINDSAY LINDBERG, AND SHIVANI DAVÉ

OUR CONNECTION TO IMPROVISED MUSIC AND THE THREAT OF RUPTURING AND FORGETTING KINSHIP RELATIONS

Šikaakwa, the city we now call Chicago, is the ancestral territory of many Indigenous peoples, including the Three Fires Peoples, the Miami, Ho-Chunk, Menominee, Sac, Fox, Kickapoo, and Illinois Nations. Chicago has been a gathering place for multiple communities since time immemorial, and those intertribal gatherings continue today.[1] Chicago is a place of music, known for blues and jazz—traditions deeply shaped through sounds carried across the Atlantic by Indigenous peoples of Africa.[2] Chicago's history as a highly segregated city shapes the music, the culture, and the media that emerge from the city and the stories told about and within this urban forest.

Moment to Moment is a collective of artists, including two percussionists, a bassist, a visual artist, and a vocalist—all based in Chicago. This collective has made music and community together for several decades. More recently, these artists have participated with us in a research project exploring the role of collaboration and improvisation in education. Ananda has been engaging in regular Zoom conversations with the group since 2021, and during this period she has travelled to Chicago three times to attend Moment to Moment performances. Lindsay was present for two of these concerts and Shivani one. Participating as audience members, educators, and researchers has shaped our connections with one another and our visions for what is pedagogically possible.

While writing this, members of the federal government were actively attempting to deploy the National Guard to Chicago. These actions, founded on false claims of Chicago as "the most dangerous city in the world,"[3] are brought to life by discursively organizing fears and inaccurately ascribing crime and violent behavior to the diversity of peoples living, teaching, learning, and gathering in urban areas.[4] Gatherings that bring together intergenerational groups of people are routinely positioned as threatening. While these politics may feel new, our ancestors tell stories of how participating in educational practices, brought to life through communal gatherings like dancing and musicking, have been and often continue to be criminalized.[5]

In the United States, the military has played a significant role in schooling as a project of "civilizing" and assimilating Native Americans and preparing African Americans for "subservient domestic and field labor."[6] These projects removed young people from their families, disrupting communal ties. We continue to live with the threat of schooling being and becoming places for rupturing kinship relationships and places for forgetting the multiple histories that are shaping present-day conditions. Designing conditions and spaces for public education that re-member relations (i.e., heal and recover kinship with people, practices, and places that have been dismembered by colonialism) while also reaching for collective thriving can be dangerous.[7] The practices of creative musicians, and in particular members of "free jazz" communities, who collectively improvise—navigate spaces that are not yet known in order to build musical worlds that "uplift humanity and enhance cultural understanding"—can provide examples of how *to story* the diversity of the relations we live within.[8]

Like drums, strings, fabric, and paint brushes, *storytelling is technology*. Although the word "technology" is often used in reference to the digital or mechanical, the Greek root word, *tekhnē*, means art or skill, as well as a "system or method for making or doing."[9] The Proto-Indo-European root word, *teks*, means "to weave." In the context of improvised music, we might understand technology to mean an artistic method for making or weaving sounds to accomplish desired goals. Technologies come to be through relations between the natural world and cultural worlds.[10] Their continued use and existence depend on systems of relations. How we use these technologies, when we use them, where we use them, and toward what ends matters. Storying possible worlds through music has long been a role that artists have played in society. Amplifying and recounting the voices and stories of improvisational musicians in Chicago is one step in a broader process of reimaging education.

UNDERSTANDING IMPROVISED MUSIC AS STORYING RELATIONS

Almost every week we encounter a story about an educator either being silenced or fired for discussing diverse ways of knowing, being, and doing in the world—particularly in relation to cultural practices from communities who have historically been marginalized. Many of these stories begin with a complaint, often brought by a learner or caretaker, who asserts that having to bring multiple perspectives alongside their own feels threatening to their dignity and safety as a person. They experience dissonance as harm and embrace the view that dignity is a commodity and therefore should only be bestowed on some. These complainants seem to believe it is possible to experience dignity without conferring respect and reverence on the personhood of others.[11]

If the pedagogical expectation is to only develop contexts for exploring what we individually know and have experienced, then the opportunity to collectively improvise—or intently searching for ways to contribute to the whole—is reduced. The moment to moment of collectively improvising, moments that stretch across time and generations, requires developing the capacity to simultaneously sit with experiences that are dissonant and reach toward resonance. As Ajay Heble and Jesse Stewart remind us, jazz festivals and public performances "can provide meaningful opportunities to recast the histories, identities, and epistemologies of diverse (and often marginalized) peoples, to stage diversity, and to promote counternarratives that invite and enable an enlargement of the base of valued knowledges."[12]

Performance spaces where people can witness the activity of collectively improvising—a kind of call and response to the diversity of sounds that are in the making—provide opportunities to listen for the story of sound and to wonder about the shape of the next possible moment alongside others.

Through our conversations with the artists and recording Moment to Moment's performances, we witnessed how the artists shared and added to each other's stories to see connections and possibilities for learning. The artists put forth the idea that learning and creating with and through improvisation is enabled by affective technologies—emotional experiences that have been in use for centuries. They also described these affective technologies as integral to enriching their shared experience and understanding themselves as artists and in relation to others.

Over the course of decades, the five artists participating in this study have worked deeply together, sharing stages, and recording studios around the world. They approach each reunion with curiosity. The expectation is that each of them has continued to develop through their interactions and experiences in the time they've been apart. They understand that their musical collaborations are grounded in their lived relations (affective, embodied, sonic, etc.) and that the how and what of musicking together shapes what they can learn from each other and build together when collaborating. These relationships and improvisations play out over decades. This in some ways parallels the improvisational dynamics of the performance, and in other senses makes possible the dynamics of the improvisational performance. Building on these musings, one of the percussionists offered the following:

> There's this constant coming together, going apart, coming together, going apart. That's very unlike what you have in a formal learning school, right? Where it's concentrated, you're together for an intense period, and then you never see each other again ever (laughs).
>
> All the relationships I've had with different musicians is that we come together. It's very intensive. You go deep, if you're fortunate enough to have a substantial time together like a long tour or recording session. And then you go away and a year, two years, three years can go by before you even see each other and meet again. And in that time, there's gestation, there's personal growth, there's personal new experiences that everyone has—musical and otherwise. And that makes what Z [the vocalist in the group] was saying about the kind of trust and that kind of openness to one another that enhances it every time. You know, the first time I play with somebody is great. The tenth time I play with somebody, it's amazing.

This percussionist is describing a relational practice of routinely coming together and apart to engage in creative processes. This practice stretches across time and space, as well as cultural, material, and natural worlds, and generates opportunities for learning together.

REENVISIONING PUBLIC EDUCATION THROUGH THE LENS OF IMPROVISED MUSIC AND PUBLIC PERFORMANCES

Public education, or education for the people, lives within communal gatherings where the goal is to understand what it means to be a human being in relation to other beings. Jazz performances and festivals often provide a space for engaging in this kind of labor.[13] Witnessing a diverse group engaging in the creative activity of improvising can provide a window into how people learn from and teach each other in the moment to moment of interaction. This space is educative in as much as both the performers and audience members can closely attend, observe, and attune to each other—listening for, watching for, feeling for, caring for—in order to create something that is more than the self. In these spaces, people take on the roles of storyteller (e.g., performer, teacher) and storylistener (e.g., audience member, learner).[14]

We invite you to consider what this looks like in practice by imagining that you are an audience member. It's June 2023, the temperature is hovering near eighty-five degrees, and you are sitting in a sunken garden with about seventy other people, waiting for the concert to begin. The artists move in a single file line, much like a processional, ringing bells carried in their hands. You understand this as the artists preparing themselves for the work they are about to collectively take part in and as a call to collectively attend. Each of the artists moves to their respective instruments. You hear a drum beat and the peal of bells. Z, a vocalist, hums in resonant tones, selecting sheaths of fabric from materials set on her table. She carefully lifts a fabric collage—twelve inches square—layered with images of the performers' ancestors, important locations, and intricate patterns. She slowly walks toward you and presents this fabric square, wordlessly inviting you to hold, witness, and pass the piece of art to the person beside you—to actively participate in this work of world-building, to bear witness to the ancestors and energy that has influenced the ongoing performance. After sixty minutes the group closes their set. Above the hush you hear bird songs and wind dancing across the leaves. Three minutes go by before an audience member says, "Thank you." This is followed by clapping from the audience, recognizing the transition in activity. H, one of the percussionists, speaks to his daughter in the audience, saying, "Are you going to say something, Ananda? If I can put you on the spot, maybe you could describe a little bit of what we've been doing over here." Ananda steps forward toward the performers, laughing softly at her father's request.

> "Thank you. My name is Ananda Marin. H is my father," she says, smiling at her father behind her. "And he's always trying to get me in front of a microphone! I'm a professor at UCLA in the Department of Education. I'm trained as a learning scientist and spend most of my time thinking about how people develop across their lifespan, how we teach and learn, and how we create learning environments in expansive ways so we can reach our full human potential. I truly believe that we have a lot to learn from artists and to learn from those that engage in the practice of improvisation and collaboration so that we can design teaching and learning spaces that allow us to be the best possible humans that we can be."

To understand education as a project of learning what it means to be a human being in relation to other beings in the world requires collectively improvising.

A PATH FORWARD WITH AFFECTIVE TECHNOLOGIES

Improvised music, specifically free jazz, and creative music, can sound unfamiliar to those who have not regularly participated in such communities. Rather than the familiar organization of a theme, chorus, and hook that many have come to expect from popular music, creative or improvised music often involves periods of time in which musicians are playing together and seem to be *searching* for something—perhaps a particular sound, a collective experience of agreement, or an experience with spirit. The process of *searching while performing* mirrored the musicians' conversations about their work together. During these meetings, they didn't rehearse for upcoming performances; instead, they shared personal stories—windows into the motivations, values, experiences, and ethical commitments that drive their artistry. In this space, they began to name the multiple kinds of technologies that are necessary for learning and communal thriving. The following composite is from a conversation in 2021 and illuminates ethical commitments held by the artists, foregrounding their understanding of and commitment to affective technologies.

Maybe we're not the dominant life force, on Earth or in the galaxy. I mean, how could we be, when there's a pandemic that's going throughout the world that's just about shut everything down. Our life here on Earth is affected drastically by climate change, but nature still goes on, you know? She regenerates herself and continues, she adapts.

History has shown us that dominance has never been the surviving thing. But we haven't learned that lesson. . . .

I think humans have shown that what has dominated us has been our ignorance and our refusal to use certain other higher technologies. Love is one of them, and compassion is one of them, tolerance, loving kindness. Tolerance, it's really a technology. You know? It's technology just like discovering electricity or something like that.

Z was speaking earlier about those divine attributes and qualities. Those are technologies that we have to learn to apply. And if we don't, we get the opposite results. I mean, compassion's not just some little, tiny slogan, you know? Loving kindness is not just a slogan. Or respecting nature. I mean, we have to develop a technology to respect our surroundings. And not just with machines, but we have to develop technologies of these qualities, attributes, that some histories have shown us that they do work. And we know, without a doubt, what happens when we institute the opposites. We're living it. You know?

We have to be more than what we perceive being a human is. We have to be more than that now. We perceived ourselves for so long, from such a limited perspective, limited place. . . . I feel we have to find out what's more than being a human—what is more than being what we have known a human to be? And humans haven't been around that long. So, maybe we're still at the beginning, you know?

Affective technologies like kindness, love, compassion, wonder, and curiosity are in part what drive us to learn. They connect us to relational systems—cultural, social, ecological, technological—that we seek to understand and become a part of.

Building connections between artists and educators, as this project has over the last four years, will continue to be an essential way to support dialogue about the role of relationality and improvisation in teaching/learning across and within educational contexts. Understanding the foundational role of affective technologies for the development of trust, the continuation of collaborations, and the deepening of relationships, can widen our visions of learning. We have begun this process by facilitating teacher-researcher focus groups, watching video clips of the three performances, reflecting on our observations of the performers' collaborations, and reenvisioning pedagogical practices for our own classrooms.

CONCLUDING THOUGHTS ON AFFECTIVE TECHNOLOGIES AND COLLECTIVE IMPROVISATION

Like the classroom, public performances can be an inclusive space for democratic public education—a form of education where both the teachers (musicians) and students (audience), learn together through affective forms of communication. The winter solstice has long been a time of reflection and pause, as the light and darkness are balanced in equilibrium, awaiting the changing of the seasons. Thirty-four years into a yearly performance and celebration of light in the darkness, in December 2024, these five artists gathered in Chicago, along with other artists, to perform together. Surrounded by instruments, paintings, and an eager audience, they waded into the unknown of this collaborative concert. In relation to improvised sounds of percussionists, a bassist, a saxophonist, and vocalist, L, a visual artist and performer, painted "Peace Now" in sharp, bold lettering on a canvas during the performance. Her painting was in response to world events and a call to building a more just future, one that recognizes the harms humans have committed. Acknowledging them, rather than forgetting them. In this hope for a more just future, affective technologies play a crucial role in helping us to recognize and acknowledge our responsibilities, re-member our relations, and build worlds for collective thriving.

Our collaboration with improvisational artists has led us to remember the importance of "higher technologies"—love, compassion, kindness—what we have referred to throughout this essay as affective technologies. The affective technologies associated with musicking and the creative arts more generally can play an important role in both imagining elsewheres and creating mini-utopias in the moment to moment of activity. These mini-utopias may be experienced as we gather, coming together, and apart, and together again. How we carry the memories of these gatherings with us and build upon them matters for ourselves, our ancestors, and our descendants (present, past, and future).

CONTINUING THE WORK ON AFFECTIVE TECHNOLOGIES AND COLLECTIVE IMPROVISATION

The reflections offered here were developed in conversation with multiple people, instruments, technologies, and texts (some of which are included in the endnotes). We close by offering the following questions for dialogue:

- What role can the arts play in building contexts to meaningfully explore what it means to be a human being?
- What role should the creative arts and improvisation play in our processes for designing curriculum and teaching/learning contexts?
- How can we draw on affective technologies to design educational systems that are grounded in relationality, creativity, and meaningful embodied practices?
- As educators, how do we prepare to engage in the work of collectively improvising?
- What role can the arts play in dreaming new futures?

CHAPTER 16

THEORIZING BACK

Reenvisioning Schools as Sites for Democratizing World-Building

MIGUEL CASAR

MY CONNECTION TO THEORIZING BACK

School began to reveal itself, therefore,
as a child's game that one could not win.

—JAMES BALDWIN,
The Fire Next Time, 1963

It's been more than twenty-three years since I was first kicked out of school. I remember bits and pieces: locked in a bathroom as punishment for refusing to dress like Emiliano Zapata; drawing my future self as a heroin addict for an assignment in my religion class; sitting across from a gray-haired man to be "evaluated"; ditching class to read HP Lovecraft (one of Dad's favorites); picking up Chomsky's *La (Des)Educación* for the first time (one of Mom's); growing increasingly troubled with the self-serving and absurd explanations, logics, and stories through which I was being "taught" to make sense of the world.

Almost two decades later, I found myself deep in dialogue with a group of young co-theorizers in a squeaky, stuffy, yet transformative classroom at a juvenile re-entry center in Los Angeles. We called this time together "Free Space"—a space collectively dreamed up to counter the silences and silencing enforced by and through schooling, ask questions relevant to our worlds, and poke holes at what Carizma, a young theorizer, once deemed "non-sense so commonsense it don't make no sense at all." For example, during one dialogue session, we interrogated the labels placed on youth who leave or are pushed out of schools:

> "Gang member. Latino, criminal, bad, don't go to school, poor, have no choices, uneducated . . . All these labels, they take the words away from us," began Francisco.
>
> "It's as if their pity or spite is a clue of what we are supposed to feel or believe, or that they are training us to blame our families, but that's not really how in fact it is," Tino affirmed.
>
> "How you going to call them dropouts, what the fuck did you do to help, what do you really know about their lives? Where is the support? The unsupported youth," CB argued.
>
> "I got one, humans that resist. Because we're humans, we have emotions and resist," Francisco suggested.[1]

Like me, these youth were forced to navigate worlds incommensurable with the stories and theories that were thrust upon them, including in school. They, too, had been punished and expelled. They had spent years in the back of a classroom or cell accumulating urgent and relevant questions about their worlds, questions where the place or space wasn't curious enough to listen, let alone germinate the power behind such questions.

Unlike me, most of them did not have the layers of unjustly accumulated capital that afforded me the privilege to rebel, make mistakes, move to "another school," and, eventually, land in a classroom where I was encouraged, not punished, for pushing back. That classroom where I first lived education as a practice of freedom.[2]

Today, as a young scholar navigating the politics (and consequences) of truth-telling within contexts committed to lies, a month away from having my first child, I reflect on the growing imperative to reconsider our institutions of "education" and their role in fighting what I consider to be a vortex of mutually compounding threats: (1) a disintegration of the relationships, practices, and institutions—albeit flawed—through which we can democratically govern and determine our futures; (2) rapidly mutating forms of accumulation, exploitation, and dispossession; and (3) a growing disjuncture between the theories and stories through which we relate to the world, the spaces and places where these stories are produced and circulated, and the realities in which we live.

As I grapple with these threats and their relationship to our systems and practices of education, I am haunted by multiple incommensurable truths: I believe in the liberatory possibilities of public schools. But I also feel a deep sense of solidarity with those subjected in public schools to endless hours of, at best, miseducation and, at worst, a barrage of violence toward their ways of knowing and being. Thus, I stand alert to the ways in which "public" education continues to be chartered toward oppressive aims and remain committed to honoring the struggles of communities who have fought for their right to education, sovereignty, and self-determination—including those that have reclaimed theory as a way forward, reimagining its purpose, practice, and meaning of theory anew.

UNDERSTANDING WHO THEORIZES AND WHY IT MATTERS

The civilization they were talking about, these theoreticians,
was evidently theirs; they owned it; they were human,
fully human, bashing, sticking, thrusting,
killing . . .

they said. What you are is a woman. Possibly not human
at all, certainly defective.
Now be quiet while we go on telling the Story of the Ascent of
Man the Hero.

—URSULA LE GUIN, 1986[3]

Theory is often understood to be the realm of those "who know"—those credentialed to explain the lives of others. As Cameroonian historian Achille Mbembe describes, theory has been the name of the West's attempt at domesticating contingency and distinguishing the theorizers from the "rest"—the theorized.[4] Over-theorizing the "other," a phenomenon plagued with voyeurism, dehumanization, and gross misrepresentation, often benefits those who "theorize." In the words of Toni Morrison, "Definitions belong to the definers—not the defined," a process crucial to the maldistribution of symbolic power and, with it, the right to world-building.[5]

State-sanctioned schools have historically played a central role in advancing and legitimizing the stories of the "definers." Through "teaching" the "official curriculum"[6]—the official story through which we are to "understand" the world—"educational" systems play a foundational role in normalizing, justifying, and exacerbating a host of oppressive projects (e.g., racial capitalism, settler colonialism, patriarchy, ableism, and carceral geographies).[7] Moreover, by assaulting marginalized people's ways of being (ontology), their knowledge and their ways of knowing (epistemology), and their values (axiology), schools tend to advance what Italian theorist Antonio Gramsci termed *hegemony*, a form of domination that operates by securing consent rather than relying solely on coercion or force.

REENVISIONING SCHOOLS AS SITES FOR THEORIZING AND WORLD-BUILDING

For when grief took to the roads
The people set out and arrived
And married new land and water
To grow their words again

—PABLO NERUDA, "The Word"

"Theory" isn't just an intellectual pursuit—it is woven
within kinetics, spiritual presence and emotion,
it is contextual and relational. . . . Most importantly,
"theory" isn't just for academics; it is for everyone. . . .
"Theory" within this context is generated from the
ground up and its power stems from its living
resonance within individuals and collectives.

—LEANNE BETASAMOSAKE SIMPSON[8]

I believe in the power of theory. But not in theory as it is normally practiced—a top-down, externally produced, capital "T" theory that severs people from the creation and sustenance of the stories through which they relate to and create their worlds. Instead, I believe in an alternative theorizing that is held together in relationships and gains power as it meaningfully characterizes and connects us to our present and to each other. Such an approach to theory gives us, in the words of Tuhiwai Smith, space to plan, strategize, and take greater control over our resistances.[9] I believe this understanding of theory pulses at the heart of a democratizing educational project. As la Paperson[10] reminds us, within the colonizing school there also exists a decolonizing education, a desire for other futures, a multiplicity of decolonizing dreamers who can wreck, scavenge, retool, and reassemble the colonizing space into decolonizing contraptions.[11]

To these purposes, steeped in long-standing traditions of struggle—including lineages that have pushed back against the ways "knowledge" production has been used to oppress—I propose theorizing back.[12] Theorizing back is a process that invites people who have been impacted by structures of injustice to use social theory as a collective tool for understanding and reimagining the world and our role within it. Theorizing back challenges the silencing and violence that robs those most marginalized from the right to world-build.

In our case, theorizing back (TB) was inspired by our elders and teachers but ultimately emerged organically as the youth and I theorized together and then reflected and revised our shared practice. Thus, TB is not a ready-made curriculum but stems from a profound trust in, and commitment to, people's ontological vocation (i.e., a fundamental desire) to be and to set each other free. TB is a methodology that reclaims the right to the word and the world and that, while seemingly abstract, is connected to everyday practices that can radically transform the ways we work alongside young people and each other. TB is shaped by a community praxis—reflection and action used to transform one's world.

My co-theorizers and I recognize that the practice of TB will differ across place and time. Yet, wherever and whenever TB is enacted, it should embody four transformative principles.

TB must be critical, interrogating how power structures actively theorize the world. This means rejecting the notion that certain perspectives are excluded by accident and that the "norm" is neither normal nor neutral. TB recognizes that we live within contexts "explained" by heavily naturalized, enforced, and coerced myths. Therefore, *critical* means giving voice to dimensions of life that too often remain unspoken, breaking silences and bringing students, educators, and communities together to purposefully disrupt the monotonous reproduction of life "as is." *Critical* means iteratively asking who the "norm" benefits and chipping away at the assumptions holding injustice together. To borrow from Walter Mignolo, *critical* means practicing epistemic disobedience—that is, actively refusing conformity to dominant knowledge systems and instead making space for alternative ways of knowing and understanding the world.[13] Last, *critical* also means transforming power relationships across educational spaces (e.g., teacher-student, school-parent-community, principal-teacher) and replacing "taken-for-granted" hierarchies with deliberate systems of responsibility and relationships.

TB must be humanizing. It must disrupt practices and pedagogies rooted in fear, punishment, and carcerality[14] and replace these with critical love and trust. It must upend a sedimented barrage of myths and assumptions that (dis)member,[15] pathologize, exoticize, and objectify. This means challenging the sociologies of deficit[16] (e.g., discourses of "high needs" and "low achievement"), refusing the logics that tell us that students are "problems" and, instead, nurturing ecologies of presence, togetherness, richness, and beauty. Humanizing tears down walls, fences, cages, and detention rooms. Instead, it looks and feels like transformative justice, spaces that care and embrace, classrooms as intergenerational community centers, seed banks, and places built to leverage each other's gifts.[17]

TB must be relational, centering reality not as "an object but a process of relationships."[18]

Thus, the goal should not be knowledge in itself but people coming together to create mutual realities (ontology), find common meanings (epistemology), and ultimately improve their worlds (axiology and methodology). This requires a paradigm shift away from what Paulo Freire terms banking methods that treat students as objects to be filled with "knowledge" created elsewhere.[19] In practice, *relational* means challenging the violence of existing temporalities and transactions (e.g., deadlines) and moving at the speed of trust. It means investing time into building relationships and organizing spaces that embody interdependence, refusing hierarchies and competition, testing and measuring mania, and instead cultivating communities where all flourishing is mutual, where we are in this together.

Last, TB must cultivate the radical imagination. It must defy the seizure of our time and energy to fulfill someone else's future and nurture possibilities and dreams already dismissed as impossible and unrealistic. In this sense, theorizing back is about practicing hope, calling something that is not yet fully present into being.[20] As Marc, a young co-theorizer, once explained: "It is a different kind of paying attention . . . like a rhythm, take time to listen and create the possibility for changing the rhythm."

A PATH FORWARD FOR DEMOCRATIZING WORLD-BUILDING

It is the word that gives form to that walk that goes on inside of us. . . .
Power uses the word to impose his empire of silence.
We use the word to renew ourselves. . . .
Let us join together in the word and the silence which liberate.

—EJÉRCITO ZAPATISTA DE LIBERACIÓN NACIONAL (EZLN)

In this section, I place TB in conversation with a strategy for democratizing world-building—especially during an epochal Zeitgeist, where our way out of this impasse is existentially entangled with the emergence of new ways of knowing and being—and offer some considerations.[21]

First, theorizing back as a broader process for world-building through and in education will require humility, courage, and solidarity as we grapple with our complicities, entanglements, and investments in the projects we are seeking to end (e.g., racial capitalism). In schools, TB must extend beyond an "after-school program" or a "fugitive classroom" that stands in opposition to the overarching logic of schooling. Instead, it must nurture a paradigmatic shift and provide entry points for a broader just transition.[22] For example, TB against carceral systems of suspensions, expulsions, and detentions entails making space for a different set of logics about conflict resolution that can then inform a broader conversation of how to better live/learn together, developing and "testing" of systems to do so, and disseminating these beyond the limits of the school systems itself. Imperatively, this cannot be done without putting most of what currently happens in schools to rest. We can do so lovingly, learning the lessons afforded by the demise, and ensuring that we build "immediate" and context-specific systems to care for those who will be impacted by their absence (e.g., rapid response and mutual aid, parallel institutions).[23]

Second, unlike the authoritarian practices of demagogues, democratizing theorizing as world-building must reflect a commitment to process and nuance (i.e., not skipping the in-between). Changing our relationship with theory means real people in real places asking real questions for substantial amounts of time, hence building the structures and rituals through which we can hold ideas/explanations/stories in ways that inform our day-to-day, our politics, and our organizing.[24] In schools, this means not only moving away from imposed "answers"; rather, it means cultivating processes through which we interrogate those answers directly (i.e., TB). Thus, as the glaring contrast between what could/should be and what actually exists rapidly expands, TB can help us return to what is our biggest source of power: the relationships, aesthetics, dreams, questions, and brilliance that once directed *back* at what is taken for granted makes transformation inevitable.[25] As a young theorizer once shared: *We think we're just another human being. . . . If we find out who we truly are, we'll fight for a whole 'nother world.*

Third, our movement will be as strong as it is deliberate. We must nurture the counter-hegemonic thinking and nuance that will inform the relationships, social processes, and institutions (i.e., the muscles) that will steer our movements. As Ella Baker said, "Strong people don't need strong leaders." A democratizing of world-building through education will require a multiplicity of opportunities across thousands of schools, classrooms, and communities to prefigure and build dissident paths. In this sense, TB will nurture a micropolitics that translates a multiplicity of realities into a politics able to shape deliberate futures and futurities. Thus, (re)claiming the "public" in public spaces (e.g., schools) is a return to the commons as a muscle through which we can counter fascistic tendencies and practice the messy and beautiful art of living together, of what the Zapatistas call making worlds where many worlds fit.[26] In practice, this means millions of hearts, eyes, and ears; questions and conversations; and stories alert toward justice, reclaiming words that had been taken hostage and setting them forth to world-build together.

CONCLUDING THOUGHTS ABOUT DEMOCRATIZING WORLD-BUILDING

If we are to step into this collective power and reenvision schools at a critical juncture in our broader struggle for justice, self-determination, and the right to world-build, I believe that theorizing back can help us reorient our focus and energy toward the processes through which we story the world. As it stands, democracy operates as a cloak for autocracy and oligarchy, transforming "I's" into fictional and abstract "we's" and thus masking subtle forms of control and domination. Conversely, democratizing can be conjured as a possibility to iteratively counter the asymmetrical accumulation and deployment of power to world-build. Similarly, TB is not an exercise of "giving" voice or power. It explicitly aims to protect and nurture voice and power within a context where these are endemically assaulted, especially for those holding intersectionality and multiply marginalized identities and locations. TB as a democratizing praxis is a node—one of many positions[27]—nurturing the good sense[28] and social formations through which we can reclaim our life force, our questions, and our words and mobilize them toward the futures we imagine for ourselves and our communities.

CONTINUING THE WORK

Though this list could be endless, here are some texts that accompanied me for this chapter:

Boaventura de Sousa Santos, *The End of the Cognitive Empire: The Coming of Age of Epistemologies of the South* (Duke University Press, 2018)

Paulo Freire, *Pedagogy of the Oppressed* (Continuum, 1970)

Robin D. G. Kelley, *Yo' Mama's Disfunktional! Fighting the Culture Wars in Urban America* (Beacon Press, 1998)

Subcomandante Insurgente Marcos, ed. Juana Ponce de León, *Nuestra Arma es Nuestra Palabra* (Seven Stories Press, 2002)

Achille Mbembe, *Out of the Dark Night: Essays on Decolonization* (Columbia University Press, 2021)

And here is a set of dialogue questions or exercises to consider in your own communities:

- In your context, what would it look like to create and nurture a school that honors the right of communities—especially those assaulted by multiple forms and systems of dehumanization and marginalization—to theorize back?
- Toward that vision, what do you need to build? What relationships, practices, pedagogies, structures, agreements, logics, and norms need to be set in motion?
- Conversely, what do we need to let go? What relationships, practices, pedagogies, structures, rules, policies, logics, and norms

trample the rights of school communities to theorize and world-build together?

- Who are your people, and how will you nurture and create the relationships necessary to move this transition forward?
- What are the fears that stop us from building these schools? How can we collectively organize to face those fears?

CHAPTER 17

TEACHING FOR DEMOCRACY IN A TIME OF DEMOCRATIC COLLAPSE

JOEL WESTHEIMER

MY CONNECTION TO EDUCATION IN A TIME OF DEMOCRATIC COLLAPSE

I lived in Argentina in the mid-1980s, just after the fall of the brutal military dictatorship that ruled from 1976 to 1983. The country was taking its first, shaky steps back toward democracy. It was a time of great hope but also of grave uncertainty—because while the generals were gone, the political culture that enabled them remained.

Like most of the nation, I was captivated by the pioneering trials of the military generals. But watching the trials, reading commentary, and witnessing the national response, I realized that even after a dictatorship collapses, its shadow can linger. Institutions that propped it up may be quick to pivot but slow to reform. And a political culture conditioned to fear, to silence, to look the other way does not snap back overnight.

In the United States, we may soon face similar challenges. But the immediate challenge is not how to recover from dictatorship but how to oppose it. The threat is clear: the authoritarian capture of education and the democratic collapse it both signals and accelerates.

Let's be clear: Fascism isn't some far-off threat—it's here. Unmarked vans and masked agents snatch students off the streets with no due process.[1] Judges and lawyers are intimidated.[2] Racist ideology is resurgent. Society's most powerful institutions—universities, tech firms, law firms, legislators—prostrate themselves to an autocrat's whims.[3] These are not warning signs. They are the thing itself. The longer we let fascism take hold, the harder it will be to recover our political culture and rebuild democracy.

There are many reasons for democratic collapse, and sociologists, historians, and political scientists suggest a number of causes, including economic inequality, weakened civil society, and social media–driven disinformation. As an educator, however, I can't help but wonder: Where have schools gone wrong? What might schools in Argentina have done differently? What, if anything, should schools today teach children about civic engagement, courage, and dissent? How can schools help young people acquire the essential knowledge, dispositions, and skills for effective democratic citizenship to withstand assault and to flourish?

For most of my career, I've written about public education—not just as voter preparation but as a foundation for cultivating critical thinking, empathy, and civic responsibility. I've argued that schools should help young people ask not only *what is* but also *what ought to be.*

That belief always felt urgent. But now it feels existential.

The old, slow threats to public education—standardization, privatization, test-based accountability—have not disappeared. But they've been joined by something darker, more aggressive, and more explicit: a coordinated effort to suppress dissent, restrict inquiry, and redefine public schooling as a tool of ideological conformity rather than democratic possibility.

And, yet, amidst this darkness, there is hope. Because if schools can be sites of authoritarian control, they can also be sites of resistance. If they can be used to suppress the truth, they can also be places where truth is defended. If they can be captured, they can also be reclaimed.

This chapter is my attempt to speak directly to that danger—and to that possibility.

UNDERSTANDING EDUCATION IN A TIME OF DEMOCRATIC COLLAPSE

The threats facing public education today are not isolated policy decisions or culture-war skirmishes—they are part of a larger, coordinated campaign to redefine the role of schools in a democratic society. Across the United States, we are witnessing the systematic dismantling of education's civic mission, replaced by a narrow, nationalistic, and ideologically rigid vision of schooling.[4] What once aimed to prepare young people for democratic participation is being conscripted to promote compliance and conformity.[5]

In Florida, teachers have faced penalties for displaying rainbow flags or assigning texts by Nobel Prize–winning author Toni Morrison.[6] In Texas, school districts have systematically removed references to civil rights leaders from curriculum materials,[7] while multiple states now require educators to present "both sides" of issues such as slavery and climate change.[8] These measures are often justified through appeals to neutrality, but in practice, "neutrality" becomes a mandate for silence in the face of injustice.[9]

What began as scattered controversies has now escalated into sweeping state-imposed censorship campaigns. In 2025, Florida school districts removed more than six hundred titles, including *The Diary of Anne Frank*, after state officials threatened legal action—a move PEN America condemned as "state-driven censorship."[10] Nationwide, the numbers are staggering: In the 2023–24 school year, there were over ten thousand recorded instances of book bans across four thousand unique titles, making clear that this is not a passing skirmish but a systemic assault on public education.[11]

The attack has also spread beyond K–12 schools. In 2025 alone, state legislatures passed more than twenty laws restricting faculty governance, diversity initiatives, and academic freedom in universities. The same tactics—vilifying teachers, surveilling classrooms, criminalizing dissent—are now being deployed to reshape higher education into an instrument of state ideology. An onslaught of new bills—for example, Texas's DEI ban or Florida's removal of sociology from general education requirements—have allowed state legislators to, as PEN notes, "cast a web of control over higher education."[12] Indiana, Texas, and Ohio are similarly exerting centralized control over governance and curricula, undermining traditional autonomy. Universities, in what Timothy Snyder calls "anticipatory obedience," are closing multicultural, women's, and LGBTQ+ resource centers—thirty-one so far across twenty-three campuses—signaling an ideological purge of inclusive spaces.[13]

This is not about balance. It's about erasure.

Public schools—especially those serving marginalized communities—have long been contested spaces, at once sites of oppression and also of struggles for social justice.[14] But the current moment is distinctive not only in the intensity and scope of attacks on public education but also in the tactics: the institutionalization of fact-free extremism that now shapes educational policy and public discourse. The silencing of dissent, surveillance of teachers, and criminalization of student protest all signal a dangerous shift from a vision of schools as democratic spaces (admittedly rarely fully realized) to schools as instruments of authoritarian ideology.[15]

The attacks on K–16 educational institutions are not only attempts to restrict knowledge—they are efforts to reshape reality. As Hannah Arendt notes, the kind of "organized lying" that is now being forced on educational institutions means that "[t]he chances of factual truth surviving the onslaught of power are very slim indeed."[16] And disinformation campaigns, amplified by social media algorithms and partisan media outlets, create parallel narratives in which educators are framed as threats to national values.[17] Public trust in education, once a cornerstone of civic life, has been eroded through a relentless drumbeat of suspicion, vilification, and political interference.

What makes the attacks on education particularly dangerous is that those attacks are not isolated. The current administration and a political party that has lost all moral grounding are hell-bent on destroying nearly every institution and arm of government that operate in the public interest and that in any way challenge the authoritarian turn. Newspapers, universities, unions, law firms, charities, museums, arts centers, and civil rights organizations are all being dismantled or forced to serve the whims of a corrupt and unaccountable leader. The Centers for Disease Control and Prevention, the Department of Justice, the Department of the Treasury—the list could go on—are being grotesquely transformed.

These assaults mirror patterns in other authoritarian regimes. In Weimar Germany, the Nazis moved quickly to control curricula, ban books, and purge teachers who resisted.[18] During Argentina's "Dirty War," intellectuals and students were targeted for repression as potential dissidents.[19] In Hungary and Turkey today, universities and schools have been brought under direct government control, their autonomy stripped away.[20]

We know where this leads.

In the face of these threats to democracy, there remains a collective responsibility to ensure that schools cultivate inquiry, dialogue, and the skills needed to challenge orthodoxy.[21]

When those functions are undermined, democracy unravels. The fight for democratic schools is inseparable from the fight for democracy itself.

REENVISIONING PUBLIC EDUCATION

What if schools were not the last places to reckon with democratic backsliding but the first? Not merely institutions that mirror society's inequalities and fears but ones that model a more just and democratic future?

To reenvision public education in this moment is to see it not as a neutral bystander or casualty of a march toward fascism but as a front-line institution in the struggle against it. This means moving beyond the narrow vision of schooling as workforce preparation or the rote transfer of "civic facts" and instead cultivating what political theorist Danielle Allen calls participatory readiness: the knowledge, habits, and courage required to participate meaningfully in a democratic society.[22]

Public education, in this reimagining, would prepare students not just to vote but to pay attention: to notice injustice, to detect manipulation, to recognize creeping authoritarianism and resist it. It would train students in what Paulo Freire called *conscientização* or *critical consciousness*—the practice of recognizing how social, political, and economic forces shape our lives, questioning whose interests they serve, and developing the courage to act against oppression.[23] This kind of public education affords students the capacity to connect personal experience with broader structures of power and to see that things could be otherwise. This is the foundation of democratic life.

In this vision, history is not flattened or sanitized to promote nationalist ideologies.

Students should study histories of struggle and resistance, from the Black Freedom Movement and labor organizing to Indigenous sovereignty movements. They should analyze the patterns by which democracies erode—not just in textbooks but in current events and, if possible, in their own communities.

Science classes would help students distinguish knowledge from opinion, understand disinformation, and ask ethical questions about emerging technologies. Media literacy would become a core practice across disciplines: how to verify a source, trace a claim, and detect efforts at indoctrination. As digital manipulation grows more sophisticated, so too must our collective capacity to see clearly. As I wrote in the book *What Kind of Citizen?*:

> The tools we might use to critically analyze our situation are themselves compromised by misinformation. The proliferation of baseless conspiracy theories . . . along with new uses of artificial intelligence make it increasingly difficult even for educated adults to distinguish reality from fiction. It is difficult to build civic, democratic discourse when a substantial number of citizens do not have accurate information on important issues that affect their lives and the lives of others.[24]

Hannah Arendt's warning still resonates: "The result of a consistent and total substitution of lies for factual truth is not that the lie will now be accepted as truth . . . but that the sense by which we take our bearings in the real world . . . is being destroyed."[25] Schools must become sites where young people reclaim those bearings.

In the vision laid out here, public education would also move away from an ideology of individualism, instead centering collective responsibility. In contrast to the neoliberal ideal of the isolated, self-interested individual, education must remind students that they live in relation to others. As Maxine Greene argued, teaching for freedom requires helping students "perceive the ways in which they are connected to others" and imagine alternative futures together.[26]

This vision does not pretend that schools can do everything. But it insists they can do something—something essential. In a moment when evidence, empathy, and justice are under siege, we need schools that prepare students to push back, to be engaged, to become courageous citizens.

A PATH FORWARD FOR EDUCATORS

The question, then, is how to chart a path forward when democracy itself is faltering.

Teaching for democracy has always been challenging, often contested. But the present moment is distinctive. White supremacist aspirations are being mainstreamed, disinformation is rampant, and the leadership of the most powerful country on earth is openly dismantling democratic norms. The rule of law, once taken for granted, now feels precarious. Schools cannot by themselves reverse these tides, but neither can they retreat into silence. The task is to ask: What can still be done in the democratic spaces that remain, and how can we prepare for the time after, when rebuilding becomes possible?

History offers guideposts. In 1964, during the Freedom Summer in Mississippi, civil rights organizers established "Freedom Schools" for African American youth. These were not ordinary schools. They taught the academic basics, but, more importantly, they taught students to question, to see themselves as agents of change, and to imagine a different society. Created in the midst of intimidation and violence, Freedom Schools modeled the possibilities of education as resistance. They remind us that even in repressive times, small-scale educational projects can nurture democratic habits and civic courage.[27]

A different lesson comes from post–World War II Germany. After the collapse of Nazi rule, the Allies made schools central to rebuilding democratic culture. They dismantled Nazi curricula, trained new teachers, and introduced civic education that emphasized tolerance, responsibility, and critical inquiry. Over time, "political education" became a core part of German schooling, coupled with Holocaust and human rights education. This was not quick or easy—nor was it uniformly successful at first. But sustained commitment over decades made public education one of the pillars of Germany's democratic renewal.[28] The lesson is that schools, if resourced and supported, can help societies not only resist authoritarianism but also rebuild democracy in its aftermath.

What do these examples suggest for the present moment? First, that teachers and students can work in the interstices of authoritarian curricula, creating spaces—however fragile—for truth-telling, dialogue, and critical inquiry.

These acts may be small: students organizing discussions about issues their schools try to silence, a teacher encouraging students to examine multiple perspectives when the official curriculum insists on one, or asking them to compare how textbooks from different countries cover the same event—where do they converge, where do they diverge, and what might these differences mean? Even modest exercises like these can become acts of resistance.

Second, collective action is essential. Teachers cannot do this alone. They need networks of solidarity, professional associations, and community partnerships to resist isolation and to sustain democratic practices. Building these alliances now will be crucial if repression deepens.

Finally, we must think ahead. Authoritarian moments do not last forever. If history is any guide, there will be a time when democratic reconstruction becomes possible. Schools that have nurtured memory, critical consciousness, and civic courage—even under duress—will be better prepared to help rebuild. That preparation is itself an act of resistance.

The stakes could not be higher. Education will either become a tool for authoritarian control or a space for resistance and renewal where democracy can still be reclaimed. Freedom Schools in Mississippi and post-war schools in Germany remind us that both resistance and rebuilding are possible. Our task now is to ensure that public education continues to plant the seeds of democracy—even amidst democratic decline.

CONCLUDING THOUGHTS ABOUT EDUCATION IN A TIME OF DEMOCRATIC COLLAPSE

When I lived in Argentina just after the fall of dictatorship, I saw how fragile democratic recovery can be. Generals may step aside, but the political culture that sustained them lingers.

That lesson echoes today: Even when authoritarian leaders falter, rebuilding democracy is slow, uncertain work.

Public education has always been at the heart of that work. Schools can reproduce fear, obedience, and conformity—but they can also nurture the courage, memory, and solidarity that democracy requires. They can prepare young people not only to live in democracy but to defend and rebuild it when it falters.

The task is not simple. Authoritarian movements are waging open assaults on schools and universities, trying to turn them into instruments of nationalist extremism. But history also shows how education can serve different roles: resisting repression, as in the Mississippi Freedom Schools, or helping to rebuild democracy, as in post-war Germany. These examples remind us that even in times of repression, schools can cultivate seeds of resistance, and in times of renewal, they can help rebuild.

Public education must not retreat into silence. It must become a vital sanctuary where democracy can be imagined, defended, and prepared for. Because democracy doesn't just protect public education—public education must also protect democracy.

CONTINUING TO WORK ON EDUCATION FOR DEMOCRATIC RENEWAL

QUESTIONS FOR REFLECTION AND DIALOGUE

1. Hannah Arendt warned that "the sense by which we take our bearings in the real world . . . is being destroyed." What helps you, or your community, *take bearings* in this moment of democratic collapse?

2. When does "staying neutral" on important matters of social concern become complicity?
3. What role should teachers, students, and other community members play when laws and/or democratic norms are flouted?

ACTIVITIES

1. **Mapping Democratic Spaces**
   In groups of three, walk around the community and create a map of institutions, organizations, and public resources where democratic practices still thrive and those where they are under threat. What patterns emerge and what actions could strengthen these spaces?

2. **Create a New Political Party**

   Tell students they are to create a new political party—the SUFF Party (Students United for the Future). Have them create (a) a political platform; (b) a slogan; and (c) strategies for effecting change. Present their new party platform, slogan, and strategies to the class.

3. **Freedom School Revisited**

   In small groups, design a one-session "Freedom School"—a short workshop or community dialogue that nurtures civic courage and democratic habits of mind. How might it foster resistance rather than compliance?

RESOURCES

Facing History & Ourselves, https://www.facinghistory.org/

The Zinn Education Project, https://www.zinnedproject.org/

SECTION 4

REASSERTING PUBLIC AND COLLECTIVE RESPONSIBILITY

CHAPTER 18

THE DANGER OF PRIVATIZATION AND NEOLIBERALISM IN PUBLIC EDUCATION

JULIAN VASQUEZ HEILIG AND NALLELY GECIK

David C. Berliner, who passed on September 25, 2025, after a lifetime of scholarship and moral clarity, once warned in his 2013 American Educational Research Association (AERA) presidential address, that "the attack on public schools is an attack on the public itself."[1] Few sentences capture more powerfully the crisis we now face. Berliner spent decades pulling back the curtain on the quiet encroachment of neoliberalism, the ideology that insists markets can manage democracy better than people can. He taught us that when education is reduced to a competition, someone must always lose, and it is rarely the powerful. Neoliberalism is not just an economic theory; it is a worldview that redefines what, and who, is valuable. It has turned our classrooms into marketplaces and our children into data points. It thrives on scarcity, convincing the public that schools can be run like businesses and teachers can be replaced like widgets. It cloaks privatization in the language of "innovation" and "choice," while starving the very institutions that once promised opportunity and belonging. As Berliner and others have reminded us, this is not reform; it is a reengineering of public purpose for private gain.[2]

The pages that follow are a reckoning. Together, we, the authors, examine how neoliberalism has transformed public education—through charter schools, vouchers, testing regimes, and other methods that foment the normalization of students as commodities. We trace how corporate philanthropy, tech ventures, and political movements have sought to take ownership over public schools. In writing this chapter, we stand on the shoulders of Berliner and a generation of scholars and educators who refused to stay silent while democracy was auctioned off piece by piece. The work ahead is to name what has been taken from us—the language of care, the commitment to equity, the understanding that public education is not a service to be purchased but a covenant to be protected. Neoliberalism has promised efficiency, but it delivered inequality. It promised innovation, but it produced standardization. It promised freedom, but it left too many communities voiceless. As we revisit the myths that sustain it, our goal is not only to critique but to reimagine, to build a public education system worthy of our children, our democracy, and the collective future we still have the power to shape.

OUR CONNECTION TO THE FIGHT AGAINST NEOLIBERALISM IN EDUCATION

Neither of us found our way to the schoolhouse as mere bystanders. We entered education as products and witnesses of its promises and its failures. Our earliest memories are laced with hope and frustration. For many Latine students, schools were not just a gateway to opportunity but also a constant reminder of how society rationed dignity and respect. Our families and communities have viewed education as a civil right and a cornerstone of American democracy. This was not an abstract principle but a lived reality for Latine children and grandchildren of immigrants, laborers, and first-generation college students. We've seen firsthand how schools have functioned as both lifelines and battlegrounds. When our parents sent us to school, they entrusted us to an institution that could help us realize the American dream. Too often, though, Latine students see dreams deferred by structural neglect, racist policies, and shifting neoliberal priorities.

In Latine communities across the country, families have witnessed fundamental shifts in public education. The mission of public schools is evolving, sometimes in ways that overlook the lived realities and aspirations of these neighborhoods. For example, charter schools have been promoted as solutions to persistent challenges that policymakers have not fully addressed.[3]

Although charter schools present polished branding and ambitious promises, they frequently lack genuine and sustained relationships with the communities they claim to serve.[4] They are often promoted as innovative, but in practice they represent a new form of privatization, one that shifts public education from communities toward private control and private management.[5]

A study by the Network for Public Education indicates that more than one in four charter schools close within five years.[6] Furthermore, the closure rate continues to climb over time, with nearly half of all charter schools closing within fifteen years.[7] These closures disrupt students' education and destabilize families and neighborhoods, leaving many communities with even fewer resources and less stability. Too often, students are viewed primarily through a financial lens, a backpack full of cash, rather than as valued members and future leaders of their neighborhoods.[8] This ongoing cycle of disruption and detachment further erodes trust in the promise of public education and underscores the urgent need for schools that are genuinely rooted in, accountable to, and governed by the communities they serve rather than private interests.

We've seen the ascendancy of standardized testing, not as a tool for equity but as a mechanism for sorting students into ability groups and blaming teachers.[9] Testing companies, flush with public dollars, grew into profit-generating assessment giants, yet the children in our care often faced narrow curricula, relentless pressure, and little space for creativity or cultural affirmation because of the constant focus on testing.[10] The language of achievement gaps replaced honest conversations about opportunity gaps and the deep roots of systemic unfairness in the US education system.[11]

Despite countless reform efforts and promises of progress from policymakers for decades, we have watched as structural inequities persist. Resources for research-based culturally responsive teaching and restorative justice approaches to school discipline remain scarce. Our histories and languages are too often erased, and our hybrid experiences as Latine students are undervalued or even dismissed. The pressure to assimilate to Eurocentric norms remains strong—schools demand conformity and convergent thinking while devaluing those who bring different languages, cultures, and perspectives.[12]

As scholars and educators, we know that public education can be a site of both exclusion and liberation. It can perpetuate the very hierarchies it claims to dismantle, or it can serve as a launching pad for young people's dreams. Our commitment is to defend the latter vision. We draw hope and inspiration from the work of scholars who insist that classrooms should elevate, not silence, the language, identity, and lived embodied experience of every child.[13]

Quite simply, for us, this is love and legacy work. The commodification of education by neoliberals is a direct attack on our communities, our histories, and our futures. We have watched as purpose gave way to profit, as children were reduced to markets, and as schools were proverbially auctioned to the highest bidder. Yet we persist. In the current moment of unprecedented political censorship, defunding, and attempted erasure of culture, we continue to teach, to resist, and to build. Education should not be intended for profit and control. It is meant for the people and democracy. Together, we remain determined to reclaim it.

UNDERSTANDING NEOLIBERALISM'S THREAT TO PUBLIC EDUCATION

The current condition of American education is the outcome of a concerted and far-reaching project of sabotage that began decades ago by Milton Friedman and many others.[14] This project of control and takeover, driven by the principles of neoliberalism, sought to reimagine public education as a commodity to be bought and sold and provided in high-quality forms primarily for the privileged.[15]

This transformation was accelerated during the Reagan era, a period marked by the systematic rollback of public investment and the ascendance of market-based ideologies. Policymakers, philanthropists, and corporate leaders promoted a new vocabulary for schools. Instead of discussing "equity" and "community," they began to speak increasingly of "choice," "competition," and "efficiency." These concepts sounded innocuous, even virtuous, but they masked a deep agenda: the dismantling of public institutions in favor of private, profit-driven alternatives.[16]

The tools of neoliberal reform, including vouchers, charter schools, and high-stakes testing, were presented as cure-alls for the perceived failures of public education. Backed by well-funded marketing campaigns and a vast ecosystem of advocacy-driven "research," their proponents promised equity, innovation, and salvation for children in so-called failing schools. Yet the evidence sustaining these claims has often been less scientific inquiry than political strategy. Much of the research that fueled market-based reform was not neutral but ideologically constructed, funded and promoted by right-wing political organizations that supported privatization.[17] These studies frequently relied on narrow quantitative metrics, such as standardized test scores, while ignoring the broader purposes of education: belonging, democracy, and community well-being.

By privileging what can be easily measured over what truly matters, neoliberal reformers reframed education as a technical problem rather than a social one. Selective publication practices and methodological blind spots reinforced this narrative, with small or short-term gains touted as proof of success while contradictory findings were minimized or dismissed. The resulting "evidence base" became an echo chamber, legitimizing reforms that redirected public funds into private hands under the guise of choice and efficiency. The language of civil rights—"saving kids from failing schools"—was weaponized to justify union busting, deepen segregation, and erode community control. In this way, neoliberal reform did not fail because it lacked data; it succeeded because it controlled the narrative about what counts as data.

Over the years, we have witnessed the emergence of entire industries eager to exploit the vulnerabilities of public schools. Testing companies, curriculum vendors, and, more recently, AI-driven ed-tech startups have flourished, frequently advancing their own interests at the expense of the very students and communities they claim to support. The language of innovation, improvement, big data, and accountability-driven student success has become omnipresent. Yet for too many students, these innovations have translated into further marginalization, unfairness, and reduced opportunities for meaningful learning.

This transformation was no accident. Policy by policy, dollar by dollar, the public purposes of education were deliberately eroded. Education "reformers" from both political parties wrapped their neoliberal agenda in alluring words.[18] Yet beneath that rhetoric lay a slow, calculated unraveling of the social contract. The deepest harm fell on those already living at the margins: the children of immigrants, children of color, and those whose lives embody hybridity and resilience. For them, the system was never built to serve. It was built to sort—much as Plato described in *The Republic* with his "Myth of the Metals," dividing society into gold, silver, and bronze, a hierarchy as old as civilization itself.[19] Thus, as neoliberalism continues to shape our schools, we must recognize that this is not simply a question of policy or finance. It is a question of democracy, of justice, and of belonging.[20]

CONCLUDING THOUGHTS ABOUT RECLAIMING EDUCATION

The future of public education, and the future of our society, depends on our willingness to name these threats and to build a different path forward. Neoliberalism has sought to turn our children into commodities and our schools into business plans. It has promoted the logic of profit over the logic of justice, efficiency over equity, and individual competition over collective care. But another world is possible. We know, from both research and lived embodied experience, that public education can be the heartbeat of a just and multiracial democracy. The ideals of equity, inclusion, and belonging matter now more than ever. These are not simply words but commitments to daily practice, collective struggle, and shared hope.

Across the United States, every state constitution enshrines a public duty to educate, treating schooling not as a marketplace luxury but as a civic obligation. The language varies, but the promise is consistent: Massachusetts commands lawmakers to "cherish" public schools;[21] Texas ties a "general diffusion of knowledge" to liberty itself;[22] Washington makes education the state's "paramount duty;"[23] Pennsylvania requires a "thorough and efficient" system;[24] Florida guarantees a "uniform, efficient, safe, secure, and high quality" system;[25] and Michigan requires the legislature to "maintain and support" free public schools.[26] These clauses aren't ornamental. They are binding commitments that anchor school funding, equity, and accountability to constitutional text and history. When policymakers flirt with privatization schemes that siphon public dollars away from public schools, they don't just test a policy preference; they test the meaning of these guarantees and the boundaries of our democratic covenant.

We know the US educational system has failed many of our students through the unequal distribution of resources; we also know that neoliberal "solutions"—marketized choice, testing, vouchers, privatization—are fool's gold, and that they deepen segregation and siphon public funds. We must hold fast to the ethics and ideals set out in state constitutions, recognizing that the work ahead will be challenging but also transformative. We are not merely defending public education. We are fighting for the right to dream, to belong, and to build a future of democracy together. Our Latine communities, our children, and our nation deserve nothing less. Education was never meant for profit in the United States. It was always meant for the people. Together, we can reclaim it and ensure that it lives up to its promise. Let us continue to teach, to organize, to fight, and to dream for our students—together.

CONTINUING TO WORK ON RECLAIMING PUBLIC EDUCATION

DIALOGUE QUESTIONS & EXERCISES

1. **Recognizing Neoliberalism's Local Footprint**

   Where do you see the influence of neoliberal policies, such as competition, privatization, or market-style accountability, in your local schools or districts? How have these policies reshaped teaching, learning, or community trust?

2. **Cultural Erasure and Affirmation**

   In what ways do your schools honor, marginalize, or erase students' languages, cultures, and hybrid identities? How might reclaiming these narratives serve as resistance to the homogenizing forces of neoliberal reform?

3. **Reimagining Democratic Schools**

   What would a truly democratic, just, and inclusive public school look like in your community? Consider how decision-making, curriculum, funding, and relationships might be restructured to center equity, belonging, and collective care over profit and performance metrics.

4. **Power, Voice, and Exclusion**

   Who currently holds power in shaping educational policy and practice where you live—and who is left out? How can educators, students, and families make decision-making processes more representative and accountable to the public good?

5. **Building Solidarity and Resistance**

   How might you and your community build or join coalitions that defend public education as a democratic right rather than a private commodity? What strategies could unite educators, families, and students in advancing educational justice and resisting privatization?

6. **Naming Hope and Next Steps**

   Amidst ongoing privatization and censorship, where do you find hope in your community's struggle for educational justice? What small, concrete actions could you take this year to move toward the vision of education "for the people and democracy"?

RESOURCES FOR DEEPER LEARNING

Frank Adamson, Björn Åstrand, and Linda Darling-Hammond, *Global Education Reform: How Privatization and Public Investment Influence Education Outcomes* (Routledge, 2016)

April Baker-Bell, *Linguistic Justice: Black Language, Literacy, Identity, and Pedagogy* (Routledge, 2020)

David C. Berliner and Carl Hermanns, eds., *Public Education: Defending a Cornerstone of American Democracy* (Teachers College Press, 2021)

Pierre Bourdieu, "Language and Symbolic Power," *Polity* (1991)

Noam Chomsky, *Profit over People: Neoliberalism and Global Order* (Seven Stories Press, 1998)

Ofelia García and Jo Anne Kleifgen, *Educating Emergent Bilinguals: Policies, Programs, and Practices for English Language Learners* (Teachers College Press, 2010)

Ofelia García and Li Wei, *Translanguaging: Language, Bilingualism and Education* (Palgrave Macmillan, 2014)

Henry A. Giroux, *Neoliberalism's War on Higher Education* (Haymarket Books, 2014)

Diane Ravitch, *Reign of Error: The Hoax of the Privatization Movement and the Danger to America's Public Schools* (Knopf, 2013)

Diane Ravitch, *Slaying Goliath: The Passionate Resistance to Privatization and the Fight to Save America's Public Schools* (Knopf, 2020)

Angela Valenzuela, *Subtractive Schooling: U.S.-Mexican Youth and the Politics of Caring* (SUNY Press, 1999)

Julian Vasquez Heilig, *Cloaking Inequity* (blog), https://cloakinginequity.com/

Julian Vasquez Heilig, *Julian Vasquez Heilig* (LinkedIn profile), https://www.linkedin.com/in/drjvh/

Julian Vasquez Heilig, *Julian Vasquez Heilig* (YouTube channel), https://www.youtube.com/user/JulianVasquezHeilig

CHAPTER 19

THREATS TO HUMANITY

Reimagining K–12 Leadership

MUHAMMAD KHALIFA

MY CONNECTION TO THE CROSSROADS OF LEADERSHIP

My earliest memories of anything "education" are intertwined with my first memories of anything "family": My father was my first principal, and my mother was my kindergarten and first-grade teacher (my siblings and I attended the school, along with three hundred other minoritized students). It was a poor private school born of Black liberation on Detroit's East Side. Much was missing in the way of the latest technologies, new textbooks and materials, and trained personnel; the building was old and empty before we moved in. But it had something that I would never experience again as a student, teacher, or faculty member: an environment of unbounded love and an undying commitment to Black excellence, success, and self-determination. The context was defiant and hopeful all at once: Our earliest shared memories were of the TV series *Shaka Zulu* and *Roots*.

By the fourth grade, I was in integrated public schools, and that love and support was gone; we were but numbers on a list of countless other Detroiters who would be neglected in school for most of our education. My siblings and I lost interest in school, and though we all graduated, many of us did not finish school on time. Thankfully, it was those earliest memories of a group of Black educators that would drive my commitments and shape my work, research, and dreams of the liberatory spaces that schools could become.

I later became a teacher and school leader in Detroit, and then a faculty member who interrogated those same urban areas where I had learned and worked. In my role as a professor, I have spent countless hours with school and district leaders across the United States. I have listened to their stories, narratives laced with both a deep commitment to justice and profound exhaustion. These leaders, many of whom are committed to humanizing students and dismantling systemic inequities, often find themselves in painful, no-win situations.

School leaders with community-oriented commitments often find themselves caught in the crosshairs of the politics of public education. They are asked to implement policies that uphold colonial legacies, reinforce anti-Blackness and anti-Indigeneity, and prioritize corporate or elite interests over student and community well-being. Time and again, I have witnessed principals, superintendents, and district leaders grapple with an impossible decision: either enforce dehumanizing mandates that betray their deepest commitments to community empowerment, or resist and risk immediate removal from leadership.

This is not an abstract dilemma. I have seen principals weep over being forced to suspend students of color under "zero tolerance" policies they knew were unjust. I have seen superintendents pressured to censor honest staff and student discussions of racism, Islamophobia, or anti-immigration practices (in particular, ICE practices in and around schools), knowing full well that silence would harm vulnerable students. I have seen leaders try to hold on to their positions long enough to make small, incremental changes for children and families, only to be castigated as "political" or "radical." One prominent example of this was the politicization of two Black female equity leaders—one in Salem-Keizer, Oregon, and the other in Bloomington, Minnesota. As they attempted to protect the students' safety and rights, and bolster the educational attainment of minoritized students, they were accused by community members and even some colleagues of being divisive and sectarian.

The choice is devastating: compromise one's principles in order to help a little, or stand firm for justice and risk removal. Both options wound the souls of leaders. Yet some principles, such as resisting student harm and dehumanization, should not be negotiable.

Unfortunately in many communities authoritarian impulses and well-funded conflict agendas have created sustained campaigns of marginalization. These campaigns have sought to strip leaders of their ability to humanize education, even as they have protected corporate power and White supremacy, and diminished community voice. School leaders committed to humanization must recognize community-based knowledges—from young people participating in hip-hop music and culture, to immigrants coming together to protect themselves from ICE harassment and oppression, to community elders sharing stories of migration and then finding a way to infuse these knowledges into schooling, curriculum, and contexts that affirm these identities and knowledges. Humanization also requires school leaders to go into communities, to humbly learn and offer support for community based-causes. Thus, we are at the intersection where we must ask: What is the true purpose of education, and whom does it serve?

UNDERSTANDING THE THREAT TO LEADERSHIP AND HUMANITY

At its core, the crisis facing educational leadership today is not simply about policy disagreements or the ebb and flow of partisan politics. It is about whether schools will continue to serve as instruments of dehumanization, or whether they can be reclaimed as sites of liberation and collective flourishing. Leadership, in this moment, is deeply entangled with broader struggles for freedom and dignity.

Schooling has always carried this dual possibility. On the one hand, it has been used as a mechanism of colonial control, enforcing hierarchies of race, culture, and class. In other words, leadership has been used to structure schools based on societies that have prioritized the lives and livelihoods of White middle- and upper-class men at the expense of minoritized communities and bodies (which are disposed of to maintain White wealth and life). On the other hand, communities, particularly Black, Indigenous, and other marginalized groups, have long insisted that education should be rooted in liberation, collective responsibility, and self-determination. In fact, in many such historic Black communities, for example, you could never serve as a leader without having community credibility and trust. The question of leadership, then, is inseparable from the question of whose humanity schools are designed to affirm.

When viewed through this lens, the problem with current educational politics becomes not about having the latest principal licensure. Indeed, leaders are pressured to disconnect schooling from the lived experiences of students and communities. They are told to reduce learning to technical compliance, to standardized test scores, and to corporate-defined metrics of "success." Yet, historically, education at its most authentic has never been about serving corporate agendas; it has been about cultivating human beings and strengthening communities.

Given these two leadership paths—either upholding the current (colonizing) status quo or serving as a community-centric leader with goals of humanization and uplift both in school and community—leaders think about their own commitments and positionality. Across time and geography, traditions of liberatory education point us toward this truth. In West African Qur'anic schools, as documented by Rudolph Ware, the purpose of learning was not only literacy but the shaping of character and communal accountability. Knowledge was embodied, tied to ethics, and meant to sustain the collective.[1] Andalusian and North African centers of learning similarly wove scholarship with community well-being, linking intellectual pursuits to the moral and spiritual development of society.[2] These traditions reveal that education is at its best when it prepares people not just to think but to live together with dignity, and to serve community.

Similarly, Black freedom struggles in the United States offer another powerful reminder. For generations, Black families and communities carved out educational spaces against the grain of state-sanctioned neglect and hostility and ever-morphing regimes of White supremacy. Freedom schools of the 1960s, for example, did more than fill curricular gaps; they cultivated political consciousness and affirmed students' worth in a society that sought to erase it. This is what Cedric Robinson described in *Black Marxism: The Making of the Black Radical Tradition*—communities imagining education beyond compliance and toward liberation.[3] Leadership is not about enforcing mandates but about protecting the conditions in which freedom dreams can be nurtured.[4]

Other scholars committed to liberation similarly remind us that the work of community is not morally neutral. As James Cone argued, to stand by without taking action in the face of oppression is to become complicit in it.[5] School leaders cannot pretend neutrality when the stakes are the dignity and survival of marginalized students. Leadership that does not resist dehumanization is leadership that legitimizes it.

Leadership linked to liberation and community uplift recognizes and shares power with leadership within multiple communities. And schools that draw on these historic traditions demonstrate the possibility of another way. In Indigenous-led schools across the US and Canada, curricula are infused with ancestral knowledge, ecological stewardship, and tribal languages, embodying the belief that education must serve the community's continuity and flourishing. In Afrocentric schools in places like Philadelphia, Toronto, and Chicago, for example, students encounter a curriculum that connects them to the histories and cultures of their ancestors, fostering both self-knowledge and collective pride. Recent Youth Participatory Action Research (or YPAR) projects show how students themselves, when given authority, can generate knowledge and push schools toward justice-oriented reform.[6] These examples echo older models of education designed not for compliance but for the improvement of humanity itself, and which traditional school leaders should recognize and co-lead with local community leadership.

Seen against this backdrop, today's threats to leadership are particularly insidious because they demand the opposite. They pressure leaders to sever education from community, to reject liberation as a goal, and to define success through the lens of efficiency and control. This is not just bad policy; it is a profound distortion of the very purpose of schooling. To strip leadership of its liberatory role is to strip education of its soul.

If we are to confront this threat, leaders must reclaim the understanding that schools are not neutral institutions but deeply moral and political spaces. And that our communities need them to be what *they* need them to be. Leaders must remember that the most enduring educational traditions—whether in Timbuktu or Tulsa, Senegal or Selma—understood knowledge as inseparable from humanity, justice, and collective life. Leadership in such a vision is not about managing compliance but about guiding schools back to their true purpose: the cultivation of human dignity and the liberation and self-determination of communities.

REENVISIONING LEADERSHIP FOR LIBERATION

Drawing on these histories and CRSL (Culturally Responsive School Leadership) research, I argue that educational leadership must be reenvisioned around community self-determination and liberation. This reenvisioning requires at least four commitments:

1. *Centering Community Voice as Power*
   Community engagement cannot be tokenistic or performative. Too often, leaders "consult" communities to fulfill compliance requirements but then exclude their voices from meaningful decision-making. In

contrast, CRSL insists that leaders must treat community voices as central sources of knowledge and authority. In one district I studied, community members helped redesign disciplinary policies—not as a symbolic gesture but as an enforceable shift in power that transformed student outcomes.

2. *Establishing Authentic Power Sharing*
Scholars such as Ann Ishimaru, Mark Warren, and John Rogers have shown that authentic power-sharing requires leaders to cede authority to families and communities, particularly those who have been historically marginalized. This is not a dilution of leadership but a reorientation toward justice and humanity. Schools must become spaces where decision-making is co-constructed and accountability flows in both directions.

3. *Building Humanizing School Climates*
Leaders must intentionally create climates where every student feels seen, valued, and safe. This includes dismantling deficit discourses, removing punitive barriers, and fostering belonging. But more importantly, leaders must become about the business of recognizing and incorporating community knowledges and student assets. It requires leaders to align policies, rituals, and daily practices with the dignity of all students.

4. *Linking Youth Agency to Structural Change*
Connected learning and YPAR demonstrate how young people can generate powerful insights and lead change when given the tools and authority to do so.[7] Leaders must not only allow but actively encourage youth-led initiatives that challenge inequitable practices and reshape school culture.

This reenvisioning acknowledges that pushback will always be present. From slavery to Jim Crow to today's anti-justice campaigns and school-centric practices, the forces of resistance to justice are deeply entrenched. Yet the Black Radical Tradition teaches us that pushback is not the end of the story. It is precisely in these moments of contestation that new forms of leadership must emerge—leadership rooted in humanity, community, justice, and love.

A PATH FORWARD FOR RESISTANCE AND HOPE IN POLICY-CONSTRAINED TIMES

If this reenvisioning seems impossible in today's political climate, we must remember that leaders have always found ways to resist—even under the harshest and most pessimistic conditions. Yes, this is a troubling moment, but please remember that Indigenous and Black territories/communities have seen far worse. Federal and state policies may be designed to restrict equity efforts, but many restorative, humanizing practices occur beneath the radar of policymakers. It can be advantageous to liberation efforts that oppressive politicians remain ignorant about the unique ways community liberation, humanization, and community empowerment can happen.

In my research, I have seen leaders comply with the formal requirements of standardized testing or reporting, while simultaneously building parallel systems of care that affirm student identity and dignity. For example, one superintendent I worked with over a three-year period in Illinois satisfied state mandates on "character education" by reframing them through an equity lens, incorporating community elders' teachings and Indigenous knowledge into the curriculum. On paper, the district met the requirements. In practice, they cultivated a radically different model of leadership.

Another education leader in Minnesota quietly reallocated discretionary funds to support undocumented students with legal services and mental health care, even though policies prohibited explicit support. The leader described this work not as defiance but as fidelity to the community's humanity.

CRSL PROVIDES A BLUEPRINT FOR THIS KIND OF TRANSGRESSIVE/SUBVERSIVE LEADERSHIP

- *Critical self-reflection*: Leaders must interrogate their own complicity in oppressive systems and commit to continual growth.[8]
- *Community knowledges*: Schools must draw from ancestral and local knowledges as foundational sources of curriculum and leadership practice.
- *System change*: Leaders must leverage their positional power to transform structures that harm students, even in small and incremental ways.
- *Solidarity and advocacy*: Leaders cannot resist alone; they must align with (and take a back seat to) educators, families, youth, and other community allies to create climates ripe for change.

They need to find local, authentic leaders and empower them. Policymakers may attempt to isolate leaders, but collective resistance generates resilience and longevity.

CONCLUDING THOUGHTS: THE NON-NEGOTIABLE STRUGGLE FOR HUMANITY

At its heart, this struggle is not about test scores, compliance, or even policy debates. It is about humanity. To lead schools today is to decide daily whether to participate in harm or to resist it. The stakes could not be higher.

Education has always been most powerful when it affirms the dignity of people and improves their material conditions. When looking at the educational histories of Black, Indigenous, and Latinx people, immigrant people, as well as communities in the global majority, territories, the most authentic schooling traditions remind us that leadership is inseparable from liberation.

Finally, in this very dangerous time, school leaders must know when to practice the politics of refusal and subversion: refuse to compromise when harm is at stake. They must root themselves in histories of resistance and in the dreams of communities who refuse to be silenced.

Above all, they must remember: Leadership is not about preserving institutions but about affirming humanity.

CONTINUING TO WORK ON REIMAGINING LEADERSHIP

REFLECTION QUESTIONS

1. How are you currently positioned at the crossroads between compliance and justice? What are the indicators or evidence? Are you reproducing oppression in your current work?
2. In what ways do your work or organization tokenize community voice rather than treat it as power? How might you truly shift power from such colonizing practices into liberating power-sharing models?
3. How might you reframe "policy compliance" as an opportunity to subvert and re-humanize the work you do?
4. Who are your allies, and how are you building collective solidarity in the face of pushback?

CHAPTER 20

WHEN CHOICE BECOMES NO CHOICE

School Boards, Democracy, and the Fight for Public Schools

CARRIE SAMPSON

MY CONNECTION TO DEMOCRATIC GOVERNANCE, SCHOOL CHOICE, AND EQUITY

Schools should be places where the local community connects, celebrates, supports each other, engages in critical dialogue, and grows together—with a focus on the well-being of people, animals, and the environment. Democratic governance is a cornerstone of this vision. It requires community participation in decision-making that is responsive, transparent, and holds those within schools and those who lead schools accountable to this vision. Equity and justice are this vision's foundation, ensuring that all voices are heard, all living beings are considered, and the concerns of those who are most marginalized are amplified.

My connection to democratic governance, school choice, and equity is as a researcher of school boards and the mother of school-age children of color navigating schools in Arizona, a place that is arguably ground zero for hypercompetitive school-choice policies. The erosion of democratic governance in education through school-choice policies has posed a serious threat to equitable and humanizing public schools that contribute to healthy communities.

My navigation of school choice began in July of 2016. We had just moved to a suburb of Phoenix, Arizona, where my children began attending daycare and preschool. After the November 2016 election and throughout the next couple of years, we dealt with several explicit racist incidents at my children's private preschools. One day my four-year-old daughter, Rose, shared that her best friend uninvited her to her birthday party. When Rose asked her friend why, her friend replied, "Because my parents don't like Brown-skinned people." Other occurrences included name-calling and hair incidents. These events were traumatic for my children, who still talk about them today with sadness and anger. My extensive expertise in education, equity, and policy could not save my children from the terror that they were experiencing at such a young age. I confronted school leadership, but their lack of cultural understanding and responsiveness created further harm.

There was no democratic governing system that would allow me to engage elected representatives and hold the school accountable. I removed my children from three schools within three years. In other words, I had to "vote with my feet"—a concept that holds the illusion of choice. Yet this was not true choice—I wanted stability for my children, not repeated transitions after experiencing harm without proper healing or justice.

UNDERSTANDING THE SCHOOL-CHOICE LANDSCAPE

School choice cannot get us to my vision of schools. It treats families like consumers rather than building strong neighboring communities, sending children outside their communities and disrupting democratic governance, equity, and justice.

Historically, we saw the consequences of students being dispersed outside their communities in the context of some school desegregation efforts. In a study that I was involved in, we found that school desegregation fractured a once thriving Black area of town in Las Vegas, Nevada. For nearly twenty years, Black children were bused far from their neighborhoods, making parental involvement difficult. Eventually, Black mothers advocated for a return to neighborhood schools for their children. After threatening a boycott by refusing to send their children to school on "count day,"[1] the school board voted in favor of returning to neighborhood schools.[2] Community advocacy and protest worked as an avenue of democratic engagement.

In this current environment, as families disperse to other schools and neighborhoods, many traditional public schools struggle to keep their doors open because of enrollment and funding decreases. In Arizona, for instance, many public schools have closed largely because of expansive school choice. For the past thirty years, this state has embraced hypercompetitive school-choice policies, including the country's first and largest universal voucher program, where the state distributes public monies toward private schools or homeschooling. These policies have contributed to an intensely competitive school environment, slowly destroying the concept of neighborhood schools.[3]

Last year, the school district where my son attended school voted to close two schools.[4] Families fought and cried for their neighborhood public school to remain open, but budget shortfalls from declining enrollment meant the district could no longer support them. Despite claims that school-choice policies give families more choices, they actually stripped away choice from these families—giving them *no choice*.

School choice, particularly open-enrollment policies, reveals additional concerns for school board governance. For example, families who send their children to schools outside of their school district forgo their rights to vote for the school board that governs their children's school, creating a barrier toward voter accountability. Additionally, these families have less incentive to vote in favor of bonds and other laws that would support their residential school district. All this exacerbates the decline of resources needed for public schools to remain a viable option for families.[5]

UNDERSTANDING DEMOCRATIC GOVERNANCE

Public schools serve as democratic institutions providing community voice through elected school boards. It is through democratic governance that communities connect, develop, and grow. They can share in the decision-making of their schools and push for equity and justice. Conservative politicians and the incentives buried in the "One Big Beautiful Bill Act" are ushering in expanded school-choice policies and vouchers.[6] As these policies and programs expand, so will the challenges and complexities that impact the sustainability of neighborhood public schools and the ability for school boards to govern equitably. Ultimately, the priorities in the "Big Beautiful Bill," and of many conservative politicians, systematically undermine local democratic governance of our schools by redirecting public funds to private entities without community accountability.[7] This is scary and dangerous.

As a scholar of educational policies and politics, I also know that school board representation is complicated.[8] Not every school board represents their community. And not all parts of the community are equally represented by their school board. School boards are both representatives of the community and trustees of local public schools. They exist to govern our local public schools, and we entrust them to do what is right by our children, even when families or communities demand otherwise. Sometimes they might have to make decisions that are not popular among the majority of the community.

The recent COVID-19 pandemic era brought unprecedented conflict to school boards.

The police murders of George Floyd and others prompted activism around the presence of school police, while political shifts opened doors for extreme conflict over COVID measures, critical race theory, LGBTQ+ rights, and equity.[9] In 2021 and 2022, police arrested or charged at least fifty-nine people for disorderly conduct at school board meetings and attempts to recall school board members reached an all-time high in 2021.[10]

Within this conflict, school boards became a target of advocates and activism from all political sides.[11] Conservative groups like Moms for Liberty recruited candidates to flip boards, while organizations like Democracy and Education supported equity-focused members.[12] And many school boards across the country have voted to sustain and advance equity efforts, even pushing back on state laws. For instance, despite the governor's ban on mask mandates, several districts in Arizona voted for mask mandates to protect vulnerable children and families, resulting in litigation.[13] Scholars have measured the national cost of this conflict during 2023–24 at nearly $3.2 billion.[14]

Some consultants focus on removing politics from schools, keeping school boards "in their lane" and narrowing board focus to test scores.[15] Unfortunately, these frameworks often contribute to excessive test preparation at the expense of children's well-being and subjects not tested. The reality is that education has always been political, and school boards are at the front lines of these political complexities.[16]

Are school boards adequately armed with the right knowledge and skills to fight these battles? Not always. Can a district operate with only a superintendent? Only until controversy arises—racist incidents, book bans, school closures. The superintendent is an education leader but also a bureaucrat whose job is to keep the district running. The school board, however, is elected and accountable to voters, and offers the public a say in public education. The superintendent relies on the school board to make the tough decisions as representatives and trustees of their communities. The school board can hold the line against the pressure to ban mask mandates or books, to remove police in schools, to close schools. And unlike with private schools, the community can engage democratically and use electoral pressure to hold their school board accountable to make equitable and sound decisions for their local schools.

REENVISIONING SCHOOL BOARDS AS A DEMOCRATIC MECHANISM FOR HUMANIZING SCHOOLS

In recent years, many communities have become increasingly aware of how essential school boards are. And while I think democratic governance through locally elected school boards is our best option when it comes to building more humanizing schools, school boards are certainly not perfect. There is room for improvement. Re-visioning democratic governance will require us to consider what has worked and what has not worked.

School board members, who are often unpaid, enter this position with various backgrounds and expertise, their training differs by state and district, and, in many school districts, board members do not reflect the demographics of the communities they are serving.[17] Although nearly 56 percent of the US student population is non-white, recent surveys suggest that 79 percent of school board members are white. Yet, studies show that school boards with more Black and Latinx members positively correlate with factors linked with higher levels of Black and Latinx student achievement;[18] higher numbers of Black, Indigenous, people of color (BIPOC) educators;[19] more bond funds proposed and approved by voters;[20] and higher levels of satisfaction among Black residents.[21] Nonetheless, school board members of color often face unique racialized challenges when running for and serving in these positions.[22] Research also shows that youth representation on boards might improve equity but their presence can be treated as symbolic and their voices often receive less validity.[23]

Voter turnout for school board elections is typically low (10–20 percent).[24] It's higher when aligned with national elections,[25] but voter turnout is less racially diverse than student populations.[26] Only a handful of localities allow undocumented residents to vote in board elections,[27] and nearly 40 percent of elections go uncontested.[28] There has been an increase in large donor contributions to school board campaigns,[29] and many school board seats are elected in at-large elections that tend to disadvantage candidates of color.[30] Yet, even given these challenges, voters tend to hold school board members accountable for student outcomes and policy decisions.[31]

Although school board effectiveness is often measured by student-achievement measures,[32] a healthy relationship between board members and the superintendent matters. School boards have been discouraged from micromanaging superintendents, yet sometimes superintendents are not transparent with their school board and expect them to rubber-stamp their decisions.[33] Also, while there is potential for community engagement and advocacy in school board meetings,[34] policy constraints, like No Child Left Behind policies, legal restrictions, and bureaucratic pressures, usually narrow community deliberation among school boards.[35] And mayoral or state takeovers, which often target majority minoritized districts,[36] show mixed results beyond decreased local control.[37]

Based on the existing evidence, reenvisioning school boards toward humanizing schools will likely require several efforts, including (1) sustaining and/or returning to locally elected school boards; (2) strengthening the school board candidate pool; (3) expanding opportunities for more diverse school board representation (i.e., compensating low-income school board members, increasing school board pipeline programs); (4) capping campaign donations; (5) aligning school board and national elections, allowing non-citizen voting, and embracing at-ward elections; (6) reconsidering ways to increase community engagement and deliberation within and beyond school board meetings; (7) validating youth representation on boards; (8) providing school boards with adequate training and administrative support to increase their capacity; (9) improving superintendent preparation to embrace democratic governance; and (10) developing measures of school board effectiveness that reflect healthy and equitable democratic engagement.

A PATH FORWARD TOWARD A DEMOCRATIC GOVERNANCE THAT FOSTERS HUMANIZING SCHOOLS

To realize democratic governance that humanizes schools, we must embrace school boards. Locally elected school boards work well when engaged and committed to the communities, families, children, and educators they serve, and these communities must be equally engaged with their boards. School boards keep the public in our public schools.[38] We must understand what's at stake. Our communities must fight to maintain this democratic avenue, despite the attempts to dismantle public education. Communities must protect public education amid school choice expansion efforts while recognizing that every child deserves a high quality, healthy, and humanizing school. This means supporting statewide policies that limit unregulated school choice, tax credits, and vouchers all while pushing for more support for public schools—including substantially higher teacher salaries, robust teacher education programs, creative curriculum, holistic accountability metrics, and safe and optimal school buildings.

We also must rethink school boards. School board members should critically reflect on their effectiveness to improve their governance. Families, youth, and residents should vocalize their dreams for how schools might contribute to humanizing communities. Educators and district leaders should consider how they can leverage democratic governance working daily with children to create a humanizing environment. What are the resources and support they need? State policymakers and leaders should consider ways to elevate and support school boards so that they can be most effective. What policies can be implemented to attract and retain diverse and qualified school board candidates, to increase voter turnout, ensure that youth voices are amplified, and protect and support public schools? Scholars and researchers from various disciplines should focus more intently on school boards to study what's working, what's not working, and what has yet to be even tried but might work—all aimed at building democratic governance that contributes to humanizing schools and local communities.

CONCLUDING THOUGHTS ABOUT DEMOCRATIC GOVERNANCE, SCHOOL CHOICE, AND ACCOUNTABILITY

The threats to public education are numerous and nuanced. Solving this complex puzzle requires many pieces. I argue that school boards are a cornerstone to this solution. School boards can help cultivate their communities' dreams. They are the critical link between the community and its school district.

We cannot solve this puzzle without waking up. Our communities must wake up to the political realities constraining our democracy, environment, public schools, and school board governance. We must change the narrative about public education and emphasize the critical importance of education as a public good.

As communities grapple with the impacts of issues like school choice and school closures, I have been inspired by how people have become activated to get involved, to speak up, and to push back. Educators, scholars, and policymakers must leverage this activation to help communities understand educational complexities and urge them to advocate at the local, state, and federal levels. We must ensure that our locally elected school boards remain a viable democratic institution, that they are prepared to effectively govern, and that one of our most important common goods—public schools—still exists for our communities to govern.

CONTINUING TO WORK ON DEMOCRACY, GOVERNANCE, AND PUBLIC SCHOOLING

DISCUSSION QUESTIONS FOR COMMUNITIES TO REFLECT ON THEIR LOCAL SCHOOL BOARDS

1. What do families and communities know about their local school board members?
2. In what ways have families and communities reached out to local school board members to share their concerns, desires, and stories? What other avenues and systems could be built to increase engagement?
3. How are local school board members accessible and responsive to their communities? How might they improve upon this? How can they prioritize parts of their communities that are most vulnerable?
4. How can states and localities increase voter turnout to school boards?
5. How can running for the school board be more attainable so that our school boards more equitably represent their communities?
6. How might we rethink the relationship and the roles of the superintendent and the school board to improve democratic governance?
7. How do we better prepare and support school board members?

Organizations that support democratic governance and public education:

Advancement Project: "Today, we envision a future where Black, Latine, and other students of color experience a liberatory education system: one where they have self-determination, power, dignity, and freedom. Our vision for liberatory education is rooted in a framework of moving from abolition to abundance." https://advancementproject.org

Alliance to Reclaim Our Schools: "Our coalition was born out of the need to shift the narrative around public education, highlighting the successes within our networks, but also elevating community solutions over corporate or legislative edicts." https://reclaimourschools.org

Democracy and Education: "Helps school board candidates and their supporters protect our public schools and stand up for democracy." https://www.democracy-education.org

H.E.A.L. Together (Honest Education Action and Leadership) via RACE Forward: "A movement of students, parents, educators, and school board members in school districts across the United States who believe that an honest, equitable, and fully funded public education is the foundation for a just, multiracial democracy." https://www.raceforward.org

Local Progress: "Working to organize school board members around a multi-issue policy agenda and create a community of practice for progressive local leaders." https://localprogress.org/issues/school-boards/

Network for Public Education: "We are an advocacy group whose mission is to preserve, promote, improve and strengthen public schools for both current and future generations of students." https://networkforpubliceducation.org/grassroots-education-network/states/

Partnership for the Future of Learning: "Brings together a diverse network of individuals and organizations with a deep commitment to an equitable, high-quality, public education system." https://futureforlearning.org

Red Wine & Blue: "A national community of over half a million diverse suburban women working together to defeat extremism, one friend at a time. We train and connect women from across the country of all political backgrounds—including many who have never been political before—to get sh*t done and have fun along the way." https://redwine.blue/troublenation/

School Board School: "We are activating a diverse coalition of education advocates and aspiring school board members to create significant and sustainable change in our school system." https://www.schoolboardschool.org

CHAPTER 21

EDUCATING AGAINST DISEMPOWERMENT

Freedom Schools as an Educational Model

VANDEEN A. CAMPBELL, MARGARET GOLDMAN, AND CHARLES M. PAYNE

Recently, some young Black people have been wearing shirts saying "Legalize Black Education." That is hardly an overstatement after the president of the United States has outlawed diversity, equity, and inclusion in education. We now have a brazen assault on the well-being of all children. For those who have been marginalized, it is a concerted effort that will undermine hope and a sense of possibility in self, community, and world. For those who identify with the mainstream it means continued immersion in the kind of misinformation that justifies white supremacy. We argue that Freedom Schools are a way through these dangers.

Historically, when the state refused to educate their children, marginalized communities have turned to alternative modes of education. One of the most powerful forms of community education we know is Freedom Schooling. We share the backgrounds that we bring to the topic then outline how communities can reenvision some of America's public schools and other spaces of learning as Freedom Schools, thereby producing students who can counter attempts to erase and disempower them.

OUR CONNECTIONS TO FREEDOM SCHOOLING AND ITS PRINCIPLES

VANDEEN: I grew up in Jamaica, where normal schooling built cultural pride, partly through studies of national heroes. Nanny of the Maroons was a favorite. She established an autonomous community deep in the mountains for people who self-emancipated from their enslavers immediately after arrival from Ghana to Jamaica. Much of what I admire in Nanny the Maroon, and what I value from schooling in Jamaica, is what Freedom Schools offer: a strong sense of dignity, hope, and possibility.

MARGARET: As a social justice educator, one of the crucial distinctions I've made is between public schooling and public education. Teaching at an abolitionist alternative school in South LA that serves youth who were excluded from public schooling crystallized this distinction. My students were critical of "school" yet eager to learn and insightfully aware of what a life-affirming education should look like. These so-called "bad kids" flourished in a space in which their humanity was affirmed, and their respect was earned. My students remind me that while public schooling belongs to the state, public education has always belonged to the community.

CHARLES: My commitment to Freedom Schools crystallized when I saw how they gave students from tough neighborhoods on the South Side of Chicago a new, stronger sense of self which changed the way they interacted with one another. It reduced "put-down" culture and gave them a space to talk about the things in life they feared. For boys, that was street violence; for girls, sexual harassment. No one could give them instant solutions, but being able to voice their fears in a supportive atmosphere meant a great deal.

UNDERSTANDING FREEDOM SCHOOLS

If you passed by the New Ark Freedom School on an afternoon in late July, you might be lucky enough to catch the sea of youngsters pouring off the front steps of the brightly colored building in preparation to rally around the neighborhood. Teachers and students gathered under the uncompromising one o'clock sun in pajamas, onesies, robes and slippers, carrying handcrafted posters that captured the theme of their National Day of Social Action: "Don't 'Sleep' on Public Education!" The posters, stretching twice as high as some of the young scholars holding them, matched the chants that ebbed and flowed in call-and-response throughout the march.

Education is the key to life and liberty!
The revolution will not be televised.
Don't sleep on public education!

As the march moved off the front steps and into the surrounding streets, you might have heard "I Can" by Nas blasting through a portable speaker carried by one of the teachers. Occasionally, someone would break out into one of the Freedom School songs—like "(Something Inside) So Strong" by Labi Siffre, the soundtrack for daily harambee circles—and the children would enthusiastically join in, belting out the lyrics they had memorized. And as the sea of youngsters made their way through the surrounding streets in protest of the assault on public education, you'd see residents looking on with admiration. A middle-aged truck driver leaned out the window of his cab and honked in approval; down the road, two young men having a hushed conversation through the tinted windows of a sports car did the same. Across from them, a woman stood in her front yard clapping and nodding, while an elderly man sitting on the porch behind her tapped his fingers to the beat of the music.

By the time the protest wound its way back to the brightly colored building, you might hear one of the scholars—a young Black girl in second grade—gently echoing the earlier collective chants, like a song lyric stuck in her head: "*Education . . . is the keeey.*"

"Freedom School" is now mostly used in reference to the schools that developed from the Mississippi Civil Rights Movement in the fateful summer of 1964, or the contemporary schools that the Children's Defense Fund (CDF) operates—nearly two hundred in 2024.[1] In 1964, as part of "Freedom Summer," a multipronged attempt to break the back of white supremacy, Charlie Cobb, a member of the Student Nonviolent Coordinating Committee (SNCC), proposed Freedom Schools to "fill an intellectual and creative vacuum in the lives of young Negro Mississippians" and to get them to understand the role they could play in building a better Mississippi.[2] The schools served over two thousand students that summer and inspired other efforts at liberatory education, including the Black Panther Liberation Schools.

In the early 1990s, the Black Student Leadership Network (BSLN)—young activists affiliated with the CDF—took up the task of addressing the unfinished work of the Civil Rights Movement, especially SNCC, with its emphasis on participatory democracy, collective leadership, and community organizing. They led a revival of SNCC Freedom Schools and built an award-winning literacy component into the model, featuring minority authors and books about children of color and social issues.

Over the past three decades, the Freedom School movement has grown. The program prioritizes student agency, building its curriculum around the idea that students can make a difference in their family, their class, their school, their neighborhood, and their world.[3] There is an annual action campaign around a selected social issue (e.g., climate change) culminating in a National Day of Action, including petitions, marches, and letter-writing campaigns. The reading materials, discussions, and staffing all maintain an eye to support positive racial/ethnic identity. The music and dance that are pervasive in Freedom Schools reflect the cultural heritage of whatever children are being served by that school.

Notwithstanding programmatic evolutions, the Mississippi schools and the CDF schools were built on a set of underlying principles that communities under fascist and racist assault have repeatedly deployed in defense of their children.[4] Communities have created educational spaces that intentionally connect education to social struggle, affirm the dignity of children, build their sense of agency, and connect them to supportive peers and elders.

Given the tenor of the times, let us be explicit about what should be obvious: In their strongest forms, Freedom Schools proceed from humanistic premises. They stand in opposition to dehumanizing contexts. For example, the curriculum for the Mississippi schools included a unit aimed at getting Black students to understand how poor whites are used as pawns in a racist system. Similarly, Charlie Cobb, who wrote the prospectus for the Mississippi schools with the legacies of Septima Clark and Ella Baker in mind, said that the whole point of the project was to get students across the state to stand up in their classrooms and ask a real question, a question of their own.[5] Freedom Schools help students find their own voice, think critically, and see the world through a variety of lenses. If we just want them to parrot what they've been told, we can leave them in the hands of MAGA.

Research on CDF Freedom Schools finds both academic and social impacts.[6] Evaluations across multiple sites—including Los Angeles,[7] Kansas City,[8] Charlotte, North Carolina,[9] and central Texas[10]—show that students improve or maintain their reading levels over the summer; a 2024 national evaluation shows that over 81 percent of CDF Freedom Schools students gained an average of nine months of learning in reading.[11] These gains are especially pronounced among scholars (how Freedom Schools intentionally refer to their students) with multiple years of participation and those in schools that implemented the program with high fidelity.

The power of Freedom Schools extends to the holistic development of scholars. Evaluations from Oakland[12] and St. Paul[13] show enhanced racial and cultural identity, improved conflict resolution and social skills, heightened self-confidence and sense of responsibility, and a deepened love of reading.

Freedom Schools have been successful with students from all kinds of backgrounds. We have not seen research on specific effects on white students, but we can extrapolate from research on ethnic studies classrooms that show benefits like "democracy outcomes" (e.g., racial understanding and perspective-taking) and increased engagement and performance for all students, including white students, especially in classrooms with cross-group interactions.[14]

REENVISIONING SCHOOLING AS FREEDOM SCHOOLS

Freedom Schools offer an appropriate response to the dumbed-down, antidemocratic education the MAGA movement is reestablishing. The age of MAGA is not a time for tinkering. We need a comprehensive response to authoritarian indoctrination, and for us that means reimagining education as transformative. We propose that the principles of Freedom Schools become the basis of a national movement to create educational spaces in the spirit of the Mississippi schools. We envision a national network of public and private schools and out-of-school programs—embracing the full spectrum of educational experiences through which young people grow—designed specifically to develop generations of children with "democracy skills," a thirst for freedom, and the confidence to use them.

The *traditions of community organizing and organizer-teaching* would guide the network, meaning an emphasis on developing the leadership potential of everyone.[15] To foster collective leadership, the network would be democratic, collaborative, and rooted in shared purpose. Schools and partner organizations would function as a community of practice, sharing strategies, co-designing curricula, and rotating leadership to build collective capacity. This same spirit would shape instruction—classrooms and programs would be organized as collective learning spaces where educators and students co-investigate their communities, cultivate critical consciousness, and practice leadership as an everyday act of civic engagement.

The network would ideally be supported by a team that includes school administrators; program directors; teachers; support staff like social workers, students, and parents/guardians; student leaders; community leaders; and other partners. The team would combine experience with Freedom Schools, teacher development, movement building, curriculum development, mental health support, and community organizing. Deep, multi-level involvement of parents and community (*community wisdom*) can help ensure the work is not bureaucratized. Parent University programs, which train parents as tutors and mentors, offer examples of how parents and community members can be mobilized as leaders in school success.[16]

A national Freedom School agenda must emphasize *academic rigor* and maintain high expectations, at the same time it prioritizes the social, emotional, and cultural dimensions of liberatory learning. This will be partly a matter of how personnel are selected. Combining Freedom Schooling with rigorous programs like International Baccalaureate (IB)—an advanced curriculum beginning in the elementary grades centered on critical thinking and global citizenship—gives children the challenging, broadening, and life-affirming environments they need and deserve.

The network would necessarily invest in *teacher preparation and professional development* models grounded in dignity-affirming practices, racial justice, and community accountability, ideally in partnerships with local teacher-preparation programs. In keeping with a spirit of *inclusivity*, Freedom School programming should take place in accessible buildings, with multilingual staff including American Sign Language, and on-demand technologies to facilitate participation for students and families who may have been excluded previously. Parents of children with disabilities should have a key role in planning.

A PATH FORWARD FOR FREEDOM SCHOOLING

The network would find ready support in traditionally underserved communities. In Blue states, Freedom Schools may be able to leverage public resources. In Red states and politically conservative locales in Blue states, Freedom Schools likely will need to operate with private support in fugitive spaces—sites where this educational work can continue outside of hostile state infrastructures—or in fugitive ways within state institutions.[17]

Some initial practical steps to develop a national Freedom School network include:

- Forming a coordinating team to connect local efforts with the network, facilitate broad collaboration, and coordinate resources and activities.
- A diverse working group would engage educators from Freedom Schools, public schools, and private schools to co-create an open-access, high-quality curriculum rooted in social justice, civic engagement, and culturally sustaining pedagogy—drawing from historical Freedom School materials and community knowledge through an iterative, collaborative process for adaptation across local contexts.
- A funding working group would build diversified, sustainable revenue through partnerships with philanthropy and mission-aligned institutions, explore endowment and long-term investment models, provide mini-grants for new sites, and pursue state funding strategies to sustain Freedom Schools beyond grant cycles.
- A working group would disseminate community education resources—such as multimedia toolkits, storytelling campaigns, and public events—to help educators, parents, policymakers, and journalists understand Freedom Schools and highlight local successes.
- A key component would be curating and expanding Freedom School research and evaluations through a coordinated research agenda with universities and evaluation centers, using participatory methods and developmental frameworks to ensure findings inform practice and policy in alignment with the work's democratic principles.
- Building a robust pool of professional development resources for educators and community youth workers, including online repositories, summer institutes, and mentorship pipelines to ensure high-quality training and sustained capacity.
- Developing rapid-response networks to provide legal, financial, and emotional support for educators and activists—along with alliances

with advocacy and civil rights organizations—will be vital to collectively defend and sustain Freedom School practices.

- Ongoing public relations and community mobilization—through social media, public forums, and journalism—will be essential to keep Freedom School work visible and central in public conversations.

Assessing barriers and mitigating risks is important to the path forward. Adult belief systems and dysfunctional organizational patterns can block meaningful implementation, and strong efforts to educate racialized youth have too often been ignored. School and program leadership turnover undermines the work, making the selection of committed teachers and principals critical. Bottom-up demand and deep community involvement help safeguard the work's core values and stabilize it amid system change, while political alliances and a legal support network can provide crucial protection.

CONCLUDING THOUGHTS ABOUT FREEDOM SCHOOLING

One of the most insidious ways that regimes of power operate is by instilling an ingrained helplessness in the people they seek to control, in part by erasing or obscuring the blueprints for liberation that *already exist*. The heterogeneous genealogy of Freedom Schooling, including both the Mississippi schools of 1964 and the contemporary CDF schools, invites us to think about the "path forward" in this moment not as building something new but as returning to and extending the paths our ancestors already created. A first step in our path forward, then, is to make accessible and *irresistible*—as Toni Cade Bambara teaches us—the rich resources and histories we have at our disposal.[18]

Rooted in such histories, there is a meaningful and arguably necessary opportunity at this historical juncture to develop a national network of schools and programs imbued with Freedom School principles. Arundathi Roy famously reimagined the COVID-19 pandemic as a *portal*: a space and invitation to reckon with and collectively refuse the unequal social order that the pandemic and its governmental response merely brought to the surface.[19] In many ways, despite some undoubtedly exceptional features, Trump's assault on public education is an escalation of the conditions against which the Freedom Schools and liberation movements of the 1960s and 1970s fought. His policies make explicit the racist and classist hostility that has long festered in American society and education.

In this way, the current political moment is also a portal—an opportunity to form networks and coalitions across people and places who have historically seen their interests as antagonistic or fractured at best. This invitation is a return to the blueprints left by Freedom Schools to disrupt American racism's hierarchies, e.g., between Blacks and poor whites.[20] This moment gives us a leg to stand on when we say that educational liberation is indeed *for everyone.*

CONTINUING TO WORK ON FREEDOM SCHOOLS

The ideas outlined in the chapter are meant to start a national effort supporting Freedom Schooling. The exercises below can help us begin to examine what this could look like in local contexts.

1. From the vantage point of your local context and thinking about learnings from liberatory education, network organizing, movement building, and other areas, what would be the building blocks for a national Freedom School movement? What is already in place?
2. In your local setting, what barriers or challenges will make it difficult to advance the work of Freedom Schools? What are strategies that you might develop for working with local stakeholders to address these challenges? Who are potential allies and what resources can you draw upon?

The Cornwall Center at Rutgers-Newark has published a Freedom School Resource Guide document; https://rutgers.app.box.com/s/mckhqy17er5nxqxkx42h1m0pvig90ysm. We also recommend the following resources as starting points:

Children's Defense Fund Freedom Schools: https://www.childrensdefense.org/programs/cdf-freedom-schools/

Mississippi Freedom School Curriculum: http://educationanddemocracy.org/ED_FSC.html; http://www.educationanddemocracy.org/FSCfiles/A_02_Introduction.htm; http://educationanddemocracy

.org/ED_FSC.html; http://www.educationanddemocracy.org/FSCfiles/A_02_Introduction.htm; http://www.educationanddemocracy.org/FSCfiles/A_02_Introduction.htm

R. P. Robinson, "Until the Revolution: Analyzing the Politics, Pedagogy, and Curriculum of the Oakland Community School," *Espacio, Tiempo y Educación* 7, no. 1 (2020): 181–203, http://dx.doi.org/10.14516/ete.273

Charles M. Payne and Carol Sills Strickland, *Teach Freedom: Education for Liberation in the African-American Tradition* (Teachers College Press, 2008)

The Brotherhood/Sister Sol and Susan Wilcox, eds., *Brother, Sister, Leader: The Official Curriculum of The Brotherhood Sister Sol* (2013), https://brotherhood-sistersol.org/product/brother-sister-leader-the-official-curriculum-of-the-brotherhood-sister-sol/

CHAPTER 22

LEAD LIKE DEMOCRACY DEPENDS ON IT

Leadership for Justice and the Public Good

MICHELLE D. YOUNG

MY CONNECTION TO LEADERSHIP FOR JUSTICE AND THE PUBLIC GOOD

Public education is the beating heart of democracy. It not only sustains, circulates, and nourishes the very conditions that allow democratic life to flourish; it also brings together students from every walk of life, to help them master ideas and skills while learning what it means to live alongside others in a shared society.

I have watched with growing alarm as public education, both K–12 and higher education, has come under intensifying attack. Authoritarian politics, market-driven reforms, and reactionary cultural backlashes have converged to erode the very idea of education as a public good. Instead of nurturing democratic possibility, schools and universities are increasingly treated as marketplaces for consumer choice, battlegrounds for ideological control, or training grounds for compliance.

All students need and deserve a public education that offers joy, justice, and opportunities for deep learning, and it is our responsibility, as education leaders, to ensure they receive it. Yet, in recent months, I've felt the ground shift beneath this responsibility. Earlier this year, for example, the president of the United States issued several executive orders mandating the termination of programs designed to support equity, inclusion, and diversity, and federal funding for education research and development has been cut significantly and, in some cases, eliminated altogether. These actions strike directly at the conditions that make educational leadership possible, and they have had a chilling effect on leaders in K–12 and higher education.

I feel this threat personally and professionally. As a scholar and as a leader of the University Council for Educational Administration and now of the Berkeley School of Education, I have spent nearly three decades working with others to reposition the field of educational leadership around leadership for learning, equity, and justice; to transform practices and structures that sustained inequity and exclusion; and to design leadership preparation programs that cultivate equity-minded educational leaders who value, respect, and engage the communities they serve. And just as the benefits of this field-transforming work were becoming more visible, a powerful backlash rose, attempting to dismantle in months what took years to achieve.

At the Berkeley School of Education, our motto is Educate Like Democracy Depends on It. The current context makes the truth of this motto palpable. It also raises the question: What does it mean to lead educational institutions like democracy depends on it? And what does such leadership demand of us in a moment when the value of higher education is questioned, curriculum is politicized, academic freedom is limited, and inclusion is cast as indoctrination? In such times, to lead as if democracy depends on it requires more than resisting the forces of censorship, erasure, and compliance. It calls for actively cultivating educational organizations as spaces of learning, belonging, inquiry, and shared purpose. It means anchoring daily decisions about curriculum, hiring, resource allocation, student support, communication, etc., not in fear or expedience but in a vision of education as a public good, a democratic right, and a shared responsibility. In other words, the charge of leadership today is not only to withstand the backlash but to advance a bolder, more inclusive vision of what education can and should be and why it matters.

UNDERSTANDING LEADERSHIP FOR JUSTICE AND THE PUBLIC GOOD

To understand what is at stake in this moment, we must first recognize that public education is not simply under-resourced or unevenly supported—it is under coordinated attack. Across the country, we are witnessing a sharp rise in efforts to delegitimize the very idea of education as a public, democratic good.

These attacks take many forms. In some states, book bans have stripped school libraries and classrooms of texts that address "divisive concepts." Politicians have targeted teachers and professors, branding them as "indoctrinators" for fostering critical inquiry or affirming the identities of LGBTQ+ students. School boards, once the most local expression of democratic participation, have become sites of intimidation, harassment, and political takeover. In higher education, faculty senates are being abolished; diversity, equity, and inclusion (DEI) offices and policies cloistered; tenure and other faculty protections eliminated; and federal funding for research, programming, and student aid held hostage for ideological purposes. Entire fields in higher education—ethnic studies, gender studies, even climate science—have been attacked or dismantled. The cumulative effect is not only to narrow what and how students can learn, what educators can teach, and what research scholars can pursue, but also to erode the democratic foundation that public education is meant to secure. This convergence of authoritarian politics, equity and inclusion backlash, and ideological pressure has produced a climate where fear, compliance, and isolationism can easily displace inquiry, justice, and inclusion.

Alongside this culture war is a quieter, more insidious threat: the redefinition of educational leadership itself. Research demonstrates that leadership for learning, equity, and justice; leadership that embraces student populations that have been historically underserved; and leadership that is practiced with integrity and in service of the public good leads to improvements in teacher performance and retention and to increases in student achievement, student and family engagement, and graduation rates. This is a very different understanding of leadership than that held in previous decades, and it was hard-won. Leadership for learning and justice, and the research on which this understanding is based, required significant investments in research, development, and efforts to embed research in national leadership performance standards, state evaluation systems, preparation programs, program accreditation standards, and professional learning opportunities. Getting to this point took several decades and considerable efforts by researchers, K–12 leaders, university faculty, state-level leaders, and professional associations.

However, in many districts, states, and institutions, leadership as the ethical stewardship of learning, equity, and access is being reshaped and diminished to focus primarily on managerial compliance—ensuring efficiency, protecting institutional reputation, and avoiding political backlash. Leaders are being asked or required to enforce policies they do not believe in, stay silent or neutral in the face of injustice, and prioritize public image over public responsibility. Many feel that they are being asked to abandon conscience and principled commitments.

This shift is not accidental, nor is the difficulty that our education organizations are having rallying to the challenge. What we are seeing today is the result of decades of market-based education reform that has eroded the moral and civic foundations of public education. In K–12, charter expansion, privatization, and punitive accountability regimes have reshaped schools into performance-based organizations rather than participatory public institutions. In higher education, it is the result of a slow, strategic erasure of the sector's civic and democratic purposes, through disinvestment, ideological attacks on the quality and purpose of a college education, and the portrayal of higher-education faculty and students as threats.

Recent examples abound. Superintendents have been fired for supporting trans students or advocating for inclusive curriculum. University leaders have been fired or disciplined for upholding free speech on campus. A culture of fear has developed within K–12 and higher-education leadership, which threatens to distort the purpose of education and the responsibilities of leadership. When school leaders are punished for defending the curriculum, their staff, and their efforts to support equity and access, we send a chilling message: Courage is costly, and compliance is safe.

The implications for students are profound. When leadership is shaped by fear rather than courage and a commitment to learning and equity, schools and universities are less likely to offer the kind of curriculum, climate, and culture that helps students develop as critical thinkers, civic participants, and agents of change. Leadership becomes an obstacle to equity rather than its catalyst, and the broader public begins to lose faith in education as a shared project—a place where all students are nurtured and developed to their full potential.

Our current reality demands more than managerial skill or procedural neutrality. It requires courage, clarity, and an unflinching commitment to justice. Leaders must do more than help their organizations survive the storm. They must be prepared to name the attacks for what they are—efforts to silence, divide, and dismantle the public—and to respond with a vision of education rooted in equity, belonging, and the public good. This requires the cultivation of leaders who have abilities and commitments that extend beyond the norm. Having a strong equity orientation, management skills, and the ability to develop human and organizational resources will be essential, but they will not be enough.

REENVISIONING LEADERSHIP

If attacks on education aim to silence, isolate, and constrain leaders, then our response must be to provide leaders with the training and support that enable them to speak truth to power, to build trust, to cultivate equity and belonging, and to advance a bolder, more inclusive vision of education. Leadership for justice and the public good encompasses aspects of collaborative, social justice, advocacy, culturally responsive, and systems leadership. These forms of leadership are not innate. They are cultivated through preparation, practice, and reflection.

To meet the current moment, leaders must be excellent problem framers, alliance builders, system thinkers, and advocates. Building these capacities requires more than a focus on content (e.g., understanding the importance of alliances) and skills (e.g., how to build alliances). It also requires what my coauthors and I refer to as critical propensities: critical reflection, critical consciousness, and multiple perspective taking.[1] Whereas critical reflection enables one to examine long-held, socially constructed ideas, beliefs, and assumptions about one's experiences[2] and scrutinize and analyze power relationships,[3] critical consciousness is a tool for thinking about and understanding education and its place in society and identify strategies for change. Multiple perspective taking involves considering issues from a variety of perspectives, pausing to check assumptions, gathering data, and seeking to understand problems, issues, and relationships with more complexity.[4] Taken together these three propensities enable a leader to understand, plan, and act in new and more profound ways. Paired with a commitment to justice and the public good, as well as opportunities to gain content knowledge and skills, these three propensities can help develop leaders who can, in turn, rethink, reimagine, and transcend current systems.

There are district and county superintendents who practice leadership for democracy and the public good, who redistribute resources to historically marginalized neighborhoods, and who model culturally responsive leadership on a daily basis. There are also higher-education leaders who stand firm in defense of inclusive pedagogy and freedom of speech. These leaders are not anomalies; they are evidence of what becomes possible when leadership is redefined for justice and the public good.

Of course, leaders must still manage budgets, follow policy, and navigate contentious politics. This is true. But ethical clarity does not replace technical skill; it anchors it. A leader grounded in justice will still balance budgets but will do so in ways that serve dignity rather than diminish it. It is also true that communities disagree about what justice or democracy looks like. But keep in mind, democracy thrives on debate. The role of educational leaders is not to eliminate conflict but to navigate it with integrity, care, and a commitment to the public good.

A PATH FORWARD

To reclaim educational leadership as a force for justice, equity, and democracy, we must reimagine how leaders are prepared, supported, and defended. Even the most talented leaders cannot lead for justice and the public good by sheer will alone. The demands of leadership today require something more. Leadership for justice and the public good must be cultivated, nurtured by institutions, protected by policy, and sustained by solidarity.

I'll begin with preparation and professional development. Leadership development must continue to cultivate essential leadership knowledge and skills, and leaders must also deeply engage issues of power, history, equity, and community. The curriculum of programs for future leaders must include and extend beyond instructional supervision, equitable decision-making, and the cultivation of communities. It must also cultivate the ability to navigate hostile conversations and meetings and organize and implement strategies used by community organizers. Leaders must understand how to employ the analytical strategies of researchers and the democratic commitments of public intellectuals. They must be able to engage in deep reflection, take multiple perspectives in their deliberations, and expand their critical consciousness. While the field has made significant gains around leadership for learning and equity, few preparation programs are designed to develop the skills and understandings needed to lead for democracy. Turning the tide will require a combination of preserving gains made in the field and making additional investments in the development of critical, analytical, and political skills.

We must also build leadership networks that nourish courage. Leaders must cultivate communities of courage within their own educational organizations, and it is equally important that they have communities of courage outside of their organizations. Networks of alumni, like UC Berkeley's Principal Leadership Institute's (PLI) twenty-five cohort-strong alumni network or UC Denver's Ritchie Program for School Leaders principals' network, provide critical spaces for reflection, shared learning, and mutual care. These networks can model how to build power through solidarity. Expanding and investing in such networks will help to ensure that leaders, especially those from marginalized identities, are not left isolated when they take principled stands.

In addition to ensuring that leaders have networks of support, we must devise ways to protect and defend them when leadership for justice and the public good is under fire. From legal defense funds to whistleblower protections, from professional association standards to formal contract language, and from community engagement to community organizing, we must be prepared to stand up for leaders who lead for democracy.

Foundations must shift funding priorities toward leadership initiatives that are justice-oriented, grounded in community building and organizing, and away from technocratic, market-driven reform. Grants should support efforts to protect and defend public education; the right to teach, learn, and discover; and the students and communities our education systems serve, particularly cross-sector collaborations among researchers, educators, and communities.

Finally, we must change how leadership is understood in the public imagination. We need stories of courageous, justice-rooted leadership to be visible and celebrated. Leadership in defense of democracy should be elevated and celebrated. This requires work in media, policy spaces, and popular discourse to elevate an understanding of education leadership as a civic responsibility and one that deserves both scrutiny and support.

Educational leadership for justice and the public good will not emerge by accident. It must be expected, prepared, supported, and defended.

CONCLUDING THOUGHTS

Reclaiming educational leadership for democracy and justice is not simply an aspirational project; it is an urgent necessity. At stake is more than the future of education; it is the health of our democracy and the possibility of a more equitable and humane society. Public education has always been contested terrain, shaped by exclusion and inequity even as it has carried the promise of opportunity and belonging. In this moment of intensifying polarization and systemic injustice, the role of leaders is to defend and reimagine that promise.

To reclaim education leadership for democracy and justice is to lead with courage, imagination, and intentionality. It is to insist that schools and universities remain places of belonging, truth-telling, and collective possibility. It is to affirm and protect the responsibility of public schools and universities to serve not only as places of learning but also as crucibles of democracy.

Leadership matters—not simply as a technical function of schooling but as a moral and political act that shapes the health of our democracy. If we are to realize the radical hope of public education, leadership must remain focused on learning, equity, and the public good.

Education leaders must be more than stewards of institutions; they must be stewards of democracy itself. To do so requires nothing less than leading and educating like democracy depends on it.

CONTINUING TO WORK ON LEADERSHIP FOR JUSTICE AND THE PUBLIC GOOD

QUESTIONS FOR REFLECTION AND DIALOGUE

- What organizational structures or traditions sustain or hinder leadership for the public good?
- Who is missing from your leadership conversations—and how might you center them?
- What would it look like to lead your organization as a site of democratic renewal and justice?
- What alliances or coalitions might you need to build inside and beyond our institution to defend and advance the public purposes of education?

MAPPING TENSIONS EXERCISE

Surface where democratic and justice-oriented ideals are upheld or constrained in one's organization. Facilitation: (1) Draw two intersecting axes: Democratic vs. Authoritarian and Equitable vs. Inequitable; (2) pick two to three troubling organizational practices or policies (e.g., graduate student teaching assignments); (3) place them on the chart where they best fit; (4) discuss why certain practices, policies, and traditions fall far from the ideals of democracy and justice.

CONSIDERING THE FUTURE EXERCISE

Imagine and plan a more democratic, justice-oriented future. Facilitation: (1) Ask participants to think of a near future (approximately ten years from now) where we have succeeded in reclaiming educational leadership for democracy and justice; (2) in groups, write a brief vignette capturing what leadership, teaching and learning, and community engagement look and feel like; (3) backward map from that future to today. What steps would we need to take in three years, one year, and the next ninety days to move in that direction?

RESOURCES

On equity leadership: *Equity Leadership Now* (podcast): https://bse.berkeley.edu/eln

On equity practice: Decoteau J. Irby and Ann M. Ishimaru, *Doing the Work of Equity Leadership for Justice and Systems Change* (Teachers College Press, 2025)

On leadership for democracy: Lauri Johnson and Yoon Pak, "Leadership for Democracy in Challenging Times: Historical Case Studies in the United States and Canada," *Educational Administration Quarterly* 54, no. 3 (2018), DOI: https://doi.org/10.1177/0013161X18761345

On preparation: Michelle Young and Angel Nash, "Aligning Frameworks and Identifying Capacities for Anti-Racist Advocacy Educational Leadership," in *Strengthening Anti-Racist Educational Leaders: Advocating for Racial Equity in Turbulent Times*, ed. Anjale Welton and Sarah Diem (Bloomsbury, 2022)

SECTION 5

CONCLUSION

CHAPTER 23

"IT'S OUR DAMN JOB"

Imagining and Building the Schools We Need

JOHN ROGERS AND GEORGE THEOHARIS

On a sunny fall Saturday in 2025, educators from across Los Angeles gathered at UCLA to share ideas about how to protect immigrant students in a very dangerous moment. John C., the proud son of immigrants, explained how an early experience with injustice motivated him to become a school leader. In his first year of teaching, John C.'s principal began the opening assembly for the new ninth-grade class with a dire warning. "Half of you," he proclaimed, "will not be here in four years—so you better work hard." John C. told us: "I could not then accept that some of our beautiful young people were expendable, and I will not accept it now. We have an obligation to help all our students fulfill their ambitions. It's our damn job."

John C.'s seemingly simple declaration powerfully conveys the charge of this book. "It's our damn job" to challenge the authoritarian turn menacing our young people and our public schools. This means we must name and confront a wide set of threats—the damnable conditions in our schools and our society writ large. But that is not enough. We must identify the threats in order to unleash generative and expansive learning and support the realization of social dreams. And because dangerous times are disorienting and too often lead to quietude, we need prophetic voices like John C.'s to remind us that we cannot be passive. We can and must act to build just schools and a better world. It's our damn job.

Many young people, educators, and community members across this nation share John C.'s moral conviction. They want change. They are frustrated with existing schooling and angry at political attacks that deepen student vulnerabilities and erode the institution of public education. Yet, often, their dissatisfaction and resistance are diffuse, and they lack a shared path forward. This book aims to offer a framework of sorts to help crystalize dissent, spark imagination, and galvanize action.

In this final chapter, we draw on insights from the authors of this book to highlight the threats facing our young people and our public schools. We then pivot to describe a set of design principles that emerge from the chapters in this book. The design principles offer starting points—grounded in moral vision and deep understanding of learning—for imagining schools that support collective flourishing. In the final section, we present a few ideas for how we might take up the shared work of building the schools we need.

THE THREATS

The authors in this book have named a wide set of threats to democracy, public education, and the well-being, learning, and humanity of our young people. Some chapters have described dynamics like censorship, sorting, and privatization. Other chapters have centered threats to particular groups—for example, transgender youth, African American girls and women, undocumented students. Looking across the chapters, we see four overarching and interlocking threats. We present these four threats below individually. But it is important to note that the threats fortify each other and should be understood as part of a shared project.

> **THREAT ONE**: *The promotion of a supremacist belief system* that construes some as more intellectually able and more deserving of development, opportunity, and love than others. This worldview justifies inequality and scarcity as inevitable and implies that a high-quality education and the right to be treated with dignity should be reserved for a select few. Threat one is driven by too much self-delusion, fear of losing status, and bigotry.

> **THREAT TWO**: *The control of diverse bodies* through surveillance, incrimination, and partition. These actions are motivated by whipped-up fear of the "other" and moralistic narratives that draw upon prevailing norms of class, race, and gender to frame student behavior as "good" or "bad." (For example, viewing some students as pulling pranks and others as committing crimes.) In the process, the developmental needs, stories, and suffering of those viewed as different and undeserving are

discounted or disregarded. This second threat highlights too much concentrated and unaccountable power policing those with little formal power. And then too many others go along.

THREAT THREE: *The silencing of inquiry* through resistance to engage the thorny, the troubling, the painful dimensions of our past and present. Relatedly, we see a reluctance to dream of possible futures. This refusal manifests in restricting or banning ideas or muzzling people with dissenting viewpoints or different backgrounds and experiences. Often, curiosity and the play of ideas are discouraged or punished. This third threat is grounded in a fear that information and knowledge will be too widely held, too controversial, or too upsetting for young people. It communicates too little faith in our collective capacity to inquire, understand, and heal.

THREAT FOUR: *The evisceration of the public* through a willful failure to recognize that our destinies are intertwined with one another and with the land that sustains us. The inability to think in collective terms leads to the recasting of education as a private good in which we all are consumers seeking to optimize our human capital (or to despair that we can't take on changing the public so we just look for small "solutions" that can be achieved with private funds). This stance both erodes and denies our relationships, our mutuality, and our shared responsibility. The fourth threat asserts too much faith in the myth of rugged individualism and the magic of the market and too little commitment to our shared democratic project.

These threats are not new. James Baldwin spoke of them (in slightly different language) six decades ago.[1] And, yet, in our current moment of rising authoritarianism, the threats have taken on enormous weight and consequence. Some groups—immigrants, transgender folks, Muslims, and more—are constantly held up as scapegoats. And many educators, as well as a diverse array of young people in our public schools, find themselves characterized as other, unworthy, and threatening. These are dangerous times for our schools, our students, and our shared endeavor to forge a multiracial democracy.

How should we respond to these dangers? Once again, James Baldwin is helpful. In 1987, Mavis Nicholson, a Welsh journalist, asked Baldwin, "Are you still in despair about the world?" Baldwin replied: "I never have been in despair about the world. I've been enraged by it. I don't think I'm in despair. I can't afford despair. I can't tell my nephew, my niece, you can't tell the children there's no hope."[2]

FORGING HOPE: REENVISIONING PUBLIC SCHOOLS IN AMERICA

Understanding the threats facing our nation's public schools, and therefore the threats to our children, is an essential step in reenvisioning public schools and the path forward. Across the chapters in this book, the authors have illuminated deeply moral claims about our shared humanity, as well as keen insights on learning and development to lift up new understandings of the purpose of education. Their images of what our schools can and should become offer a powerful counterpoint to the overarching threats shared above. They also present compelling ways to build toward a society that no longer is defined by those threats.

Looking across the chapters, we discern four design principles, or *core commitments*, for reenvisioning public schools. We used these principles to organize the sections of the book. To dream and create the schools we all need, we must begin by:

1. Asserting the brilliance of all students
2. Affirming diverse students and leveraging difference
3. Leaning into problems
4. Reasserting collective responsibility and the public good

The chapters in this book lay out the case that the reenvisioning begins with recognizing the *brilliance of our students* and a steadfast commitment to cultivate the breadth of their interests and capabilities. All students, but particularly those living or placed on the margins and those who challenge our systems, imagination, and (at times) patience, must experience the reenvisioned school as safe, supportive, and attentive to their distinctive genius. And, yes, that means the genius of each and every one.

The authors in this book assert that a reenvisioned school routinely and deeply *affirms the diversity of students*. Of course, this means rejecting attacks on the humanity of particular students (trans, immigrant, Black, Muslim, disabled, etc.). But it also means educators moving beyond a soft notion of tolerance toward the dynamism of support, delight, and love. Students feel support when adults express interest in who they are and take action to help them become who they want to be; young people experience delight when educators purposefully make space (over and over and over) for their playful ideas, provocative thinking, and out of the ordinary preferences; students encounter love when adults stand with them during moments of joy and through hard times—regardless of the forces aligned against them or whether they have made a mistake. Different student experiences, ways of being, and perspectives become resources for curiosity, questioning, and translation. In such spaces, *diversity is essential to learning and an educated public*. And, yes, this means listening to Black families, reading queer stories, and studying the movement of young people across borders (and then taking up the question of why we have borders).

The chapters call for a reenvisioned public education that requires *leaning into the problems we face and a deep commitment to inquiry*. Our schools should uplift dissenting views, silenced voices, and marginalized experiences. Schools should become spaces that invite young people to unleash their curiosity, wrestle with ideas, and engage difficult and thorny local, national, and global problems. This entails learning about the history and current manifestations and presence of discrimination, hate, and bigotry, as well as the many beautiful ways that people join together to express care, provide aid, and heal. And, yes, that also means students learn about and play a role in addressing challenging issues and problems affecting them, their communities, and the natural world.

The authors from across this book assert that a reenvisioned education fosters interdependence and *collective responsibility—moving away from an idealization of the isolated individual*. Our public schools should become spaces of mutuality and shared interests. Rejecting both the privatization of public schooling and the sale of our children's future to markets and billionaires, *leadership and democratic governance reasserts relational bonds, the public good, and the shared responsibility* for each other and our schools. And, yes, shared public responsibility means not allowing any of us to hoard opportunities for our own children.

REENVISIONING SCHOOLING

In reenvisioning education, the authors in this book advance the four design principles in relationship to school climate (the way the school feels);

the curriculum and instruction our kids experience (what they learn and how educators facilitate that); the organization of the school (how we structure and arrange children and adults); the role of educators (how teachers and leaders approach the work); and issues beyond the school level (civil rights, funding, and governance). We pull those ideas together here. The ideas we present next are not a prescriptive blueprint for new schools but rather guides to support inquiry and engagement. We think this is useful for a democratic process of charting a path forward, and we recognize it is also frustrating for those of us who want to know exactly what to do next.

REENVISIONING SCHOOL CLIMATE

Reenvisioned school climate is fundamentally humanizing. Schools become places that uplift trans, Muslim, disabled, system-impacted, immigrant, Black, queer, and poor students—as well as students who hold a range of identities. Schooling in America becomes a place of collective work, cooperative struggle, and shared joy—moving away from a winner-takes-all approach that emphasizes individual reward.

REENVISIONING CURRICULUM AND INSTRUCTION

A reenvisioned curriculum and instruction emerge from the foundational ideas of student brilliance and collective responsibility. At the core is the need for students to learn the critical skills to understand and explain the world around them. Young people need opportunities to grapple with the distinction between knowledge and opinion, identify propaganda and its sources, and build courageous capacity for speaking up to power. This means embracing Freire's problem posing education that enables students to question the taken-for-granted, notice injustice, detect manipulation, recognize creeping authoritarianism, and (ultimately) resist it.

A reenvisioned curriculum is purposefully inclusive. Mathematics moves from narrow computation toward problem-solving and listening. Historical inquiry becomes an opportunity to examine the concerns, struggles, and contributions of the full diversity of the United States.

Literacy is transformed into a project of forging radical empathy, as reading and discussing stories become ways to understand and uphold the dignity of neighbors near and far.

REENVISIONING THE ORGANIZATION OF SCHOOL

Across the chapters of this book, the authors call for reenvisioning the structure and organization of public schools. First, they highlight the need to shift away from sorting, classifying, and excluding students toward bringing students together to listen, engage, and learn in classrooms rich in mathematical, linguistic, and experiential diversity. Moving away from sorting requires challenging typical practices that cluster by ability, speed, capacity to sit still, and more. It relies on creative solutions to integrate groups and classrooms. Second, the authors push for replacing taken-for-granted hierarchies between adults and students, between administrators and teachers, and between educators and community with new relationships and structures that foster mutuality across traditional boundaries of power.

These organizational changes cannot be relegated simply to "fugitive classrooms," afterschool programs, community spaces, or alternative schools. As important as these spaces are for some students and some educators in fighting for and creating humanizing education, relegating these changes to the margins allows the system to ignore the brilliance, diversity, and issues of too many students and avoids shared responsibility for their future. These organizational changes must become the backbone structure for schooling in this dangerous time.

REENVISIONING THE ROLE FOR EDUCATORS

A reenvisioned public school is only possible if teachers and school leaders take on new roles. Educators need a deep understanding of the systemic nature of problems experienced in their schools, and this entails grappling with economic inequality, racism, homophobia, and more. It is important for critically conscious educators both to clearly communicate insights and to attend to the wisdom in the communities they serve. They can support inquiry and deliberation by engaging, listening, and taking up ideas from young people and their families. This work, as well as collaboration with other educators, should be relational, improvisational, and democratic. Educators should play a role in democratic governance of public schools alongside young people, community members, and other leaders.

To enact these new roles, educators will need our educational system to support their development in ways that are consistent with our design principles. We must ask: What are the conditions necessary for a teacher to *assert the brilliance of all students*? What do teachers require to *affirm diverse students and leverage difference?* What is needed in order for all teachers *to lean into problems?* How do communities and school systems create spaces for teachers to be part of *reasserting collective responsibility and the public good?*

The design principles of *asserting the brilliance of all students* and *affirming diverse students* position school leadership as inseparable from the question of whose humanity gets recognized at school. Leadership in this space is neither neutral nor obsessed with maintaining the false patina of balance. Enacting the four principles means leadership creates conditions for equal opportunities, the equitable distribution of resources, and collective responsibility. In this regard, leadership is political. And courageous. Such leadership encourages members of the school community to reconsider unquestioned practices and systems that reproduce inequality. And, in so doing, it encourages mutual accountability by inviting students, family members, and educators to raise challenging questions about leadership practices.

REENVISIONING BEYOND THE LEVEL OF THE SCHOOL

The project of reenvisioning public schools cannot stop at the school level. Right now, many governmental bodies (at the local, state, or national level) are at best indifferent and at worst openly hostile to our design principles. For a broad cross section of schools to become sites where brilliance is recognized, diversity affirmed, problems engaged, and collective responsibility enacted, governmental systems and structures must be transformed.

The authors in this book highlight three essential changes for educational governance.

First, we need more inclusive and participatory structures for decision-making so that our schools are informed by the diverse perspectives and experiences of all members of our communities. Second, we need vigorous civil rights protections. Such protections ensure all members of our school communities have equitable access to high-quality learning, fair treatment, and meaningful opportunities to exercise voice. Third, we need public funding that distributes resources according to the learning and developmental needs of young people. Such robust public funding negates the outsized influence of private philanthropy and reaffirms the ideal that public education is our shared project.

In coming back to the four design principles, we ask: What do our school systems need for each school to *assert the brilliance of all students*? What decision-making structures and protections are needed to *affirm diverse students and leverage difference?* What protocols for civil rights enforcement, funding, and governance foster *leaning into problems?* How can communities and school systems create participatory processes and financial commitments that *reassert collective responsibility and the public good?* The threats we are facing now and those we will face on the path toward these schools are real and pernicious. We are each called to do our part to see this reenvisioning take hold.

BUILDING THE SCHOOLS WE NEED

Throughout this book, education scholars have presented ideas for reenvisioning public schools in dangerous times. "Reenvisioning" can be understood as coming to see something differently than before, and in the process visualizing a possible future. Certainly, there is a cognitive dimension to this task—some of the work of reenvisioning entails reading about and reflecting on the purpose and practice of education. But this book also seeks to prompt social engagement and action. We aim to foster a shared moral and civic project through which we join together to dream and build new schools.

How can this book help us reenvision schools? The authors in this book have expressed a variety of hopes for our schools—they want educators to enact less sorting, more problem-posing, and a greater commitment to student dignity. We would like you to think of these ideas as tools or starting points that motivate and help you and others to join in the process of collectively imagining new ways of being and new practices in our schools.

What does reenvisioning look like? The ways of being and commitments that we hope to realize in some distant future become guideposts for our practices today. For our purposes, this means a participatory process with spaces for dialogue, reflection, and political learning that look and feel a lot like the schools we hope to create.

What is the role of our design principles in this participatory process? As we join together to reenvision and remake schools, we must look for the brilliance of one another. The diverse experiences and identities of our fellow participants are sources for collective learning. Such learning requires us to engage with difficult and sometimes painful problems. And always, we must enact this work with care and shared responsibility toward one another.

Does having design principles mean that change will be easy? Unfortunately, no. Where threats abound and where new and unpredictable challenges are constantly emerging, there is no straightforward or easy way to enact the design principles. We must constantly assess and reassess the conditions that we face and respond accordingly. And we must deal with the fact that long and troubling histories of inequality and oppression have led some folks to turn off to the possibility of change. We need to find ways to acknowledge the pain of these histories, to treat one another with dignity, to heal, and to move forward. We also will need to embed learning into our collective efforts. We are sure to make missteps and outright mistakes as we reimagine and create schools. Thus, our learning through reflection, reconsideration, and revision must be ongoing.

How do we begin? This book is an invitation for you and your people (and people who you do not yet know as your people) to imagine and work for new schools together. A key starting point will be joining together to engage generative questions about schools and the purpose of education. Generative questions both rely upon and promote democracy-enhancing conditions—curiosity, a willingness to learn from those with different life experiences, and a belief in one another's capacity for problem-solving.

How do we identify and take up generative questions? All the chapters in this book close with a set of questions. The authors present four different types of questions, inviting participants to (1) share learning experiences; (2) analyze why schooling looks this way and how it might be different; (3) investigate whether prevailing educational practices privilege particular groups; and (4) dream collectively about possible futures. Each form of question plays an important role in the project of reenvisioning schools.

1. *Share learning experiences.* A first type of question encourages participants to narrate their own experiences learning in schools and in the broader community. For example, Arshad Ali asks: "What examples of community learning already exist around you, such as study circles, mutual aid efforts, art collectives, land-based education, or gatherings in faith and friendship?" Because everyone has stories about their own learning, this type of question opens up opportunities for broad engagement. Similarly, we all can respond to questions about learning in our past, like that asked by Shirin Vossoughi: "What memories do you hold about the people and places that taught you how to think about the world?" Such questions bring forth tales of family members and deeply held values, supporting diverse participants to recognize one another's full humanity.
2. *Analyze schooling.* A second kind of question motivates participants to reexamine their schools in light of some overarching idea or framework. For example, Julian Vasquez Heilig and Nallely Gecik ask: "Where do you see the influence of neoliberal policies, such as competition, privatization, or market-style accountability, in your local schools or districts? How have these policies reshaped teaching, learning, or community trust?" Such questions are critical in the sense that they push people to reflect on the ways that broad forces—often driven by systems of power—shape taken-for-granted aspects of how we experience public schools. They remind us that things don't need to be as they are. Often questions that prompt analysis about our assumptions also invite inference and speculation about what might be possible. Christy Ashby and Beth Myers query: "Are there reasons why you think a student might not be able to participate in an inclusive classroom right now? How could you imagine that differently?"
3. *Investigate and identify patterns.* A third sort of question calls for us to observe, count, and compare so as to better understand experiences in our schools and communities. Judy Alston pushes us to inquire about: "Which voices are prioritized in lessons? Are Black queer figures included across subjects?" Closely examining existing practices can help us identify biases and other problem areas. Investigations also may provide data to help us have

different conversations about previously unrecognized forms of privilege or exclusion. This is part of the purpose behind Antero Garcia, Christián Pena, and Alix Dick's call for us to document "the invisible costs incurred by individuals labeled undocumented"—what they refer to as "*La Cuenta*," or "the bill" in Spanish. Similarly, Joel Westheimer suggests that we walk around our communities in small groups and create maps "of institutions, organizations, and public resources where democratic practices still thrive and those where they are under threat." Westheimer imagines us using these maps to consider "what patterns emerge and what actions could strengthen these spaces."

4. *Dream collectively.* A final variety of question propels far-reaching conversations about the sort of schools we want to build and how we can achieve these goals. Megan Franke aims to initiate such a process by calling for us to talk about what school math can accomplish. She then asks us to "consider how the goals we have for school math are going to enable us to solve the problems of today and the future." Nicole Mirra sets up a similar dynamic by asking us to "imagine that all the class sets of books in your local high school [have] disappeared." She invites us to reflect together on "what sorts of activities, assignments, or projects—beyond reading classic literature . . . would be meaningful and useful for students?"

   Collective dreaming also demands strategic questions about how we realize our dreams. Pedro Noguera encourages us to examine the steps needed for change—including information about the impact of our efforts and a reckoning with "what skills might be necessary." Building on this theme, Muhammad Khalifa implores us to ask: "Who are your allies, and how are you building collective solidarity in the face of pushback?" And Miguel Casar Rodriguez reminds us to account for the obstacles within us all. He invites us to consider: "What are the fears that stop us from building these schools? How can we collectively organize to face those fears?"

By asking and engaging such questions in community, we will assert our collective brilliance, affirm the value of diversity, lean into problems, and fortify the public good.

A CLOSING NOTE AND A WAY FORWARD: LISTENING TO YOUNG PEOPLE

We started the book with an epigraph from James Baldwin's 1963 essay "A Talk to Teachers," which foretells the story of our own moment. "Let's begin," Baldwin exhorts, "by saying that we are living through a very dangerous time."[3] A central message of this book is that the threats to our students and our schools right now are very real, but so too are the possibilities for reenvisioning. Baldwin acknowledged this duality as well. In that same 1963 essay, he encourages readers to recognize that social change is possible if we center the voices and vitality of young people. "[I]f America is going to become a nation, she must find a way—and this child must help her to find a way to use the tremendous potential and tremendous energy which this child represents." Six decades later, the time has come to heed James Baldwin. If we act, new schools and a better future lie ahead. Let's begin.

ACKNOWLEDGMENTS

This book is about an unwavering hope for public education—a belief in the power of schools, a commitment to the ideals of educational equity, a humility to question ourselves along the way, and a spirit of collective action. Too often, good books are looked upon as individual endeavors, not as collaborative works. This project stands in direct opposition to that idea—challenging the notion that one writer, one department head, one bureaucrat, one superintendent, one professor, or one teacher will save the day. Indeed, as we have learned from working in schools, the best work stands side by side with, on the shoulders of, and in relationship to a great many people. And, thus, it is a community of people that has enabled and produced this book.

Our first debt of gratitude is to the chapter authors. They have demonstrated career-long commitments to the brilliance of all students, affirming the diversity of our children, leaning into problems, and reasserting collective responsibility to public education. Your work and words are both provocative and reassuring. We ask the nation to engage with your ideas.

We are deeply appreciative of Rachael Marks, Rebecca Johnson, Ella Rose Morgan, Susan Lumenello, and the team at Beacon. Your enthusiasm for this project is deeply felt, and your willingness to collaborate with us has produced a better book.

We cannot express the importance of the community of our closest intellectual collaborators and what that has given to us and to this work—thank you, Christy Ashby, Tom Bull, Megan Franke, Gretchen Givens Generett, Leela George, Mark Gooden, Joseph Kahne, Rebecca Lowenhaupt, Georgia Lazo, Ernest Morrell, Beth Myers, Jeannie Oakes, Nancy Parachini, Sharon Radd, Sylvia Rousseau, Martin Scanlan, Veronica Terriquez, and Joel Westheimer.

We appreciate Jeanne Theoharis and Samuel Stern for their careful work, as well as the time and energy they put into supporting this book.

We do not have sufficient space to name the multitude of amazing teachers and leaders we have partnered with over our decades working in and working with public schools. Nor can we name the thousands of our own students who are part of the heart and soul of public schools. We appreciate your passion and service. We need and expect great things from you. Our children are counting on that.

These acknowledgments would not be complete without our offering of appreciation and gratitude to our families, who have so deeply shaped our personal commitment to social justice and whose actions to create a more just and equitable world serve as inspiration for us personally and are a reminder of the constant vigilance needed to enact social change. We offer our most heartfelt appreciation.

EDITOR BIOS

GEORGE THEOHARIS (PhD, University of Wisconsin-Madison; BS, Macalester College) is a professor in educational leadership and inclusive education at Syracuse University. Starting as a kindergarten teacher, he worked as a teacher, principal, university faculty, and university administrator focused on educational equity. Theoharis served as department chair, associate dean, and director of field relations. His work emphasizes issues of inclusion, university-school partnerships, and leadership for social justice. He has written hundreds of op-eds, book chapters, practitioner magazine pieces, and peer-reviewed articles, as well as thirteen books. He grew up in Wisconsin in an activist family and has two ebullient young-adult children and an inspiring partner.

JOHN ROGERS (PhD, Stanford University; BA, Princeton University) is a professor of education and associate dean for research and public scholarship in the UCLA School of Education and Information Studies. He directs UCLA's Institute for Democracy, Education, and Access. Rogers studies issues of democracy and education, and he has written widely about the role of students, parents, and school leaders in educating toward a multiracial democracy. Rogers is the recipient of the American Educational Research Association's Presidential Citation.

EDITOR BIOS

CONTRIBUTOR BIOS

JUDY ALSTON, PhD, is professor and chair of the Department of Educational Leadership at Miami (OH) University, and co–executive editor of the journal *Educational Administration Quarterly*. An accomplished author, she has published books including *Herstories: Leading with the Lessons of the Lives of Black Women Activists*; *School Leadership and Administration: Important Concepts, Case Studies, & Simulations*; *Purveyors of Change: School Leaders of Color Share Narratives of Student, School, and Community Success*; *The Undivided Life: Faculty of Color Bringing Our Whole Selves to the Academy*; and *Leading with Soul: Examining the Praxis of Critical Servant Leadership Theory and Spiritual Leadership for School Administrators*.

ARSHAD IMTIAZ ALI is an associate professor of education and affiliate faculty in critical race and ethnic studies at the University of California, Santa Cruz. He is concerned with educational possibility, liberatory moments/movements, and methodological approaches that attend to the interpretive practices and knowledge relations researchers build with youth and communities. He has written extensively on the cultural geography of Muslim student surveillance, citizenship, governmentality, and the colonial conditions shaping Muslim life in Western contexts. His current work draws on Muslim and non-Western storywork to cultivate science learning environments where students' ways of knowing inform how they inquire, interpret, and make sense of the world.

CHRISTINE ASHBY, PhD, is professor of inclusive education and disability studies and director of the Center on Disability and Inclusion at Syracuse University. Her teaching and research focus on inclusive education, communicative diversity, disability studies, and inclusive teacher preparation, with specific emphasis on the experiences of autistic and neurodivergent students. Her co-edited book, *Enacting Change from Within: Disability Studies Meets*

Teaching and Teacher Education, explores how disability studies can inform the practical work of teachers.

VANDEEN CAMPBELL, PhD, is an assistant research professor in the Department of Urban Education and associate director of the Joseph C. Cornwall Center for Metropolitan Studies at Rutgers University–Newark. Her research interests include segregation and the distribution of educational opportunity, STEM pathways, dual enrollment and college access, parental engagement, and community-engaged approaches to data, including the development of local data infrastructures to support school improvement and community empowerment. Campbell works in the context of research-practice partnerships.

MIGUEL CASAR, PhD, is an assistant professor at the University of Alabama specializing in critical qualitative methodologies, the sociology of education, and educational justice. His scholarship explores how research can contribute to a collective praxis through which those resisting oppression can ask critical questions about our realities, build power, and author more just and humanizing futures.

VINCENT CHO, PhD, is associate professor of educational leadership at Boston College, where he directs its EdD program in educational leadership. A former teacher and administrator, he aims his research at supporting school leaders in the digital age. Drawing upon theories of sociotechnical systems and sensemaking, his recent projects explore states' AI policies, teachers' AI practices, and the impact of classroom-management apps on parent-teacher relationships and data-informed improvement. Cho is also co-author of *Supervision: A Redefinition* (9th ed.) with Thomas J. Sergiovanni and Robert J. Starratt.

SHIVANI DAVÉ is a PhD candidate in the Department of Education at UCLA. She holds a BA in biochemistry from Vassar College and an MAT in general and special education from Relay Graduate School of Education. Prior to beginning her doctoral journey, Shivani taught special education in New York City for five years. Currently, Shivani's research is situated within the co-design and implementation of a special education credentialing pathway within the Teacher Education Program (TEP) at UCLA. She centers affect in the design of research methods that also serve as learning opportunities around teachers' noticing practices toward responding in ethical and just ways.

KATIE DAVIS is a professor at the University of Washington (UW) Information School, where she is co-director of the UW Center for Digital Youth. She investigates the impact of digital technologies on young people's learning, development, and well-being, and co-designs positive technology experiences for youth and their families. Her work bridges the fields of human development, human-computer interaction, and the learning sciences.

ALIX DICK is a filmmaker, researcher, and writer originally from Sinaloa, Mexico. She is the coauthor of *The Cost of Being Undocumented: One Woman's Reckoning with America's Inhumane Math*. Alix has worked closely with multiple immigrant-rights organizations and was named an Artist Disruptor by the Center for Cultural Power. She is an in-demand presenter and the co-editor and founder of *La Cuenta*, an online publication centering the perspectives of individuals labeled undocumented. Alix has authored numerous essays and op-eds for publications across the United States. Alix lives in Los Angeles.

MANUEL LUIS ESPINOZA is a writer and scholar of education. He is the director of research for the Right2Learn Dignity Lab and a member of Zion Baptist Church in the Five Points neighborhood of Denver. He writes about the fulfillment of the universal right to education and the role of dignity as a design principle for learning environments.

MEGAN FRANKE is a professor of education at UCLA. Megan and her colleagues support and study teachers as they make use of research-based information about the development of children's mathematical thinking and consider how attention to students' mathematical thinking can help challenge existing school structures and create opportunities for marginalized students to learn with understanding. Her research work to support teachers, schools, and communities was recognized with the AERA Research into Practice Award, and she was elected to the National Academy of Education.

ANTERO GARCIA is a professor in the Graduate School of Education at Stanford University. His research explores the possibilities of speculative imagination and healing in educational research. He has authored or edited more than two dozen books about the possibilities of literacies, play, and civics in transforming schooling in America. Antero currently co-edits *La Cuenta*, an online publication centering the voices and perspectives of individuals labeled undocumented in the US.

NALLELY GECIK is a Holmes Scholar and faculty member dedicated to equity in education and the success of first-generation college students from immigrant backgrounds. She teaches at the College of Southern Nevada and at Southwestern College, supporting binational students commuting from Tijuana, Mexico. A San Diego native raised in a border community, she connects deeply with students through shared bicultural experiences. Her research examines how cultivating supportive educational environments is essential for vulnerable students facing systemic barriers, including epistemic injustice and the coloniality of power. She is pursuing a doctorate in education for social justice at the University of San Diego.

MARGARET GOLDMAN, PhD, is a postdoctoral associate at the Joseph C. Cornwall Center for Metropolitan Studies at Rutgers University–Newark and a former high school educator. Her research, teaching, and organizing focus on the entanglements between schooling and carceral regimes, on one hand, and the necessary intersections between abolitionist and educational justice, on the other. She believes firmly that the young people most impacted by carceral and criminalizing systems possess indispensable blueprints for social and educational transformation, and this belief guides her work.

MARCELLE HADDIX is the Dean and Karen A. Falk Distinguished Chair in the University of Wisconsin–Madison School of Education. Previously, she held leadership positions at Syracuse University, including associate provost for strategic initiatives and department chair. She is a leading scholar in literacy education with a focus on the experiences of students and teachers of color. Her book *Cultivating Racial and Linguistic Diversity in Literacy Teacher Education: Teachers Like Me* received the 2018 Outstanding Book Award from the American Association of Colleges for Teacher Education. She earned a doctorate in education from Boston College.

KEVIN LAWRENCE HENRY JR. is an associate professor in the Department of Educational Leadership and Policy Analysis at the University of Wisconsin–Madison. His interdisciplinary scholarship investigates the politics of education, specifically privatization (school choice/market-based approaches) in education, and considers how the perspectives and practices of Black educational actors can reshape and transform the field of education to be more just, humanizing, and liberatory. He is the co-author with Colleen Capper of *Organizational Theory for Equity and Diversity*, 2nd ed., and co-editor with Kevin Clay of *The Promise of Youth Anti-Citizenship: Race and Revolt in Education*.

TYRONE C. HOWARD is the Pritzker Family Endowed Chair and professor of education in the School of Education at UCLA. A leading expert on race, culture, and educational equity, he is the faculty co-director of the UCLA Center for the Transformation of Schools and the co-faculty director of the UCLA Pritzker Center. He is a fellow of the American Educational Research Association and an elected member to the National Academy of Education and the American Academy of Arts and Science. He is also a past president of the American Educational Research Association.

LINDSAY LINDBERG is an educational researcher, dance educator, and learning scientist based in Los Angeles. She earned a PhD from UCLA's School of Education and Information Studies, and is a graduate of NYU's master of arts in dance education program. Lindsay has been a K–12 dance educator in New York City and Los Angeles, and she teaches the dance methods course at CSUN for credential candidates. She currently serves as a postdoctoral researcher at UCLA and as an arts and education consultant. Her research uses dance-based qualitative methods and looks critically at the role of the body in education.

MUHAMMAD KHALIFA is a professor of educational administration and executive director for Urban Education Initiatives at the Ohio State University. He also serves as president and CEO of the Culturally Responsive School Leadership Institute (crsli.org). His book *Culturally Responsive School Leadership* (Harvard Education Press, 2018) is a top seller and used in over five hundred leadership-preparation programs around the world. His new book, *Culturally Responsive Instructional Leadership*, is due out in 2026. Through

CRSLI, he and colleagues developed academies, equity audits, and online modules that help leaders become culturally responsive. Formerly an educator and administrator in Detroit schools, he's contributed to leadership and anti-colonial works throughout Africa, Asia, and other global majority contexts.

ANANDA MARIN is associate professor in the Department of Education and faculty in American Indian studies at the University of California, Los Angeles. She brings research on the socio-ecological and cultural nature of learning alongside efforts to co-design teaching-learning environments. Broadly speaking, she explores the diversity of ways that multigenerational groups of people organize attention and observation to participate in joint activities, collaborate, and improvise across contexts. A goal of her work is to broaden research methodologies and theories of teaching-learning in ways that are consequential to the communities she partners with and the field of education.

MOLLIE MCQUILLAN is an associate professor in educational leadership and policy analysis at the University of Wisconsin–Madison. Their research examines how gender, sexuality, and educational policy shape school climate, health, and educational achievement. A W. T. Grant Scholar, they've published in top education and health journals and have received national recognition for their research advancing gender-inclusive educational leadership and policy.

NICOLE MIRRA is an associate professor of teacher education in UCLA's Department of Education and faculty director of the UCLA Teacher Education Program (TEP). Her research utilizes participatory design methods in classroom, community, and digital spaces to collaboratively create learning environments with teachers and youth that disrupt structures of social injustice and creatively compose liberatory futures. She previously taught English language arts and debate in Brooklyn, New York, and Los Angeles, California.

JULISSA O. MUÑIZ, PhD, is an assistant professor at the School of Education and Information Studies at the University of California, Los Angeles. Her scholarship examines how people and communities of color—specifically Latinx and Black communities—navigate, negotiate, and resist racialized organizations and systems of power such as the education, criminal legal, and juvenile legal systems. Dr. Muñiz earned both her PhD and MA in human development and social policy from Northwestern University. Dr. Muñiz is a first-generation borderlands scholar from San Ysidro, California, and has spent numerous years volunteering, teaching, and researching at correctional facilities across the US.

BETH MYERS is an associate professor of inclusive education and executive director of the Taishoff Center of Inclusive Higher Education at Syracuse University. She is the chair of the National State of the Art Conference on Inclusive Postsecondary Education and editor of the *Journal of Inclusive Postsecondary Education*. She serves as a founding member of the board of the Inclusive Postsecondary Education Association. Her books include *Autobiography on the Spectrum: Disrupting the Autism Narrative* and *Creating Our Own Lives: Students with Intellectual Disability in College* (edited and co-authored with M. Gill). Beth lives in Syracuse with her four fabulous children.

PEDRO NOGUERA is the dean of the Rossier School of Education and a Distinguished Professor of Education at USC. He is the author of fifteen books and hundreds of articles and editorials, and he serves as an advisor to several states, school districts, foundations, NGOs, and nonprofits. He was born in New York City to Caribbean immigrants and is the father of five children and grandfather to five.

CHARLES M. PAYNE is the Henry Rutgers Distinguished Professor of African American Studies at Rutgers University–Newark, where he also directs the Joseph C. Cornwall Center for Metropolitan Studies. His seven books include *So Much Reform, So Little Change: The Persistence of Failure in Urban Schools* and *I've Got the Light of Freedom: The Organizing Tradition in the Mississippi Civil Rights Movement*. His most recent book (co-edited) is *Dignity-Affirming Education: Cultivating the Somebodiness of Students and Educators*. He has taught at Southern University, Northwestern, Duke, and the University of Chicago and has won multiple teaching awards.

CHRISTIÁN PEÑA is an immigrant mother, a writer, and a storyteller. She runs a newsletter, *Matrixial*, where she explores the intersections of motherhood, memory, and migration through personal essays, poetry, and other forms of storytelling. She co-runs *La Cuenta*, a publication dedicated to the exploration of the costs incurred by roughly eleven million individuals in the US who are labeled undocumented. She is a 2025 Ann Friedman Fellow.

CARRIE SAMPSON is an associate professor in the Division for Advancing Education Policy, Practice, and Leadership at Arizona State University. Her research focuses on K–12 educational leadership and equity, examining school boards, district policymaking, and community advocacy. Sampson's recent book, *Navigating School Board Politics: A Framework for Advancing Equity*, explores how education leaders, school board members, and community advocates can advance equity-focused policies amid our complex and often contentious political climate in education. Sampson also serves as a fellow for the National Education Policy Center and the Black Education Research Center.

JULIAN VASQUEZ HEILIG is a professor of educational leadership, research, and technology at Western Michigan University and the creator of the award-winning education policy blog *Cloaking Inequity*. A nationally recognized scholar and public voice on K–12 equity, he has authored more than eighty publications and presented his work across North America, Europe, Asia, and Latin America. His research and commentary have appeared in *The New York Times*, *The Washington Post*, *Education Week*, NPR, and MSNBC. A former NAACP Education Chair and adviser to policymakers, he is widely regarded for advancing community-centered approaches to equity, justice, and educational opportunity. His full curriculum vitae is accessible at bit.ly/ProfJVHcv.

SHIRIN VOSSOUGHI is an educator, a mother, a writer, and an associate professor of learning sciences at Northwestern University, where she studies the cultural, sociopolitical, and ethical dimensions of human learning. Vossoughi's research centers on learning environments that support young people to develop, question, and expand disciplinary and artistic knowledge in ways that nourish educational self-determination. She is particularly concerned with understanding the pedagogies, ethical relations, and developmental trajectories that take shape within these settings. She takes a collaborative approach to research and design, partnering with teachers, families, and students to study the conditions that foster educational dignity and possibility.

JOEL WESTHEIMER is professor of democracy and education at the University of Ottawa and an education columnist for the Canadian Broadcasting Company. His current work focuses on youth perceptions of democracy at a time of rising populist nationalism. His books include *What Kind of Citizen? Educating Our Children for the Common Good*, 2nd ed., and *Pledging Allegiance: The Politics of Patriotism in American Schools* (foreword by Howard Zinn). Westheimer is a member of the National Academy of Education and a fellow of the Royal Society of Canada. He can be reached at joelwestheimer@mac.com. Find out more at joelwestheimer.org.

MICHELLE D. YOUNG is dean of the Berkeley School of Education. A scholar of educational policy and leadership, Young focuses on leveraging educational programs, policies, and practices to foster equitable and quality experiences for the students and adults who learn and work in schools. She has published eleven books and more than a hundred peer-reviewed articles and book chapters. Among her awards and honors are the William J. Davis Award for most outstanding article, an Emerald Literati Award for Excellence in Scholarship, and the prestigious Edwin M. Bridges Award, for her contributions to research on the preparation of education leaders.

NOTES

CHAPTER 1: THE PURPOSE OF PUBLIC EDUCATION IN DANGEROUS TIMES

1. James Baldwin, "A Talk to Teachers" (1963), in *Multi-Cultural Literacy: Opening the American Mind*, ed. Rick Simonson and Scott Walker (Graywolf Press, 1988), 3–12.

2. Eve L. Ewing, *Original Sins: The (Mis)education of Black and Native Children and the Construction of American Racism* (One World, 2025); Jarvis Givens, *American Grammar: Race, Education, and the Building of a Nation* (Harper, 2025).

3. Gary Orfield, *Public School Desegregation in the United States, 1968–1980* (Joint Center for Political Studies, 1983).

4. David Hursh, "The Growth of High-Stakes Testing in the USA: Accountability, Markets and the Decline in Educational Equality," *British Educational Research Journal* 31, no. 5 (2005): 605–22.

5. Joseph Kahne, John Rogers, and Alexander Kwako, "The New Politics of Education and the Pursuit of a Diverse Democracy," *AERA Open* 11 (2025): 23328584241311819.

6. Mica Pollock, John Rogers, Alexander Kwako, Andrew Matschiner, Reed Kendall, Cicely Bingener, Erika Reece et al., *The Conflict Campaign: Exploring Local Experiences of the Campaign to Ban "Critical Race Theory" in Public K–12 Education in the US, 2020–2021* (UCLA Institute for Democracy, Education, and Access, 2022).

7. Carlin Borsheim-Black, "'This Is My Hill to Die On': Effects of Far-Right Conservative Pushback on US English Teachers and Their Classroom Practice," *English Teaching: Practice & Critique* 23, no. 3 (2024): 317–31; John Rogers, Joseph Kahne, Michael Ishimoto, Alexander Kwako, Samuel C. Stern, Cicely Bingener, Leah Raphael et al., *Educating for a Diverse Democracy: The Chilling Role of Political Conflict in Blue, Purple, and Red Communities* (UCLA Institute for Democracy, Education, and Access, 2022).

8. John Rogers, Joseph Kahne, Deborah La Torre, Charity Castro, Samuel Stern, Micaela Bronstein, and Michael Ishimoto, *"The Fear is Everywhere": U.S. High School Principals Report Widespread Effects of Immigration Enforcement* (UCLA Institute for Democracy, Education, and Access, 2025).

CHAPTER 2: DIGNITY AND BEAUTIFUL LEARNING ENVIRONMENTS

1. See, generally, Martha Nussbaum, *Creating Capabilities: The Human Development Approach* (Harvard University Press, 2011), providing an overview of the approach and identifying the "central" capabilities.

2. Martin Buber, *I and Thou*, trans. Walter Kaufmann (Charles Scribner's Sons, 1970), 24, explaining how humane interpersonal relations forge enduring bonds of social solidarity.

3. John Dewey, *Democracy and Education: An Introduction to the Philosophy of Education* (MacMillan, 1916), 384, arguing that the "educative arts" work hand-in-glove with "philosophy" in a generative manner to guide human life.

4. Mike Rose, *Possible Lives: The Promise of Public Education in America* (Houghton Mifflin, 1995), 5, asserting that the classroom is a "fundamental unit" of both school and democratic life.

5. C. Wright Mills, *The Sociological Imagination* (Oxford University Press, 1959), 5, arguing for a social science that connects biography and history.

6. Compare Marx Wartofsky, "Perception, Representation, and the Forms of Action," in *Models: Representation and the Scientific Understanding*, ed. R. S. Cohen and Marx Wartofsky (Springer, 1979), 188 (explaining how humans create the future through environments that offer emancipatory experiences), with Kris Gutiérrez, "Developing a Sociocritical Literacy in the Third Space," *Reading Research Quarterly* 43, no. 2 (2008): 148–64 (discussing learning ecologies that provide opportunities for adolescents to reconceive who they are through the development of sociocritical literacies); Carol Lee, "Is October Brown Chinese? A Cultural Modeling Activity System for Underachieving Students," *American Educational Research Journal* 38, no. 1 (2001), 97–141 (analyzing the development of literary reasoning in underachieving Black high school students); and Shirin Vossoughi, Ava Jackson, Suzanne Chen, Wendy Roldan, and Meg Escudé, "Embodied Pathways and Ethical Trails: Studying Learning in and Through Relational Histories," *Journal of the Learning Sciences* 29, no. 2 (2020): 183–223 (examining the role of assistance in creating environments that enact educational dignity).

7. Over the last five centuries, the notion of the individual as the subject of international law has developed into a foundational tenet, e.g., Hersch Lauterpacht, *An International Bill of the Rights of Man* (Columbia University Press, 1945), 28–29, arguing that "the sanctity of the individual human being as the ultimate subject of all law asserts its full vigour" only within a restructured system of international law; and Philip C. Jessup, *A Modern Law of Nations* (MacMillan, 1959), 2, arguing for the keystone principle that "international law . . . must be directly applicable to the individual." See also Francisci de Victoria and De Indis Et De Iure Belli Relectiones, "Being Part of Relectiones Theologicae," trans. John Pawley Bate (Cosimo Classics, 1917), 143, arguing, in part, that the "aborigines . . . were true owners [of their lands], before the Spaniards came among them, both from the public and private point of view"; Hugo Grotius, *De Jure Belli Ac Pacis* (1625), trans. Louise R. Loomis (Classics Club, 1949), reasoning that matters of law and justice between nations are inherently related to the integrity of the individual; and Samuel Pufendorf, *De Jure Naturae Et Gentium Libri Octo* (1688), trans. C. H. and W. A. Oldfather (1995), arguing for a law of nations built upon natural law and human equality. Today, a complex and asymmetrical latticework of local, national, and international structures—e.g., declarations, covenants, treaties, statutes, rules, and norms—supports the daily and uneven realization of this central tenet of international law. With respect to the schools, if children and adolescents are to feel themselves subjects of international law, the general pattern of education law within a country or region, coupled to the prudent use of existing resources, must result in the creation of educational sanctuaries where they may experience freedom of thought, inquiry, and creativity.

8. UN Department of Economic and Social Affairs, *The Sustainable Development Goals Report 2023, Special Edition* 20 (2023).

9. Pope Francis, *Fratelli Tutti: Sobre La Fraternidad y La Amistad Social* (US Conference of Catholic Bishops, 2020), explaining the role of dignity in religious, social, and political life.

10. See European Commission for Democracy Through Law, "The Principle of Respect for Human Dignity" (September 1999), presenting international perspectives on dignity as the foundation of law and modern society.

11. Mike Rose, *When The Light Goes On: The Life-Changing Wonder of Learning in an Age of Metrics, Screens, and Diminished Human Connection* (Beacon Press, 2022), 195, presenting detailed case studies of individual transformation through learning.

12. See, generally, Robert Coles, *The Moral Life of Children* (Houghton Mifflin, 1986), demonstrating through interviews how children grapple with moral dilemmas; Rose, *Possible Lives*, providing detailed accounts of robust public school classrooms across the US; Eftychia Stamkou et al., "Awe Sparks Prosociality in Children," *Psychological Science* 34, no. 4 (2023): 455–67, explaining empirical research regarding the relation between experiences of awe and generosity.

13. See, generally, Coles, *The Moral Life of Children*, demonstrating through interviews how children grapple with moral dilemmas; Rose, *Possible Lives*; Stamkou et al., "Awe Sparks Prosociality in Children," 455–67.

CHAPTER 3: LEVERAGING THE COLLECTIVE POWER OF YOUNG PEOPLE'S MATHEMATICAL IDEAS

1. Maisie L. Gholson and Charles E. Wilkes, "(Mis)Taken Identities: Reclaiming Identities of the 'Collective Black' in Mathematics Education Research Through an Exercise in Black Specificity," *Review of Research in Education* 41, no. 1 (2017): 228–52; Danny Bernard Martin, "Race, Racial Projects, and Mathematics Education," *Journal for Research in Mathematics Education* 44, no. 1 (2013): 316–33; Jeannie Oakes, *Keeping Track: How Schools Structure Inequality* (Yale University Press, 1985); Tesha Sengupta-Irving and Shirin Vossoughi, "Not in Their Name: Re-Interpreting Discourses of STEM Learning Through the Subjective Experiences of Minoritized Girls," *Race Ethnicity and Education* 22, no. 4 (2019): 479–501.

2. Megan Franke, Juliet Lee, and Christine Roberts, "'I See Her Able to Stay on Track': How School Structures Shape Elementary Teachers' Reported Characterizations and Supports for Students in Mathematics," *Teachers College Record: The Voice of Scholarship in Education* 126, no. 1 (2024): 89–114; Jennifer Langer-Osuna, Jen Munson, Emma Gargroetzi, Immanuel Williams, and Rosa Chavez, "'So What Are We Working On?': How Student Authority Relations Shift During Collaborative Mathematics Activity," *Educational Studies in Mathematics* 104, no. 3 (2020): 333–49; Paul T. von Hippel and Ana P. Cañedo, "Is Kindergarten Ability Group Placement Biased? New Data, New Methods, New Answers," *American Educational Research Journal* 59, no. 4 (2022): 820–57.

3. John B. Diamond, Antonia Randolph, and James P. Spillane, "Teachers' Expectations and Sense of Responsibility for Student Learning: The Importance of Race, Class, and Organizational Habitus," *Anthropology & Education Quarterly* 35 (2004): 75–98; Jan N. Hughes, Katie A. Gleason, and Duan Zhang, "Relationship Influences on Teachers' Perceptions of Academic Competence in Academically at-Risk Minority and Majority First Grade Students," *Journal of School Psychology* 43, no. 4 (2005): 303–20; Catherine Riegle-Crumb and Melissa Humphries, "Exploring Bias in Math Teachers'

Perceptions of Students' Ability by Gender and Race/Ethnicity," *Gender & Society* 26, no. 2 (2012): 290–322.

4. Hervé Varenne and Ray McDermott, *Successful Failure: The School America Builds* (Westview Press, 1998).

CHAPTER 4: ALL REALLY MEANS ALL

1. *Regular Lives*, Gerardine Wurzburg, dir., State of the Art, 1987, https://www.kanopy.com/en/product/regular-lives.

2. Endrew F. v. Douglas County School District RE-1, 580 U.S. ___ (2017).

3. Douglas Biklen, *Schooling Without Labels: Parents, Educators, and Inclusive Education* (Temple University Press, 1992), 85.

4. Cassandra M. Cole, Nancy Waldron, and Massoumeh Majd, "Academic Progress of Students Across Inclusive and Traditional Settings," *Mental Retardation* 42, no. 2 (2004): 136–44.

5. Laura Schifter, "Using Survival Analysis to Understand Graduation of Students with Disabilities," *Exceptional Children* 82, no. 4 (2016): 479–96; Sandy Cole, Hardy Murphy, Michael Frisby, and James Robinson, "The Relationship Between Special Education Placement and High School Outcomes," *Journal of Special Education* 57, no. 1 (2023): 13–23.

6. David W. Test, Valerie L. Mazzotti, April L. Mustian, Catherine H. Fowler, Larry Kortering, and Paula Kohler, "Evidence-Based Secondary Transition Predictors for Improving Postschool Outcomes for Students with Disabilities," *Career Development for Exceptional Individuals* 32, no. 3 (2009): 160–81.

7. Harold Kleinert, Elizabeth Towles-Reeves, Rachel Quenemoen, Martha Thurlow, Lauren Fluegge, Laura Weseman, and Allison Kerbel, "Where Students with the Most Significant Cognitive Disabilities Are Taught: Implications for General Curriculum Access," *Exceptional Children* 81, no. 3 (2015): 312–28.

8. Rachel Sermier Dessemontet and Gérard Bless, "The Impact of Including Children with Intellectual Disability in General Education Classrooms on the Academic Achievement of Their Low-, Average-, and High-Achieving Peers," *Journal of Intellectual & Developmental Disability* 38, no. 1 (2013): 23–30; Grzegorz Szumski, Joanna Smogorzewska, and Maciej Karwowski, "Academic Achievement of Students Without Special Educational Needs in Inclusive Classrooms: A Meta-Analysis," *Educational Research Review* 21 (June 2017): 33–54.

9. James McLeskey, Nancy L. Waldron, and Lacy Redd, "A Case Study of a Highly Effective, Inclusive Elementary School," *Journal of Special Education* 48, no. 1 (2014): 59–70.

10. James Trent, *Inventing the Feeble Mind: A History of Intellectual Disability in the United States* (Oxford University Press, 2016).

11. Nirmala Erevelles, "Crippin' Jim Crow: Disability, Dis-location, and the School-to-Prison Pipeline," in *Disability Incarcerated: Imprisonment and Disability in the United States and Canada*, ed. Liat Ben-Moshe, Chris Chapman, and Allison C. Carey (Palgrave Macmillan US, 2014), 81–99; Da'Shay Templeton, "The Immovable Veil of Black Disability: An Introduction to Black Disability Threat Theory and Its Application to the School to Prison Nexus," *Race Ethnicity and Education* 28, no. 4 (2025): 518–42.

12. Jess Davidson, "Leading Disability Organizations: President Trump's Blame of Deadly Crash on Disabled Federal Workers Is Baseless, Irresponsible," Disability Rights Education & Defense Fund (DREDF), January 31, 2025.

13. Django Paris and H. Samy Alim, eds., *Culturally Sustaining Pedagogies: Teaching and Learning for Justice in a Changing World* (Teachers College Press, 2017).

14. Saili S. Kulkarni, Amanda L. Miller, Emily A. Nusbaum, Holly Pearson, and Lydia XZ Brown, "Toward Disability-Centered, Culturally Sustaining Pedagogies in Teacher Education," *Critical Studies in Education* 65, no. 2 (2024): 107–27.

CHAPTER 5: SEEING THE GENIUS IN THOSE LABELED "SYSTEM IMPACTED"

1. Vanessa Siddle Walker, *Their Highest Potential: An African American School Community In The Segregated South* (University of North Carolina Press, 1996).

2. Dorothy Roberts, *Torn Apart: How The Child Welfare System Destroys Black Families—and How Abolition Can Build a Safer World* (Basic Books, 2002).

3. Tyrone C. Howard, *Equity Now: Justice, Repair and Belonging in Schools* (Corwin Press, 2024).

4. Carla Shalaby, *Troublemakers: Lessons in Freedom from Young Children at School* (New Press, 2017).

5. James Baldwin, "A Talk to Teachers" (1963), in *Multi-Cultural Literacy: Opening the American Mind*, ed. Rick Simonson and Scott Walker (Graywolf Press, 1988), 3–12.

6. Bettina L. Love, *Punished for Dreaming: How School Reform Harms Black Children and How We Heal* (St. Martin's Publishing Group, 2023).

CHAPTER 6: BEYOND CLASSROOM BORDERS AND UNDOCUMENTED SCHOOLING

1. David Graeber, "The Possibility of Political Pleasure: David Graeber at TEDx Whitechapel," 2013, https://www.youtube.com/watch?v=5eR_95slEFw.

2. Hakim Bey, *T.A.Z.: The Temporary Autonomous Zone, Ontological Anarchy, Poetic Terrorism* (Autonomedia, 1991).

3. David Graeber, *Possibilities: Essays on Hierarchy, Rebellion, and Desire* (AK Press, 2007).

4. Alix Dick and Antero Garcia, *The Cost of Being Undocumented: One Woman's Reckoning with America's Inhumane Math* (Beacon Press, 2015).

CHAPTER 7: SEARCHING FOR A SAFE SPACE IN AN UNSAFE SYSTEM

1. Judy A. Alston, "Standing (Out)side of the Circle: The Politics of Identity and Leadership in the Life of a Black Lesbian Professor," in *Black Women & Social Justice Education: Legacies and Lessons*, ed. Stephanie Y. Evans, Andrea D. Domingue, and Tania D. Mitchell (SUNY Press, 2019), 67.

2. Kimberlé W. Crenshaw, "Mapping the Margins: Intersectionality, Identity Politics, and Violence Against Women of Color," in *The Public Nature of Private Violence* (Routledge, 2013), 93–118; Shannon D. Snapp, Ryan J. Watson, Stephen T. Russell, Rafael M. Diaz, and Caitlin Ryan, "Social Support Networks for LGBT Young Adults: Low Cost Strategies for Positive Adjustment," *Family Relations* 64, no. 3 (2015): 420–30.

3. Human Rights Campaign, *2024 Black LGBTQ+ Youth Report*, February 2024, https://hrc-prod-requests.s3-us-west-2.amazonaws.com/2024-Black-LGBTQ-Youth-Report.cleaned.pdf.

4. Center for American Progress and Movement Advancement Project, *Unjust: How the Broken Criminal Justice System Fails LGBT People*, 2016, https://www.lgbtmap.org/policy-and-issue-analysis/lgbt-criminal-justice.

5. Kimberlé Crenshaw, "Demarginalizing the Intersection of Race and Sex: A Black Feminist Critique of Antidiscrimination Doctrine, Feminist Theory and Antiracist Politics," *University of Chicago Legal Forum* 1989, Article 8 (1989), available at https://chicago unbound.uchicago.edu/uclf/vol1989/iss1/8.

6. Andrea Ritchie, *Invisible No More: Police Violence Against Black Women and Women of Color* (Beacon Press, 2017).

7. Nhan L. Truong, Adrian D. Zongrone, and Joseph G. Kosciw, *Erasure and Resilience: The Experiences of LGBTQ Students of Color. Black LGBTQ Youth in US Schools* (Gay, Lesbian and Straight Education Network, 2020), 13.

8. Snapp et al., "Social Support Networks for LGBT Young Adults," 420–30.

9. Kimberlé W. Crenshaw, Priscilla Ocen, and Jyoti Nanda, *Black Girls Matter: Pushed Out, Overpoliced and Underprotected* (African American Policy Forum, 2015).

10. Bettina L. Love, *We Want to Do More Than Survive: Abolitionist Teaching and the Pursuit of Educational Freedom* (Beacon Press, 2019).

11. Ilan H. Meyer, "Prejudice, Social Stress, and Mental Health in Lesbian, Gay, and Bisexual Populations: Conceptual Issues and Research Evidence," *Psychological Bulletin* 129, no. 5 (2003): 674.

12. Love, *We Want to Do More Than Survive.*

13. Ann Arnett Ferguson, *Bad Boys: Public Schools in the Making of Black Masculinity* (University of Michigan Press, 2020).

14. William P. Banks, "Literacy, Sexuality, and the Value(s) of Queer Young Adult Literatures," *English Journal* 98, no. 4 (2009): 33–36, https://doi.org/10.58680/ej20087020.

15. Tara J. Yosso, "Whose Culture Has Capital? A Critical Race Theory Discussion of Community Cultural Wealth," *Race Ethnicity and Education* 8, no. 1 (2005): 69–91.

16. Love, *We Want to Do More Than Survive.*

CHAPTER 8: WHAT SCHOOLS CANNOT HOLD

1. Human Rights Watch, *"We Need to Take Away Children": Zero Accountability Six Years After "Zero Tolerance,"* December 16, 2024, https://www.hrw.org/report/2024/12/16/we-need-take-away-children/zero-accountability-six-years-after-zero-tolerance.

2. Costs of War Project, *Human Costs of Post-9/11 Wars: Direct Deaths and Displacement Caused by the United States' Post-9/11 Wars*, Watson Institute for International and Public Affairs, Brown University, 2021.

3. Louise A. Cainkar, *Homeland Insecurity: The Arab American and Muslim American Experience After 9/11* (Russell Sage Foundation, 2009).

4. Matt Apuzzo and Adam Goldman, *Enemies Within: Inside the NYPD's Secret Spying Unit and Bin Laden's Final Plot Against America* (Simon and Schuster, 2013).

5. Arshad Imitaz Ali, "Citizens Under Suspicion: Responsive Research with Community Under Surveillance," *Anthropology & Education Quarterly* 47, no. 1 (2016): 78–95.

6. Sylviane A. Diouf, *Servants of Allah: African Muslims Enslaved in the Americas* (New York University Press, 2013); Michael A. Gomez, *Black Crescent: The Experience and Legacy of African Muslims in the Americas* (Cambridge University Press, 2005); Edward E. Curtis IV, *Black Muslim Religion in the Nation of Islam, 1960–1975* (University of North Carolina Press, 2009).

7. Wayne Au, *A Marxist Education* (Haymarket Books, 2018).

8. Hannah Natanson, "Schools Shut Down Some Students, Teachers Who Comment on the Gaza War," *Washington Post*, December 19, 2023; Kanishka Singh,

"Pro-Palestinian US High School Students Accuse School of Censoring Speech," Reuters, April 24, 2024.

9. Ali, "Citizens Under Suspicion," 78–95.

10. Ali, "Citizens Under Suspicion," 78–95; "The Campus as Crucible: A Critical Race Analysis of Campus Climate in the Experiences of American Muslim Undergraduates," *Teachers College Record* 121, no. 5 (2019): 1–38.

11. Thea Renda Abu El-Haj, *Unsettled Belonging: Educating Palestinian American Youth After 9/11* (University of Chicago Press, 2015); Leigh Patel, *No Study Without Struggle: Confronting Settler Colonialism in Higher Education* (Beacon Press, 2021).

12. Patel, *No Study Without Struggle.*

13. Eve L. Ewing, *Ghosts in the Schoolyard: Racism and School Closings on Chicago's South Side* (University of Chicago Press, 2018).

14. Stefano Harney and Fred Moten, *The Undercommons: Fugitive Planning & Black Study* (Minor Compositions, 2013).

CHAPTER 9: A MENACE TO SOCIETY

1. "Queer" is a dynamic, umbrella term that describes sexualities, genders, and ways of being that resist or exist outside heterosexual and cisgender norms. It often names identities, politics, and practices that challenge fixed categories, affirm fluidity, and critique systems that enforce boundaries around what is seen as "normal."

2. Mollie T. McQuillan, Benjamin A. Lebovitz, and Lashanda Harbin, "The Disruptive Power of Policy Erasure: How State Legislators and School Boards Fail to Take Up Trans-Affirming Policies While Leaning into Anti-LGBTQ+ Policies," *Educational Policy* 38, no. 3 (2024): 642–99; Mollie T. McQuillan, "A Starting Point: Gender, Hot Cognition, and Trans-Informed Administrative Guidance," *Educational Researcher* 51, no. 5 (2022): 336–51.

3. McQuillan et al., "The Disruptive Power of Policy Erasure"; Mollie T. McQuillan, Joseph R. Cimpian, Benjamin A. Lebovitz, and Erin K. Gill, "Transgender Adolescent School Climate, Mental Health, and Adult Social Support," *JAMA Pediatrics* 178, no. 10 (2024): 1082–84; Joseph R. Cimpian and Mollie T. McQuillan, "Masking the Health Impacts of Anti-LGBTQ+ Policies by Political Suppression of Data and Informational Erasure," *American Journal of Public Health* 115, no. 7 (2025): 982–84.

4. T. Jameson Brewer, "School 'Choice' as a Method of Division: Leveraging Fear to Promote White Supremacy and Christian Nationalism," in *Resisting Divide-And-Conquer Strategies In Education: Pathways And Possibilities*, ed. Dennis L. Rudnick (Myers Education Press, 2024), 37–52.

5. Mollie T. McQuillan, Suzanne Eckes, and Maria M. Lewis, "A Solution in Search of a Problem: Justice Demands More for Trans Student-Athletes to Fulfill the Promise of Title IX," *Marquette Sports Law Review* 33 (2022): 195; Julie F. Mead and Suzanne E. Eckes, "Vouchers as a Mechanism for State-Sanctioned Private," in *The School Voucher Illusion: Exposing the Pretense of Equity*, ed. Kevin Welner, Gary Orfield, and Luis A. Huerta (Teachers College Press, 2023), 87.

6. McQuillan et al., "The Disruptive Power of Policy Erasure"; McQuillan, "A Starting Point"; Kevin Lawrence Henry Jr., "Zones of Nonbeing: Abjection, White Accumulation, and Neoliberal School Reform," *Teachers College Record* 123, no. 14 (2021): 129–49.

7. Cris Mayo and Mollie T. McQuillan, "History on Repeat: Silencing Trans-Related Health Information and Violating Health Professionals' Ethical Obligations," *Health Education Journal* 84, no. 6 (2025), 582–93.

8. Mayo and McQuillan, "History on Repeat."

9. Michael Feola, "'You Will Not Replace Us': The Melancholic Nationalism of Whiteness," *Political Theory* 49, no. 4 (2021): 528–53.

10. "Conservative Political Action Conference Former President Donald Trump," C-SPAN, August 6, 2022.

11. Beth Hawkins, "As The LGBTQ Youth Population Doubles, Number of Bills Targeting Them Triples," *The 74 Million*, September 23, 2025, https://www.the74million.org/article/as-the-lgbtq-youth-population-doubles-number-of-bills-targeting-them-triples/.

12. Hawkins, "As the LGBTQ Youth Population Doubles, Number of Bills Targeting Them Triples."

13. Samuel L. Perry, Joshua T. Davis, And Joshua B. Grubbs, "Controlling the Past to Control the Future: Christian Nationalism and Mandatory Patriotic Education in Public Schools," *Journal for the Scientific Study of Religion* 62, no. 3 (2023): 694–708.

14. Shannon D. Snapp, Jack K. Day, and Stephen T. Russell, "School Pushout: The Role of Supportive Strategies Versus Punitive Practices for LGBT Youth of Color," *Journal of Research on Adolescence* 32, no. 4 (2022): 1470–83; Ceema Samimi, Labibah Buraik, Quinn Oteman, and Scott Marsalis, "What Is Known About LGBTQ Youth and Exclusionary Discipline? A Scoping Review," *Journal of Homosexuality* 72, no. 11 (2025): 2195–220.

15. Snapp et al., "School Pushout," 1470–83; Samimi et al., "What Is Known About LGBTQ Youth and Exclusionary Discipline?" 2195–220.

16. Mayo & McQuillan, "History on Repeat."

17. Michael Apple, *Educating the Right Way: Markets, Standards, God, and Inequality* (Routledge, 2013); Catherine A. Lugg, "Reading, Writing, and Reconstructionism: The Christian Right and the Politics of Public Education," *Educational Policy* 14, no. 5 (2000): 622–37; Brandon D. Mitchell, *Education Censorship: Elite Capture of the Public Educational System* (Springer Nature, 2025).

18. Mollie T. McQuillan, Janel Anderson, and Lydia Gandy-Fastovich, "'Sometimes It's Hard to Do the Right Thing': The Gender-Inclusivity Leadership Spectrum of How PK–12 Administrators Understand Gender Diversity Laws, Policies, and Implementation," *American Educational Research Journal* 62, no. 1 (2025): 14–52; McQuillan, "A Starting Point"; Mollie McQuillan, "Scaling Gender and Sexual Diversity Policies in K–12 Schools," *Educational Policy* 37, no. 4 (2023): 910–52; Melinda M. Mangin, "Transgender Students in Elementary Schools: How Supportive Principals Lead," *Educational Administration Quarterly* 56, no. 2 (2020): 255–88.

19. Lisa Bardach, Sebastian Röhl, Sophie Oczlon, Aki Schumacher, Marko Lüftenegger, Rosa Lavelle-Hill, Miriam Schwarzenthal, and Steffen Zitzmann, "Cultural Diversity Climate in School: A Meta-Analytic Review of Its Relationships with Intergroup, Academic, and Socioemotional Outcomes," *Psychological Bulletin* 150, no. 12 (2024): 1397; Mollie T. McQuillan, Erin K. Gill, and Xue Gong, "LGBTQ+-Inclusive Professional Development in Elementary Schools: Does It Matter to Schoolwide Discipline?" *Journal of School Leadership* 33, no. 4 (2023): 382–408; Hilary Malatino, "Pedagogies of Becoming: Trans Inclusivity and the Crafting of Being," *Transgender Studies Quarterly* 2, no. 3 (2015): 395–410; Cal Horton and Anna Carlile, "'We Just Think of Her as One of the Girls': Applying a Trans Inclusion Staged Model to the Experiences of Trans Children and Youth in UK Primary and Secondary Schools," *Teachers College Record* 124, no. 8 (2022): 168–91; Jacqueline Ullman, "Breaking Out of the (Anti) Bullying 'Box': NYC Educators Discuss Trans/Gender Diversity-Inclusive Policies and Curriculum," *Sex Education* 18, no. 5

(2018): 495–510; Mollie T. McQuillan and Cris Mayo, "School Leaders and Transphobia: Direct, Facilitative, Accommodative, and Resistant Forms of Gender-Based Bias and Bullying," *Educational Administration Quarterly* 60, no. 1 (2024): 37–73.

20. bell hooks, *Teaching to Transgress: Education as the Practice of Freedom* (Routledge, 2014).

21. McQuillan et al., "'Sometimes It's Hard to Do the Right Thing'"; McQuillan, "A Starting Point."

22. McQuillan et al., "LGBTQ+-Inclusive Professional Development in Elementary Schools."

23. Colleen A. Capper and Michelle D. Young, "The Equity Audit as the Core of Leading Increasingly Diverse Schools and Districts," in *Leadership for Increasingly Diverse Schools* (Routledge, 2015), 212–23.

24. Terrance L. Green, "Community-Based Equity Audits: A Practical Approach for Educational Leaders to Support Equitable Community-School Improvements," *Educational Administration Quarterly* 53, no. 1 (2017): 3–39.

25. John Dewey, "The Need for an Industrial Education in an Industrial Democracy," in *John Dewey: The Middle Works, 1899–1924, Vol. 10: 1916–1917*, ed. J. A. Boydston (Southern Illinois University Press, 1980), 139.

CHAPTER 10: THE COMPASS AND THE ALGORITHM

1. Vincent Cho, "Administrators' Professional Learning via Twitter: The Dissonance Between Beliefs and Actions," *Journal of Educational Administration* 54, no. 3 (2016); Alice E. Marwick, "Instafame: Luxury Selfies in the Attention Economy," *Public Culture* 27, no. 1 (2015): 137–60.

2. Associated Press, "Massachusetts 19-Year-Old Pleading Guilty to Stealing, Extorting Teacher and Student Private Data," May 21, 2025; Howard Blume, "L.A. Unified Data Breach Last Year Includes at Least 2,000 Student Records, Officials Say," *Los Angeles Times*, February 23, 2023.

3. Center for Internet Security, *2025 CIS MS-ISAC K-12 Cybersecurity Report: Where Education Meets Community Resilience* (Center for Internet Security, 2025).

4. Vincent Cho and Sofia Dueñas, "Surprises from the Shadows: Confronting Intrusions from Bots & Generative AI in Survey Research," *Journal of Educational Research and Practice* 15, no. 1 (2025): 1–21, https://scholarworks.waldenu.edu/cgi/viewcontent.cgi?article=2091&context=jerap.

5. James Rundle, "The AI Effect: Amazon Sees Nearly 1 Billion Cyber Threats a Day," *Wall Street Journal*, November 21, 2024.

6. Lakshmi Varanasi, "Here's How Far We Are from AGI, According to the People Developing It," *Business Insider*, April 23, 2025.

7. Ethan Mollick, *Co-Intelligence: Living and Working with AI* (Penguin, 2024), 208.

8. Sam Altman, "The Gentle Singularity," *Sam Altman*, June 10, 2025, https://blog.samaltman.com/the-gentle-singularity.

9. Kevin Roose et al., "A.I. School Is in Session: Two Takes on the Future of Education," *Hard Fork*, podcast, *New York Times*, September 5, 2025.

10. Ruha Benjamin, "The New Artificial Intelligentsia," *Los Angeles Review of Books*, October 18, 2024; Meredith Broussard, *More Than a Glitch: Confronting Race, Gender, and Ability Bias in Tech* (MIT Press, 2023); Melanie Mitchell, "Why AI Chatbots Lie to Us," *Science* 389, no. 6758 (2025).

11. Benjamin, "The New Artificial Intelligentsia"; Broussard, *More Than a Glitch.*

12. Emily M. Bender and Alex Hanna, *The AI Con: How to Fight Big Tech's Hype and Create the Future We Want* (Harper, 2025); Jillian Fisher et al., "Biased LLMs Can Influence Political Decision-Making," in *Proceedings of the 63rd Annual Meeting of the Association for Computational Linguistics, Volume 1: Long Papers*, ed. Wanxiang Che, Joyce Nabende, Ekaterina Shutova, and Mohammad Taher Pilehvar (Association for Computational Linguistics, 2025); Mollick, *Co-Intelligence.*

13. Jeff Horwitz, "Meta's AI Rules Have Let Bots Hold 'Sensual' Chats with Children," Reuters, August 14, 2025.

14. Kate Conger, "Grok Chatbot Mirrored X Users' 'Extremist Views' in Antisemitic Posts, xAI Says," *New York Times*, July 12, 2025.

15. Will Oremus, "Trump Is Targeting 'Woke AI.' Here's What That Means," *Washington Post*, July 24, 2025.

16. Mateusz Łabuz and Christopher Nehring, "On the Way to Deep Fake Democracy? Deep Fakes in Election Campaigns in 2023," *European Political Science* 23, no. 4 (2024): 454–73.

17. Thomas H. Costello, Gordon Pennycook, and David G. Rand, "Durably Reducing Conspiracy Beliefs Through Dialogues with AI," *Science* 385, no. 6714 (2024).

18. Fisher et al., "Biased LLMs Can Influence Political Decision-Making."

19. Gad Levanon, Matt Sigelman, Mariano Mamertino, Mels de Zeeuw, and Gwynn Guilford, *No Country for Young Grads: The Structural Forces That Are Reshaping Entry-Level Employment* (Burning Glass Institute, 2025); Matthew Martin, *Educated but Unemployed, a Rising Reality for College Grads* (Oxford Economics, 2025).

20. Jean-Christophe Bélisle-Pipon, "AI, Universal Basic Income, and Power: Symbolic Violence in the Tech Elite's Narrative," *Frontiers in Artificial Intelligence* (February 8, 2025).

21. Binny Jose, Jaya Cherian, Alie Molly Verghis, Sony Mary Varghise, Mumthas S., and Sibichan Joseph, "The Cognitive Paradox of AI in Education: Between Enhancement and Erosion," *Frontiers in Psychology* 16 (April 2025); Nataliya Kosmyna, Eugene Hauptmann, Ye Tong Yuan, and Jessica Situ, "Your Brain on ChatGPT: Accumulation of Cognitive Debt When Using an AI Assistant for Essay Writing Task," arXiv:2506.08872; preprint, arXiv, June 10, 2025, https://doi.org/10.48550/arXiv.2506.08872; Hao-Ping (Hank) Lee, Advait Sarkar, Lev Tankelevitch et al. "The Impact of Generative AI on Critical Thinking: Self-Reported Reductions in Cognitive Effort and Confidence Effects from a Survey of Knowledge Workers," *Proceedings of the 2025 CHI Conference on Human Factors in Computing Systems* (ACM, 2025), 1–22.

22. Derek Thompson, "Will AI Usher In the End of Deep Thinking?" *Plain English with Derek Thompson*, August 6, 2025, retrieved August 19, 2025.

23. Mollick, *Co-Intelligence.*

24. Alicia Martín, Amir Globerson, Amy Wang, et al., "Towards an AI-Augmented Textbook," arXiv:2509.13348, preprint, arXiv, September 30, 2025, https://doi.org/10.48550/arXiv.2509.13348.

25. Ricardo Fitas, "Inclusive Education with AI: Supporting Special Needs and Tackling Language Barriers," preprint, arXiv, April 19, 2025.

26. Cho and Dueñas, "Surprises from the Shadows: Confronting Intrusions from Bots & Generative AI in Survey Research," 1–21.

27. Aayushi Dangol et al., "Relief or Displacement? How Teachers Are Negotiating Generative AI's Role in Their Professional Practice," in *Proceedings of the CHI Conference on Human Factors in Computing Systems (CHI 2026)* (Association for Computing Machinery, 2026).

28. Center for Humane Technology, "The Attention Economy: Why Do Tech Companies Fight for Our Attention?" *Center for Humane Technology Youth Toolkit* (Center for Humane Technology, n.d.); Howard Gardner and Katie Davis, *The App Generation: How Today's Youth Navigate Identity, Intimacy, and Imagination in a Digital World* (Yale University Press, 2013).

29. Kashmir Hill, "They Asked an A.I. Chatbot Questions. The Answers Sent Them Spiraling," *New York Times*, June 13, 2025; Kashmir Hill and Dylan Freedman, "Chatbots Can Go into a Delusional Spiral. Here's How It Happens," *New York Times*, August 8, 2025; Benjamin Weiser and Nate Schweber, "The ChatGPT Lawyer Explains Himself," *New York Times*, June 8, 2023.

30. TAKE IT DOWN Act, Pub. L. No. 119–12, 139 Stat. 55 (2025).

31. Gregory Smith, Karlyn D. Stanley, Krystyna Marcinek, Paul Cormarie, and Salil Gunashekar, *Liability for Harms from AI Systems: The Application of U.S. Tort Law and Liability to Harms from Artificial Intelligence Systems* (RAND, 2024).

32. Elizabeth Laird, Maddy Dwyer, and Hannah Quay-de la Vallee, *Hand in Hand: Schools' Embrace of AI Connected to Increased Risks to Students* (Center for Democracy and Technology, 2025), https://cdt.org/insights/hand-in-hand-schools-embrace-of-ai-connected-to-increased-risks-to-students/.

33. John Seely Brown and Paul Duguid, "Organizational Learning and Communities-of-Practice: Toward a Unified View of Working, Learning, and Innovation," *Organization Science* 2, no. 1 (1991): 40–57; Michelle D. Van Lare and S. David Brazer, "Analyzing Learning in Professional Learning Communities: A Conceptual Framework," *Leadership and Policy in Schools* 12, no. 4 (2013): 374–96.

34. Elizabeth A. City, Melissa Kagle, and Mark B. Teoh, "Examining Instruction," in *Data Wise*, ed. Kathryn Parker Boudett, Elizabeth A. City, and Richard J. Murnane (Harper, 2013), 109–30; Marnie Curry, "Critical Friends Groups: The Possibilities and Limitations Embedded in Teacher Professional Communities Aimed at Instructional Improvement and School Reform," *Teachers College Record* 110, no. 4 (2008): 733–74; Kim Schildkamp, Cindy L. Poortman, and Adam Handelzalts, "Data Teams for School Improvement," *School Effectiveness and School Improvement* 27, no. 2 (2016): 228–54.

35. Gallup/Walton Family Foundation, *Teaching for Tomorrow: Unlocking Six Weeks a Year with AI* (Gallup, 2025).

36. American Federation of Teachers, "AFT to Launch National Academy for AI Instruction with Microsoft, OpenAI, Anthropic and United Federation of Teachers," press release, July 7, 2025.

37. Laird, Dwyer, and Quay-de la Vallee, *Hand in Hand*.

CHAPTER 11: WE'VE BEEN HERE BEFORE

1. National Women's Law Center, "Terrifying Reasons 300K Black Women Lost Jobs in 2025," July 29, 2025.

2. Sherdell Baker, "Black Women See Highest Job Losses in April 2025," *Ebony*, May 26, 2025.

3. Claudine Gay, "What Just Happened at Harvard Is Bigger Than Me," *New York Times*, January 3, 2024.

4. Menah Pratt-Clarke and Johanna B. Maes, eds., *Journeys of Social Justice: Women of Color Presidents in the Academy*, vol. 88, Black Studies and Critical Thinking (Peter Lang, 2017).

5. Octavia E. Butler, *Parable of the Sower* (Grand Central Publishing, 2023).

6. Stephanie E. Jones-Rogers, *They Were Her Property: White Women as Slave Owners in the American South* (Yale University Press, 2019).

CHAPTER 12: LEARNING FOR A NEW WORLD

1. Ken Robinson and Kate Robinson, "4 Core Purposes of Education," *Edutopia*, March 2, 2022.

2. The Federal Bureau of Investigation (FBI) advises schools and other institutions to regularly practice active-shooter drills. See FBI Active Shooter Safety Resources, https://www.fbi.gov/how-we-can-help-you/active-shooter-safety-resources.

3. Bertrand Russell and Albert Einstein, "Russell-Einstein Manifesto," July 9, 1955.

4. Yuval Noah Harari, *Nexus: A Brief History of Information Networks, from the Stone Age to AI* (Penguin Random House, 2024), 39.

5. Erica Meltzer, "Trump Moved Fast and Broke Things in Education. But What He's Creating Isn't Clear," *Chalkbeat*, June 20, 2025, https://www.chalkbeat.org/2025/06/20/trump-education-strategy-anti-dei-fervor-pushes-schools-toward-fork-in-road/.

6. Bayo Akomolafe is a philosopher, a writer, an activist, and a professor of psychology. He currently lectures at Pacifica Graduate Institute in California and the University of Vermont in Burlington. He sits on the boards of many organizations, including Science and Nonduality and Unashay Sanctuary. For this essay I referenced his book *These Wilds Beyond Our Fences: Letters to My Daughter on Humanity's Search for Home* (North Atlantic Books, 2017).

7. Jonathan Haidt, *The Anxious Generation: How the Great Rewiring of Childhood Is Causing an Epidemic of Mental Illness* (Penguin, 2024).

8. Eckhart Tolle, *A New Earth: Awakening to Your Life's Purpose* (Penguin, 2008).

9. Paulo Freire, *Pedagogy of the Oppressed*, trans. Myra Bergman Ramos (Continuum, 1970). I had the privilege of studying with Freire when he taught a seminar at Stanford University in 1983 (education economist Martin Carnoy served as the co-convener with Freire).

10. Freire, *Pedagogy of the Oppressed.*

CHAPTER 13: REENVISIONING POWERFUL LITERACY EDUCATION

1. Carol Lee, Gregory White, and Dian Dong, eds., *Educating for Civic Reasoning and Discourse* (National Academy of Education, 2021).

2. Samuel Thurber, "English in Secondary Schools: Some Considerations as to Its Aims and Its Needs," *School Review* 2, no. 8 (1894): 471.

3. Matthew Arnold, *Culture and Anarchy* (1869; Oxford University Press, 2009).

4. Kyungae Chae and Ricki Ginsberg, *The State of Literature Use in U.S. Secondary English Classrooms* (National Council of Teachers of English, 2025).

5. Sarah Mervosh, "White House Will Release $5.5 Billion for Schools, After Surprise Delay," *New York Times*, July 25, 2025.

6. American Library Association, "2024 Book Ban Data," 2025.

7. Kasey Meehan, Jonathan Friedman, Sabrina Baêta, and Tasslyn Magnusson, *Banned in the USA: The Mounting Pressure to Censor* (PEN America, 2023), 4.

8. Marcelo Goncalves, Isabelle Langrock, Jack LaViolette, and Katie Spoon, "Book Bans in Political Context: Evidence from U.S. Schools," *PNAS Nexus* 3, no. 6 (2024): 197–222.

9. Nicole Mirra, *Educating for Empathy: Literacy Learning and Civic Engagement* (Teachers College Press, 2018).

10. Nicole Mirra and Antero Garcia, *Civics for the World to Come: Committing to Democracy in Every Classroom* (W. W. Norton, 2023); Ernest Morrell, *Critical Literacy and Urban Youth: Pedagogies of Access, Dissent and Liberation* (Routledge, 2008).

11. Maxine Greene, *Releasing the Imagination: Essays on Education, the Arts, and Social Change* (Jossey-Bass, 2000).

12. Rose Horowitch, "The Elite College Students Who Can't Read Books," *The Atlantic*, October 1, 2024.

13. Gallup/Walton Family Foundation, "2025 Report Card: Student Perspective on U.S. Schools," 2025.

CHAPTER 14: POLITICAL EDUCATION, REPRESSION, AND THE PURPOSES OF LEARNING

1. Daniel Morales-Doyle, Tiffany Childress Price, and Mindy J. Chappell, "Chemicals Are Contaminants Too: Teaching Appreciation and Critique of Science in the Era of Next Generation Science Standards (NGSS)," *Science Education* 103, no. 6 (2019): 1347–66; Maxine McKinney de Royston and Tesha Sengupta-Irving, "Another Step Forward: Engaging the Political in Learning," *Cognition and Instruction* 37, no. 3 (2019): 277–84; Sepehr Vakil and Rick Ayers, "The Racial Politics of STEM Education in the USA: Interrogations and Explorations," *Race Ethnicity and Education* 22, no. 4 (2019): 449–58.

2. Sepehr Vakil, "Ethics, Identity, and Political Vision: Toward a Justice-Centered Approach to Equity in Computer Science Education," *Harvard Educational Review* 88, no. 1 (2018): 26–52.

3. Cynthia Enloe, "Womenandchildren: Making Feminist Sense of the Persian Gulf Crisis," *Village Voice* 25, no. 9 (1990).

4. Maya Mikdashi, "Can Palestinian Men Be Victims? Gendering Israel's War on Gaza," *Jadaliyya*, August 26, 2014.

5. Mohammed El-Kurd, *Perfect Victims and the Politics of Appeal* (Haymarket Books, 2025).

6. Adom Getachew, "The New Black Internationalism," *Dissent* (Fall 2021).

7. Carol D. Lee and Susan R. Goldman, "Assessing Literary Reasoning: Text and Task Complexities," *Theory into Practice* 54, no. 3 (2015): 213–27.

8. Beth Warren, Shirin Vossoughi, Ann S. Roseberry, Megan Bang, and Edd V. Taylor, "Disciplinary Learning and Epistemic Heterogeneity," in *Handbook of the Cultural Foundations of Learning*, ed. N. S. Nasir, C. D. Lee, R. Pea, and M. McKinney de Royston (Routledge, 2020), 277–93.

9. Megan Bang and Shirin Vossoughi, "Participatory Design Research and Educational Justice: Studying Learning and Relations Within Social Change Making," *Cognition and Instruction* 34, no. 3 (2016): 173–93; Anna Lees, "Roles of Urban Indigenous Community Members in Collaborative Field-Based Teacher Preparation," *Journal of Teacher Education* 67, no. 5 (2016): 363–78; Ann M. Ishimaru, *Just Schools: Building Equitable Collaborations with Families and Communities* (Teachers College Press, 2019).

10. April Baker-Bell, *Linguistic Justice: Black Language, Literacy, Identity, and Pedagogy* (Routledge, 2020); Nelson Flores and Jonathan Rosa, "Undoing Appropriateness: Raciolinguistic Ideologies and Language Diversity in Education," *Harvard Educational Review* 85, no. 2 (2015): 149–71; Kris D. Gutiérrez, Patricia Baquedano-López, and Carlos Tejeda, "Rethinking Diversity: Hybridity and Hybrid Language Practices in the Third Space," *Mind, Culture, and Activity* 6, no. 4 (1999): 286–303; Carol D. Lee, "Is October Brown Chinese? A Cultural Modeling Activity System for Underachieving Students," *American Educational Research Journal* 38, no. 1 (2001): 97–141; Teresa L. McCarty and Sheilah E. Nicholas, "Reclaiming Indigenous Languages: A Reconsideration of the Roles and Responsibilities of Schools," *Review of Research in Education* 38, no. 1 (2014): 106–36.

11. Megan Bang, Carrie Tzou, Leah Bricker, Jordan Sherry-Wagner, and Priya Pugh, "Attunements to Socioecological Histories of Places in Learning and Decision-Making in Complex Socioecological Systems," in *Proceedings of the 16th International Conference of the Learning Sciences-ICLS 2022* (International Society of the Learning Sciences, 2022), 1605–8.

12. Megan Bang and Ananda Marin, "Nature–Culture Constructs in Science Learning: Human/Non-Human Agency and Intentionality," *Journal of Research in Science Teaching* 52, no. 4 (2015): 530–44; Anna Lees and Megan Bang, "We're Not Migrating Yet: Engaging Children's Geographies and Learning with Lands and Waters," *Occasional Paper Series*, no. 48 (2022): 33–47; Jordan D. Sherry-Wagner, *Wondering with People, Places, and More-Than-Humans as an Ontological Orientation to Ethical Socio-Ecological Education: Towards More Just & Livable Futures Through Design-Based, Mediational, and Quantitative Analyses* (University of Washington, 2023); Carrie Tzou, Megan Bang, and Leah Bricker, "Commentary: Designing Science Instructional Materials That Contribute to More Just, Equitable, and Culturally Thriving Learning and Teaching in Science Education," *Journal of Science Teacher Education* 32, no. 7 (2021): 858–64.

13. Shirin Vossoughi, Ananda Marin, and Megan Bang, "Toward Just and Sustainable Futures: Human Learning and Relationality Within Socio-Ecological Systems," *Review of Research in Education* 47, no. 1 (2023): 218–73.

14. adrienne marie brown, *We Will Not Cancel Us: And Other Dreams of Transformative Justice* (AK Press, 2020); Shirin Vossoughi, Kalonji Nzinga, Allena Berry, Faith Irvine, Christopher Mayorga, and Mari Gashaw, "Writing as a Social Act: The Feedback Relation as a Context for Political and Ethical Becoming," *Research in the Teaching of English* 56, no. 2 (2021): 200–222.

15. Melita Morales, Mya Franklin, Shirin Vossoughi, Sam Carroll, Onam Lansana, Megan Bang, and Sahibzada Mayed, "World-Making Through a Feminist Abolitionist Lens in a STEAM Middle School Program," *Reading Research Quarterly* 59, no. 3 (2024): 257–81.

16. Decoteau Irby, *Stuck Improving: Racial Equity and School Leadership* (Harvard Education Press, 2022); Ann M. Ishimaru and Megan Bang, "Designing with Families for Just Futures," *Journal of Family Diversity in Education* 4, no. 2 (2022): 130–40; Muhammad Khalifa, *Culturally Responsive School Leadership* (Harvard Education Press, 2020).

17. James D. Anderson, Megan Bang, Bryan McKinley Jones Brayboy, Cati V. de los Ríos, Kris D. Gutiérrez, Deborah Hicks, Li-Ching Ho, Carol D. Lee, Stacey J. Lee, Maribel Santiago, Vanessa Siddle Walker, and Joy Ann Williamson-Lott, "Agency and

Resilience in the Face of Challenge as Civic Action: Lessons Learned from Across Ethnic Communities," *Educating for Civic Reasoning and Discourse* (2021): 157–243; Bryan McKinley Jones Brayboy, Susan C. Faircloth, Tiffany S. Lee, Margaret J. Maaka, and Troy A. Richardson, "Sovereignty and Education: An Overview of the Unique Nature of Indigenous Education," *Journal of American Indian Education* 54, no. 1 (2015): 1–9; Eve L. Ewing, *Original Sins: The (Mis)education of Black and Native Children and the Construction of American Racism* (One World, 2025).

18. Na'ilah Suad Nasir, Carol D. Lee, Roy Pea, and Maxine McKinney de Royston, *Handbook of the Cultural Foundations of Learning* (Taylor & Francis, 2020); National Academies of Sciences, Engineering, and Medicine, *Science and Engineering in Preschool Through Elementary Grades: The Brilliance of Children and the Strengths of Educators* (National Academies Press, 2022); Carla Shalaby, *Troublemakers: Lessons in Freedom from Young Children at School* (New Press, 2017).

19. Warren et al., "Disciplinary Learning and Epistemic Heterogeneity."

20. Savannah Shange, *Progressive Dystopia: Abolition, Antiblackness, and Schooling in San Francisco* (Duke University Press, 2020).

21. Isabelle Bates, "Fury as Aston University Cuts Ceremony Livestream as Graduate Dedicates Degree to Murdered Child," *Birmingham Live*, July 19, 2025, https://www.birminghammail.co.uk/news/midlands-news/fury-aston-university-cuts-ceremony-32088619.

22. James M. Pierce, "A Manifesto for Speculative Relations," in *Five Manifestos for the Beautiful World:* The Alchemy Lecture (Penguin Random House, 2024).

CHAPTER 15: LEARNING ALONGSIDE CREATIVE ARTISTS

1. Megan Bang, Lawrence Curley, Adam Kessel, Ananda Marin, Eli S. Suzukovich III, and George Strack, "Muskrat Theories, Tobacco in the Streets, and Living Chicago as Indigenous Land," *Environmental Education Research* 20, no. 1 (2014): 37–55.

2. In this chapter we use the terms "jazz" and "free jazz" because they are familiar to the public; however, they are not without complication. As partnering artists explained, "What is commonly known as jazz by the public is associated with a certain modality. However, the name jazz does not reflect the diversity of activities pursued by creative musicians and artists. Similarly, free jazz is a term that has been used by music critics to describe a shift in form among jazz musicians beginning with Ornette Coleman, John Coltrane, Cecil Taylor, and many others who collectively improvised, expanding the soundscape beyond jazz standards. What we are doing is leaping beyond traditional boundaries of technique and the mental activity of what is form or non-form, right or wrong, to allow ourselves to courageously explore. Motivated by a search for open space or the placeless place, the goal is seeing where the individual and the collective can travel, by playing with chordal structures, rhythm, color, sound, silence, and processes of stepping forward and stepping back."

3. Megan De Mar, "Trump Again Claims Chicago Is 'Most Dangerous' City, but the Data Doesn't Agree," CBS News, October 14, 2025, https://www.cbsnews.com/chicago/news/trump-chicago-dangerous-city-data/.

4. Bryan McKinley Jones Brayboy and Jeremiah Chin, "On the Development of Terrortory," *Contexts* 19, no. 3 (2020): 22–27; Inmaculada M. García-Sánchez and Chantral Tetreault, "Arabic and the Discursive Contours of Islamo-Linguistic-Phobia in Spain and France," *Language and Social Justice: Global Perspectives* (2024): 211.

5. See, for example, Andre Bouchard, "Native American Dance: A Perspective from the Field," Indigenous Performance Productions, September 1, 2023; Harmony Holiday, "A Brief History of the Policing of Black Music. Harmony Holiday Dreams of a Black Sound Unfettered by White Desire," *Literary Hub*, June 19, 2020; Michelle Joffroy, "Inventing the Crime of Dancing," *A History of Domestic Work and Worker Organizing*, accessed January 4, 2026.

6. K. Tsianina Lomawaima and Jeffrey Ostler, "Reconsidering Richard Henry Pratt: Cultural Genocide and Native Liberation in an Era of Racial Oppression," *Journal of American Indian Education* 57, no. 1 (2018): 83.

7. Ngũgĩ wa Thiong'o, *Something Torn and New: An African Renaissance* (Civitas Books, 2009).

8. Association for the Advancement of Creative Musicians (AACM), https://www.aacmchicago.org/, accessed October 14, 2025.

9. etymonline, "Origin and History of *Technology*," https://www.etymonline.com/word/technology, accessed January 4, 2026.

10. Megan Bang, Ananda Marin, Lori Faber, and Eli S. Suzukovich III, "Repatriating Indigenous Technologies in an Urban Indian Community," *Urban Education* 48, no. 5 (2013): 705–33.

11. Manuel Luis Espinoza and Shirin Vossoughi, "Perceiving Learning Anew: Social Interaction, Dignity, and Educational Rights," *Harvard Educational Review* 84, no. 3 (2014): 285–313.

12. Ajay Heble and Jesse Stewart, *Jamming The Classroom: Musical Improvisation and Pedagogical Practice* (University of Michigan Press, 2023), 37.

13. Heble and Stewart, *Jamming The Classroom.*

14. Jo-Ann Archibald, *Indigenous Storywork: Educating the Heart, Mind, Body, and Spirit* (UBC Press, 2008); Ananda Marin, Kyle Halle-Erby, Megan Bang, Nikki McDaid-Morgan, Mario Guerra, Kalonji Nzinga, Meixi, Emma Elliot-Groves, and Angela Booker, "The Power of Storytelling and Storylistening for Human Learning and Becoming," in *14th International Conference of the Learning Sciences: The Interdisciplinarity of the Learning Sciences, ICLS 2020—Conference Proceedings*, vol. 4, ed. M. Gresalfi and I. S. Horn, Computer-Supported Collaborative Learning Conference (International Society of the Learning Sciences, 2020), 2199–206; Stephanie R. Toliver, *Recovering Black Storytelling in Qualitative Research: Endarkened Storywork* (Routledge, 2021).

CHAPTER 16: THEORIZING BACK

1. An edited assemblage of several conversations that took place during Theorizing Back sessions. For more, see M. Casar Rodriguez, "Homies Theorizing Back: Reclaiming the Right to the Word and the World," PhD diss., UCLA, 2022.

2. bell hooks, *Teaching to Transgress: Education as the Practice of Freedom* (Routledge, 2014).

3. Ursula K. Le Guin, "The Carrier Bag Theory of Fiction," in *The Ecocriticism Reader: Landmarks in Literary Ecology*, ed. Cheryll Glotfelty and Harold Fromm (University of Georgia Press, 1996), 149–54.

4. Achille Mbembe, *Out of the Dark Night: Essays on Decolonization* (Columbia University Press, 2021).

5. Stuart Hall, ed., *Representation: Cultural Representations and Signifying Practices* (Sage, 1997).

6. See also Michael W. Apple, "The Politics of Official Knowledge: Does a National Curriculum Make Sense?" *Teachers College Record* 95, no. 2 (1993): 222–41; Eve Tuck and Rubén A. Gaztambide-Fernández, "Curriculum, Replacement, and Settler Futurity," *Journal of Curriculum Theorizing* 29, no. 1 (2013): 72–89.

7. For more, see K. Tsianina Lomawaima and Teresa L. McCarty, *"To Remain an Indian": Lessons in Democracy from a Century of Native American Education* (Teachers College Press, 2025); Louis Althusser, "Ideology and Ideological State Apparatuses (Notes Towards an Investigation) (1970)," in *Cultural Theory: An Anthology*, ed. Imre Szeman and Timothy Kaposy (Wiley, 2010), 204–22; Michael W. Apple, *Can Education Change Society?* (Routledge, 2012); Pierre Bourdieu and Jean-Claude Passeron, *Reproduction in Education, Society and Culture*, vol. 4. (Sage, 1990); Samuel Bowles and Herbert Gintis, *Schooling in Capitalist America*, vol. 57 (Basic Books, 1976); Henry A. Giroux, *Theory and Resistance in Education: A Pedagogy for the Opposition* (Bergin & Garvey, 1983); Peter McLaren and Adriana Puiggrós, *Pedagogía Crítica, Resistencia Cultural y la Producción del Deseo* (Aique Grupo Editor, 1994); Sonia Nieto, "Public Education in the Twentieth Century and Beyond: High Hopes, Broken Promises, and an Uncertain Future," *Harvard Educational Review* 75, no. 1 (2005): 43–64; Angela Davis, *Are Prisons Obsolete?* (Seven Stories Press, 2003); Erica Meiners, *A Right to Be Hostile: Schools, Prisons, and the Making of Public Enemies* (Routledge, 2007); Damien Sojoyner, *First Strike: Educational Enclosures in Black Los Angeles* (University of Minnesota Press, 2016); Loïc Wacquant, "The New Peculiar Institution': On the Prison as Surrogate Ghetto," *Theoretical Criminology* 4, no. 3 (2000): 377–89; Walter D. Mignolo, *Local Histories–Global Designs: Coloniality, Subaltern Knowledges, and Border Thinking* (Princeton University Press, 2012).

8. Leanne Betasamosake Simpson, "Land as Pedagogy: Nishnaabeg Intelligence and Rebellious Transformation," *Decolonization: Indigeneity, Education & Society* 3, no. 3 (2014): 7.

9. Linda Tuhiwai Smith, *Decolonizing Methodologies: Research and Indigenous Peoples* (Zed Books, 2012).

10. la paperson, *A Third University Is Possible* (University of Minnesota Press, 2017).

11. paperson, *A Third University Is Possible*. See also Fred Moten and Stefano Harney, "The University and the Undercommons: Seven Theses," *Social Text* 22, no. 2 (2004): 101–15.

12. Eve Tuck, "Theorizing Back: An Approach to Participatory Policy Analysis," in *Theory and Educational Research*, ed. Jean Anyon (Routledge, 2008), 121–40; Smith, *Decolonizing Methodologies*; Sandy Grande, *Red Pedagogy: Native American Social and Political Thought* (Rowman and Littlefield, 2004); Boaventura de Sousa Santos, *The End of the Cognitive Empire: The Coming of Age of Epistemologies of the South* (Duke University Press, 2018); Arjun Appadurai, "The Right to Research," *Globalisation, Societies and Education* 4, no. 2 (2006): 167–77.

13. Walter D. Mignolo, "Epistemic Disobedience, Independent Thought and Decolonial Freedom," *Theory, Culture & Society* 26, nos. 7–8 (2009): 159–81.

14. Dominique Moran, *Carceral Geography: Spaces and Practices of Incarceration* (Routledge, 2016); Danfeng Koon, Soto-Vigil, Hoang Pham, Cecelia Jordan, Seenae Chong, Bianca N. Haro, Jamelia N. Harris, Danielle Huddlestun, and Jeremy Prim, "Racial Capitalism and Student Disposability in an Era of School Discipline Reform," *American Journal of Education* 130, no. 2 (2024): 207–37.

15. Ngũgĩ wa Thiong'o, *Re-membering Africa* (East African Educational Publishers, 2009).

16. de Sousa Santos, *The End of the Cognitive Empire*. See also Robin D. G. Kelley, *Yo' Mama's Disfunktional! Fighting the Culture Wars in Urban America* (Beacon Press, 1998); Gloria Ladson-Billings, "Through a Glass Darkly: The Persistence of Race in Education Research & Scholarship," *Educational Researcher* 41, no. 4 (2012): 115–20; Django Paris, "'A Friend Who Understand Fully': Notes on Humanizing Research in a Multiethnic Youth Community," *International Journal of Qualitative Studies in Education* 24, no. 2 (2011): 137–49.

17. Maisha T. Winn, *Justice on Both Sides: Transforming Education Through Restorative Justice* (Harvard Education Press, 2020); Mariame Kaba, *We Do This 'Til We Free Us: Abolitionist Organizing and Transforming Justice*, vol. 1 (Haymarket Books, 2021).

18. Shawn Wilson, *Research Is Ceremony: Indigenous Research Methods* (Fernwood Publishing, 2020).

19. Paulo Freire, *Pedagogy of the Oppressed*, trans. Myra Bergman Ramos (Continuum, 1970).

20. See Alex Khasnabish and Max Haiven, *The Radical Imagination: Social Movement Research in the Age of Austerity* (Bloomsbury, 2014).

21. de Sousa Santos, *The End of the Cognitive Empire*.

22. Movement Generation, *From Banks and Tanks to Cooperation and Caring; A Strategic Framework for a Just Transition* (2017), https://movementgeneration.org/wp-content/uploads/2016/11/JT_booklet_English_SPREADs_web.pdf.

23. Vanessa Machado De Oliveira, *Hospicing Modernity: Facing Humanity's Wrongs and the Implications for Social Activism* (North Atlantic Books, 2021).

24. See also Michael Hardt, "The Militancy of Theory," *South Atlantic Quarterly* 110, no. 1 (2011): 19–35.

25. As further explored by Derrida, displacement of a material-discursive structure enables something else to be thought and to happen, and, in that way, deconstruction, too, can be called a practice of freedom. In Jacques Derrida, *Positions* (University of Chicago Press, 1972).

26. For more, see *Cuadernos del primer grade de la Escuelita de la Libertad según lxs Zapatistas*, Radio Zapatista, https://radiozapatista.org/?page_id=20465&lang=en, accessed January 4, 2026; Subcomandante Insurgente Marcos, *Our Word Is Our Weapon: Selected Writings*, ed. Juana Ponce de León (Seven Stories Press, 2002).

27. Referring to a war of positions, a concept by Gramsci that describes a revolutionary process, a participatory and cultural form of struggle aiming to destroy the appearance of a "natural order" and formulate a new, more just, and democratic hegemony. For more, see Antonio Gramsci, *Prison Notebooks*, vol. 2 (Columbia University Press, 2011).

28. Gramsci, *Prison Notebooks*, vol. 2. For Gramsci, "good sense" referred to the potentially transformative elements embedded within the broader, often contradictory, and sometimes misleading "common sense" of the masses; not a separate form of knowledge but, rather, a critical capacity within everyday understanding that can be directed toward social change.

CHAPTER 17: TEACHING FOR DEMOCRACY IN A TIME OF DEMOCRATIC COLLAPSE

1. Democracy Now! "'Arrest Now, Ask Questions Later': Why Did L.A. ICE Agents Arrest and Jail U.S. Citizen Andrea Velez?" July 2, 2025.

2. Nate Raymond, "U.S. Judges Recount Death Threats, 'Swatting' After Rulings Against Trump," Reuters, July 31, 2025; Gregory Svirnovskiy, "'Stop Fanning These Flames': Judges Say White House Needs to Tone Down Attacks," *Politico*, July 31, 2025.

3. Steven Greenhouse, "Trump's Presidential Philosophy Is Government by Shakedown," *The Guardian*, August 22, 2025.

4. Robert Reich, "Public Education After Neoliberalism," *Stanford Social Innovation Review* (Summer 2024).

5. Michael W. Apple, *Ideology and Curriculum*, 4th ed. (Routledge, 2018); Akilah Alleyne, "Book Banning, Curriculum Restrictions, and the Politicization of U.S. Schools," Center for American Progress, July 18, 2022.

6. James Ross Gardner, "How a Culture War Over Race Engulfed a School District," *New Yorker*, September 13, 2023; US House Committee on Education and Labor, "Curriculum Sabotage and Classroom Censorship Hearing," transcript (US Government Publishing Office, 2022).

7. Jaden Edison, "How Some Texas Parents and Historians Say a New Texas Curriculum Glosses Over Slavery and Racism," *Texas Tribune*, November 18, 2024.

8. National Education Association, "Know Your Rights: Texas," July 8, 2023.

9. Bruce Maxwell, "Teacher Neutrality, Pedagogical Impartiality, and Democratic Education," in *The Cambridge Handbook of Democratic Education*, ed. Julian Culp, Johannes Drerup, and Douglas Yacek (Cambridge University Press, 2023), 607–27; Joel Westheimer, *What Kind of Citizen? Educating Our Children for the Common Good*, 2nd ed. (Teachers College Press, 2024); Howard Zinn, *You Can't Be Neutral on a Moving Train: A Personal History* (Beacon Press, 2002).

10. Olivia Empson, "'State-Driven Censorship': New Wave of Book Bans Hits Florida School Districts," *The Guardian*, August 16, 2025.

11. PEN America, *Banned in the USA: Beyond the Shelves*, November 1, 2024.

12. Laura Benitez, Amy Reid, and Jonathan Friedman, "With a Wave of New Bills in 2025, State Legislators Cast a Web of Control Over Higher Education," PEN America, July 24, 2025.

13. Erin Gretzinger, Maggie Hicks, Christa Dutton, Jasper Smith, Sonel Cutler, and Aisha Baiocchi, "Tracking Higher Ed's Dismantling of DEI," *Chronicle of Higher Education*, August 18, 2025; Timothy Snyder, *On Tyranny: Twenty Lessons from the Twentieth Century* (Crown, 2017).

14. Kevin K. Kumashiro, *Against Common Sense: Teaching and Learning Toward Social Justice* (Routledge, 2024).

15. See, for example, Claire Partain, "ACLU Texas Questions Houston ISD Suspensions After 'Disruptive' Immigration Protest," *Houston Chronicle*, February 13, 2025.

16. Hannah Arendt, *Between Past and Future* (Viking Press, 1961), 231.

17. Edward Graham, "Who Is Behind the Attacks on Educators and Public Schools?" *NEA Today*, December 14, 2021.

18. Ellen W. Schrecker, *No Ivory Tower: McCarthyism and the Universities* (Oxford University Press, 1986).

19. Marguerite Feitlowitz, "A Lexicon of Terror: Argentina and the Legacies of Torture," in *Emotions: A Social Science Reader*, ed. Monica Greco and Paul Stenner (Routledge, 2013), 429–33.

20. Michael Ignatieff, "An Authoritarian Came for My University. His Objective Was Clear," *Washington Post*, June 2, 2025; Endangered Scholars Worldwide, "New Law

Reaffirms Presidential Control over Turkish Higher Education," August 20, 2025, https://www.endangeredscholarsworldwide.net/post/new-law-reaffirms-presidential-control-over-turkish-higher-education.

21. John Dewey, *Democracy & Education* (Macmillan, 1916); Walter C. Parker, *Teaching Democracy: Unity and Diversity in Public Life* (Teachers College Press, 2003).

22. Danielle Allen, "Response to Commentators," *Education and Equality* (University of Chicago Press, 2016).

23. Paulo Freire, *Pedagogy of the Oppressed*, trans. Myra Bergman Ramos (Continuum, 1970).

24. Joel Westheimer, *What Kind of Citizen? Educating Our Children for the Common Good*, 2nd ed. (Teachers College Press, 2024), xvii. The COVID-19 pandemic offers a salient example. See, for example, Sander van Der Linden, "Misinformation: Susceptibility, Spread, and Interventions to Immunize the Public," *Nature Medicine* 28, no. 3 (2022): 460–67.

25. Arendt, *Between Past and Future*, 252.

26. Maxine Greene, *Releasing the Imagination: Essays on Education, the Arts, and Social Change* (Jossey-Bass, 1995).

27. Jon N. Hale, *The Freedom Schools: Student Activists in the Mississippi Civil Rights Movement* (Columbia University Press, 2016).

28. Brian Puaca, *Learning Democracy: Education Reform in West Germany, 1945–1965* (Berghahn Books, 2022).

CHAPTER 18: THE DANGER OF PRIVATIZATION AND NEOLIBERALISM IN PUBLIC EDUCATION

1. David C. Berliner, "The Context for Educational Research: The End of the World as We Know It?" presidential address, American Educational Research Association Annual Meeting, San Francisco, April 27, 2013.

2. David C. Berliner, "Public Education Is Still the Cornerstone of American Democracy," in *Public Education: Defending a Cornerstone of American Democracy*, ed. David C. Berliner and Carl Hermanns (Teachers College Press, 2021), 3–5.

3. Julian Vasquez Heilig, "Reframing the Refrain: Choice as a Civil Rights Issue," *Texas Education Review* 1, no. 1 (2013): 83–94.

4. Julian Vasquez Heilig, Jameson Brewer, and Yohuru Williams, "Choice Without Inclusion? Comparing the Intensity of Racial Segregation in Charters and Public Schools at the Local, State and National Levels," *Education Sciences* 9, no. 3 (2019): 1–17.

5. Julian Vasquez Heilig, Amanda Williams, Linda McNeil, and Christopher Lee, "Is Choice a Panacea? An Analysis of Black Secondary Student Attrition from KIPP, Other Private Charters, and Urban Districts," *Berkeley Review of Education* 2, no. 2 (2011): 153–78.

6. Network for Public Education, *Doomed to Fail: An Analysis of Charter School Closures From 1998–2022* (Network for Public Education, 2024), https://networkforpubliceducation.org/wp-content/uploads/2024/11/DTM-Final.pdf.

7. Network for Public Education, *Doomed to Fail.*

8. *Backpack Full of Cash*, Sarah Mondale, dir. (Stone Lantern Films, 2016).

9. Julian Vasquez Heilig and Linda Darling-Hammond, "Accountability Texas-Style: The Progress and Learning of Urban Minority Students in a High-Stakes Testing Context," *Educational Evaluation and Policy Analysis* 30, no. 2 (2008): 75–110.

10. Julian Vasquez Heilig, T. Jameson Brewer, and Terrenda White, "What Instead? Reframing the Debate about Charter Schools, Teach For America, and Testing," in *Assault on Kids and Teachers: Countering Privatization, Deficit Ideologies, and Standardization of U.S. Schools*, ed. R. Ahlquist, P. Gorski, and T. Montaño (Peter Lang, 2018), 201–17.

11. Julian Vasquez Heilig, T. Jameson Brewer, and Jimmy Ojeda Pedraza, "Examining the Myth of Accountability, High-Stakes Testing, and the Achievement Gap," *Journal of Family Strengths* 18, no. 1 (2018): 1–14.

12. Angela Valenzuela, *Subtractive Schooling: U.S.–Mexican Youth and the Politics of Caring* (State University of New York Press, 1999).

13. Dolores Delgado Bernal, "Using a Chicana Feminist Epistemology in Educational Research," *Harvard Educational Review* 68, no. 4 (Winter 1998): 555–82.

14. Julian Vasquez Heilig, "Scrutinizing the School Choice Equity Ethos for Black Parents," in *Public Education: The Cornerstone of American Democracy*, ed. David Berliner and Carl Hermanns (Teachers College Press, 2021), 255–67.

15. Julian Vasquez Heilig, "The Seductive Allures of School Choice," *Cloaking Inequity*, March 14, 2016, https://cloakinginequity.com/2016/03/14/the-seductive-allures-of-school-choice/.

16. Robert Reich, "The Four Horsemen of the Neoliberal Apocalypse," *Eurasia Review* (February 8, 2022).

17. Julian Vasquez Heilig, Julian Brewer, and Frank Adamson, "The Politics of Market-Based School Choice Research: A Commingling of Ideology, Methods, and Funding," in *Handbook of Research on School Choice*, 2nd ed., ed. Mark Berends, R. Joseph Waddington, and Matthew Springer (Routledge, 2019), 335–50.

18. Julian Vasquez Heilig and Brent Clark, "New Insights and Directions: Considering the Impact of Charter School Attributes on Communities of Color," *Journal of Transformative Leadership and Policy Studies* 7, no. 1 (2018): 3–9.

19. Plato, *The Republic*, trans. Allan Bloom (Basic Books, 1991).

20. Pauline Lipman, *The New Political Economy of Urban Education: Neoliberalism, Race, and the Right to the City* (Routledge, 2011).

21. Massachusetts Constitution, Part the Second, Chapter V, Section II ("The Encouragement of Literature, Etc."), https://malegislature.gov/Laws/Constitution, accessed January 4, 2026.

22. Texas Constitution, art. VII, "Education," Sec. 1. Support and Maintenance of System of Public Free Schools, https://statutes.capitol.texas.gov/Docs/CN/htm/CN.7.htm, accessed January 4, 2026.

23. Washington State Constitution, Article IX, "Education," Section 1, https://leg.wa.gov/state-laws-and-rules/washington-state-constitution, accessed January 4, 2026.

24. Constitution of Pennsylvania, Article III, "Legislation," B. Education, Section 14, "Public School System," https://www.palegis.us/statutes/consolidated/view-statute?chapter=3&section=14, accessed January 4, 2026.

25. Constitution of the State of Florida, Article IX, "Education," Section 1. Public Education, (a) https://www.flsenate.gov/Laws/Constitution#A9S01, accessed January 4, 2026.

26. Constitution of the State of Florida, Article IX, "Education," Section 1. Public Education (a).

CHAPTER 19: THREATS TO HUMANITY

1. Rudolph T. Ware, *The Walking Qur'an: Islamic Education, Embodied Knowledge, and History in West Africa* (University of North Carolina Press, 2014).

2. Zachary V. Wright, *Realizing Islam: The Tijaniyya in North Africa and the Eighteenth-Century Muslim World* (University of North Carolina Press, 2015).

3. Cedric J. Robinson, *Black Marxism: The Making of the Black Radical Tradition* (University of North Carolina Press, 1983).

4. Robin D. G. Kelley, *Freedom Dreams: The Black Radical Imagination* (Beacon Press, 2002).

5. James H. Cone, *God of the Oppressed* (Orbis Books, 1997).

6. Nicole Mirra, Ernest Morrell, and Danielle Filipiak, "From Critical Research to Collaborative Praxis: Negotiating Partnerships to Advance Youth Participatory Action Research," *Review of Research in Education* 42, no. 1 (2018): 1–33.

7. Mirra, Morrell, and Filipiak, "From Critical Research to Collaborative Praxis."

8. Muhammad A. Khalifa, Mark Anthony Gooden, and James Earl Davis, "Culturally Responsive School Leadership: A Synthesis of the Literature," *Review of Educational Research* 86, no. 4 (2016): 1272–1311.

CHAPTER 20: WHEN CHOICE BECOMES NO CHOICE

1. "Count day" refers to when schools report their attendance, which is used to help calculate funding that school will receive according to the number of students enrolled.

2. Sonya Douglass Horsford, Carrie Sampson, Felicia Forletta, "School Resegregation in the Mississippi of the West: Community Counternarratives on the Return to Neighborhood Schools in Las Vegas, 1968–1994," *Teachers College Record* 115, no. 11 (2013): 1–28.

3. Carrie Sampson, David R. Garcia, Matthew O. Hom, and Melanie Bertrand, "Open Enrollment and Disrupting the Political Ecology of US Public Education," *Peabody Journal of Education* 97, no. 1 (2022): 62–73; Jeanne M. Powers, Amelia M. Topper, and Michael Silver, "Public School Choice and Student Mobility in Metropolitan Phoenix," *Journal of School Choice* 6, no. 2 (2012): 209–34; Save Our Schools Arizona Network, *The Impacts of Universal ESA Vouchers: Arizona's Cautionary Tale* (Save Our Schools Arizona Network, 2023); Ryan Suppe, "Blueprint or Cautionary Tale? Arizona's $800 Million School Choice Program Is Popular but Unruly," *Idaho Capital Sun*, December 18, 2024.

4. Carrie Sampson, "School Closures Threaten the Heart of Arizona Communities," *AZ Mirror*, January 29, 2025; Beth Lewis, "Neighborhood Schools Are Closing Across Arizona. It's Because of Vouchers," *AZ Mirror*, October 6, 2025.

5. Sampson et al., "Open Enrollment and Disrupting the Political Ecology of US Public Education."

6. Jamie Klinenberg, Jon Valant, and Nicolas Zerbino, "Arizona's 'Universal' Education Savings Account Program Has Become a Handout to the Wealthy," Brookings, May 7, 2024.

7. Emily Young, "What the Federal Voucher Program Means for Students in Your State," EdTrust, July 21, 2025, https://edtrust.org/blog/what-the-federal-voucher-program-means-for-students-in-your-state/?emci=95b5b52d-527c-f011-b481-6045bdfe8e9c&emdi=54a8c7f1-737c-f011-b481-6045bdfe8e9c&ceid=417053.

8. Carrie Sampson, *Navigating School Board Politics: A Framework for Advancing Equity* (Harvard Education Press, 2024); Carrie Sampson, "(Im) Possibilities of Latinx School Board Members' Educational Leadership Toward Equity," *Educational Administration Quarterly* 55, no. 2 (2019): 296–327.

9. Maya Riser-Kositsky, Stephen Sawchuk, and Holly Peele, "School Police: Which Districts Cut Them? Which Brought Them Back?" *Education Week*, June 4, 2021, https://www.edweek.org/leadership/which-districts-have-cut-school-policing-programs/2021/06.

10. Gabriela López and Carrie Sampson, "The Politics of the 2021 School Board Recall Attempts," *Theory into Practice* 63, no. 3 (2024): 313–22; Nicole Carr and Lucas Waldron, "How School Board Meetings Became Flashpoints for Anger and Chaos Across the Country," *ProPublica*, July 19, 2023.

11. Jami Carmichael, Jasmine Pham, Carrie Sampson, and Ruth M. López, "How Whiteness Shapes Public Narratives: A Critical Discourse Analysis of Media and the NSBA Letter," *Educational Administration Quarterly* 61, no. 5 (2025): 843–72.

12. Sana Sinha, Nicolas Zerbino, Jon Valant, and Rachel M. Perera, "Moms for Liberty: Where Are They, and Are They Winning?" *Brookings*, October 10, 2023.

13. Save Our Schools Arizona Network, "Arizona Educators Battle Ducey's Ban on Mask Mandates," October 23, 2021.

14. John Rogers, Rachel White, Robert Shand, and Joseph Kahne with Samuel C. Stern, Charity Castro, and Alison Yoshimoto-Towery, *The Costs of Conflict: The Fiscal Impact of Culturally Divisive Conflict on Public Schools in the United States* (UCLA Institute for Democracy, Education, and Access, 2024).

15. Sampson, *Navigating School Board Politics.*

16. David B. Tyack, *Seeking Common Ground: Public Schools in a Diverse Society* (Harvard University Press, 2003), 145.

17. Michael Ford and Douglas Ihrke, "Uncontested: Electoral Competition in American School Board Elections," *Journal of Educational Administration* 58, no. 6 (2020): 661–75.

18. Kenneth Meier and Eric G. Juenke, "Electoral Structure and the Quality of Representation on School Boards," in *Besieged: School Boards and the Future of Education Politics*, ed. William G. Howell (Brookings Institution Press, 2005), 199–227; Vladimir Kogan, Stéphane Lavertu, and Zachary Peskowitz, "How Does Minority Political Representation Affect School District Administration and Student Outcomes?" *American Journal of Political Science* 65, no. 3 (2021): 699–716.

19. Luis Fraga and Rachel Elis, "Interests and Representation: Ethnic Advocacy on California School Boards," *Teachers College Record* 111, no. 3 (2009): 659–82; Benjamin Fischer, "No Spending Without Representation: School Boards and the Racial Gap in Education Finance," *SSRN Electronic Journal* (2020); Kenneth J. Meier, Eric G. Juenke, Robert D. Wrinkle, and J. L. Polinard, "Structural Choices and Representational Biases: The Post-Election Color of Representation," *American Journal of Political Science* 49, no. 4 (2005): 758–68; Kogan et al., "How Does Minority Political Representation Affect School District Administration and Student Outcomes?"

20. Kogan et al., "How Does Minority Political Representation Affect School District Administration and Student Outcomes?"

21. Melissa Marschall, "Minority Incorporation and Local School Boards," in Howell, *Besieged*, 173–98.

22. Sampson, "(Im) Possibilities of Latinx School Board Members' Educational Leadership Toward Equity"; Julie Corbett, "Seats of Change: An Examination of How Equity-Focused Pipelines Mitigate the Disproportionate Racial Representation of School Boards," EdD diss., American University, 2025; Luis Fraga, David Krimm, Max Neiman, and Belinda Reyes, *Examining Latino Representation on California's School Boards: Their Impact on Perceptions About District Problems, Priorities and Policies* (Public Policy Institute of California, 2010).

23. Van Lac and Katherine Mansfield, "What Do Students Have to Do with Educational Leadership? Making a Case for Centering Student Voice," *Journal of Research on Leadership Education* 13, no. 1 (2018): 38–58; Katherine Mansfield and Maria Lambrinou, "'This Is Not Who We Are': Students Leading for Anti-Racist Policy Changes in Alexandria City Public Schools, Virginia," *Politics of Education Association* 36, no. 1 (2021); Allison Mattheis, Yanin Ardila, and Sivan Levaton, "'We Think Differently': Student Representation and Voice at the Los Angeles Unified School District Board of Education," *Journal of Ethical Educational Leadership* 5, no. 2 (2018): 1–25.

24. Howell, ed., *Besieged*; Margaret Plecki, Jennifer McCleery, and Michael Knapp, "Redefining and Improving School District Governance," Center for the Study of Teaching and Policy, 2006.

25. J. Kenneth Blackwell, "On-Cycle School Board Elections Make It Easier to Vote," America First Policy Institute, July 25, 2022; Arnold F. Shober and Michael T. Hartney, *Does School Board Leadership Matter?* (Thomas B. Fordham Institute, 2014).

26. Vladimir Kogan, Stéphane Lavertu, and Zachary Peskowitz, "The Democratic Deficit in U.S. Education Governance," *American Political Science Review* 115, no. 3 (2021): 1082–89.

27. Joshua Butwin, "Putting Students First: Why Noncitizen Parents Should Be Allowed to Vote in School Board Elections," *Fordham Law Review Online* 87 (2018); Tara Kini, "Sharing the Vote: Noncitizen Voting Rights in Local School Board Elections," *California Law Review* 93, no. 1 (2005): 271–321; López and Sampson, "The Politics of the 2021 School Board Recall Attempts."

28. Ford and Ihrke, "Uncontested."

29. Jeffrey R. Henig, Rebecca Jacobsen, and Sarah Reckhow, *Outside Money in School Board Elections: The Nationalization of Education Politics* (Harvard Education Press, 2019); Sarah Reckhow, Jeffrey R. Henig, Rebecca Jacobsen, and Jamie Alter Litt, "'Outsiders with Deep Pockets': The Nationalization of Local School Board Elections," *Urban Affairs Review* 53, no. 5 (2017): 783–811.

30. David L. Leal, Valerie Martinez-Ebers, and Kenneth J. Meier, "The Politics of Latino Education: The Biases of At-Large Elections," *Journal of Politics* 66, no. 4 (2004): 1224–44; Meier et al., "Structural Choices and Representational Biases."

31. Thomas L. Alsbury, "School Board Member and Superintendent Turnover and the Influence on Student Achievement: An Application of the Dissatisfaction Theory," *Leadership and Policy in Schools* 7, no. 2 (2008): 202–29; López and Sampson, "The Politics of the 2021 School Board Recall Attempts"; Christopher Berry and William Howell, "Democratic Accountability in Public Education," in Howell, *Besieged*; Vladimir Kogan, Stéphane Lavertu, and Zachary Peskowitz, "Do School Report Cards Produce Accountability Through the Ballot Box?" *Journal of Policy Analysis and Management* 35, no. 3 (2016): 639–61.

32. Deborah Land, "Local School Boards Under Review: Their Role and Effectiveness in Relation to Students' Academic Achievement," *Review of Educational Research* 72, no. 2 (2002): 229–78.

33. Carrie Sampson, "From a Lighthouse to a Foghorn: A School Board's Navigation Toward Equity for English Learners," *American Journal of Education* 125, no. 4 (2019): 521–46; Sampson, *Navigating School Board Politics*; Dale H. Sutherland, "'Tell Them Local Control Is Important': A Case Study of Democratic, Community-Centered School Boards," *Education Policy Analysis Archives* 30, no. 178 (2022); Brenda DeHart and Daniel Ganley, "A Descriptive Case Study of Discord & Dissent: The Story of a School Board's Act of Non-Compliance to State and Federal Law," in *The Future of School Board Governance: Relevancy and Revelation*, ed. Thomas L. Alsbury (Rowman & Littlefield Education, 2008); Meredith Mountford, "Systemic Leadership Amidst Turbulence: Superintendent-School—Board Relations Under Pressure," in *The Future of School Board Governance: Relevancy and Revelation*, ed. Thomas L. Alsbury (Rowman & Littlefield Education, 2008); Robert S. White and Mindy Y. Lineburg, "Backtalk: School Boards and Superintendents Should Work in Concert," *Phi Delta Kappan* 103, no. 1 (2021): 67–68.

34. Carrie Sampson and Melanie Bertrand, "'This Is Civil Disobedience. I'll Continue.': The Racialization of School Board Meeting Rules," *Journal of Education Policy* 37, no. 2 (2022); Carrie Sampson and Melanie Bertrand, "Counter-Storytelling, Metaphors, and Rhetorical Questioning: Discursive Strategies of Advocacy toward Racial Equity in School Board Meetings," *Discourse* (2021); James Collins, "Does the Meeting Style Matter? The Effects of Exposure to Participatory and Deliberative School Board Meetings," *American Political Science Review* 115, no. 3 (2021): 790–804; Margaret Durfy and Karen Tracy, "Speaking Out in Public: Citizen Participation in Contentious School Board Meetings," *Discourse and Communication* 1, no. 2 (2007): 223–49.

35. Sarah Diem, Erica Frankenberg, and Cristóbal Cleary, "Factors That Influence School Board Policy Making: The Political Context of Student Diversity in Urban-Suburban Districts," *Educational Administration Quarterly* 51, no. 5 (2015): 712–52; Rochelle Freelon, "Transformational Resistance and Parent Leadership: Black Parents in a School District Decision-Making Process," *Urban Education* 57, no. 8 (2022): 1329–57; Muhammad A. Khalifa, Monique E. Jennings, Felecia Briscoe, Ashley M. Oleszweski, and Nadifo Abdi, "Racism? Administrative and Community Perspectives in Data-Driven Decision Making: Systemic Perspectives Versus Technical-Rational Perspectives," *Urban Education* 49, no. 2 (2014): 147–81; Tina M. Trujillo, "The Disproportionate Erosion of Local Control: Urban School Boards, High-Stakes Accountability, and Democracy," *Educational Policy* 27, no. 2 (2013): 334–59.

36. Jamilah Wright, Raquel W. Whitaker, Muhammad Khalifa, and Felecia Briscoe, "The Color of Neoliberal Reform: A Critical Race Policy Analysis of School District Takeovers in Michigan," *Urban Education* 55, no. 3 (2020): 424–47; Domingo Morel, "The Effects of Centralized Government Authority on Black and Latino Political Empowerment," *Political Research Quarterly* 69, no. 2 (2016): 347–60.

37. Gary A. Hoover, "Elected Versus Appointed School District Officials: Is There a Difference in Student Outcomes?" *Public Finance Review* 36, no. 5 (2008): 635–47; Michael P. O'Malley, Donyell L. Roseboro, and Joseph Hunt, "Accountability, Fiscal Management, and Student Achievement in East St. Louis, Illinois 1994–2006: Implications

for Urban Educational Reform Policy," *Urban Education* 47, no. 1 (2012): 117–43; Kenneth Wong and Francis Shen, "When Mayors Lead Urban Schools: Assessing the Effects of Takeover," in Howell, *Besieged*.

38. Carrie Sampson and Sonya Horsford, "Putting the Public Back in Public Education: Community Advocacy and Every Student Succeeds Act," *Journal of School Leadership* 27 (September 2017): 725–54.

CHAPTER 21: EDUCATING AGAINST DISEMPOWERMENT

1. Children's Defense Fund, "2024 Program Description" (February 2025).

2. Charles E. Cobb Jr., *On the Road to Freedom: A Guided Tour of the Civil Rights Trail* (Algonquin Books, 2008), 67–68.

3. Referencing Marian Wright Edelman, "The Best of What Education Can Be" (Children's Defense Fund, n.d.), https://www.childrensdefense.org/the-best-of-what-education-can-be/.

4. Charity Anderson and Charles M. Payne, "The Radical Affirmation of Dignity: Septima Clark, Ella Baker, and Educating the Disenfranchised," in *Dignity-Affirming Education: Cultivating the Somebodiness of Students and Educators*, ed. Decoteau J. Irby, Charity Anderson, Charles M. Payne, William Ayers, and Therese Quinn (Teachers College Press, 2022), chapter 2.

5. Charles E. Cobb Jr., "Some Notes on Education" (n.d.), retrieved from https://www.crmvet.org/info/cobb_education.pdf.

6. Thomas S. Dee and Emily K. Penner, "The Causal Effects of Cultural Relevance: Evidence from an Ethnic Studies Curriculum," *American Educational Research Journal* 54, no. 1 (2017): 127–66; Diane Hughes, James Rodriguez, Emilie P. Smith, Deborah J. Johnson, Howard C. Stevenson, and Paul Spicer, "Parents' Ethnic-Racial Socialization Practices: A Review of Research and Directions for Future Study," *Developmental Psychology* 42, no. 5 (2006): 747.

7. Gwen C. Uman, Tyrone C. Howard, and Rachael Thomas, *Children's Defense Fund Freedom Schools® in Los Angeles County's Second District: Evaluation Report, Summer 2015* (Vital Research, 2015).

8. Philliber Research Associates, *Evaluation of the Kansas City CDF Freedom Schools® Initiative* (Children's Defense Fund, 2008).

9. D. Bruce Taylor, Adrian L. Medina, and Sandraluz Lara-Cinisomo, *Evaluation Report: Freedom School Partners Children's Defense Fund Freedom Schools® Program* (Center for Adolescent Literacies, UNC Charlotte, 2010).

10. Lakia M. Scott, Rachel Renbarger, and Yasmin Laird, "Examining the Children's Defense Fund Freedom Schools Model on Middle School Students' Reading Achievement," *Journal of Multicultural Affairs* 5, no. 2 (2020), article 3.

11. Children's Defense Fund, "2024 Program Description."

12. Sharon L. Bethea, "The Impact of Oakland Freedom School's Summer Youth Program on The Psychosocial Development of African American Youth," *Journal of Black Psychology* 38, no. 4 (2012): 442–54.

13. Edith Gozali-Lee and Amanda J. Petersen, *Evaluation of 2013 Summer Learning Freedom School Program* (Wilder Research, 2013).

14. Christine E. Sleeter, *The Academic and Social Value of Ethnic Studies: A Research Review* (National Education Association Research Department, 2011); Christine E.

Sleeter and Miguel Zavala, "What the Research Says About Ethnic Studies," in *Transformative Ethnic Studies in Schools: Curriculum, Pedagogy, and Research* (Teachers College Press, 2020), chapter 3.

15. Charles M. Payne, "'Give Light and the People Will Find a Way': Ella Baker and Teaching as Politics," in *Teach Freedom: Education for Liberation in the African-American Tradition*, ed. Charles M. Payne and Carol Sills Strickland (Teachers College Press, 2008).

16. Anne T. Henderson, Karen L. Mapp, Vivian R. Johnson, and Don Davies, *Beyond the Bake Sale: The Essential Guide to Family-School Partnerships*, 2nd ed. (New Press, 2022).

17. Jarvis R. Givens, *Fugitive Pedagogy: Carter G. Woodson and the Art of Black Teaching* (Harvard University Press, 2021).

18. Toni Cade Bambara, *Conversations with Toni Cade Bambara*, ed. Thabiti Lewis (University Press of Mississippi, 2017).

19. Arundhati Roy, "The Pandemic Is a Portal," *Financial Times*, April 3, 2020.

20. W. E. B. Du Bois, *Black Reconstruction in America: An Essay Toward a History of the Part Which Black Folk Played in the Attempt to Reconstruct Democracy in America, 1860–1880* (Harcourt, 1935); Robin D. G. Kelley, "Interview with Robin D. G. Kelley," *Race: The Power of an Illusion*, 2002, California Newsreel, the Othering & Belonging Institute, the UC Berkeley Library, and the American Cultures Center at UC Berkeley.

CHAPTER 22: LEAD LIKE DEMOCRACY DEPENDS ON IT

1. Michelle D. Young, Erin Anderson, and Angel Miles Nash, "Preparing School Leaders: Standards-Based Curriculum in the United States," *Leadership and Policy in Schools* 16, no. 2 (2017): 228–71.

2. Jack Mezirow, "Transformative Learning: Theory to Practice," *New Directions for Adult and Continuing Education* 74 (1997): 5–12.

3. Sharan B. Merriam and Lisa M. Baumgartner, *Learning in Adulthood: A Comprehensive Guide* (John Wiley & Sons, 2020).

4. Michelle D. Young and Angel Miles Nash, "Aligning Frameworks and Identifying Capacities for Anti-Racist Advocacy Educational Leadership," in *Strengthening Anti-Racist Educational Leaders: Advocating for Racial Equity in Turbulent Times*, ed. Anjalé D. Welton and Sarah Diem (Bloomsbury, 2022), 109–20.

CHAPTER 23: "IT'S OUR DAMN JOB"

1. James Baldwin, "A Talk to Teachers" (1963), in *Multi-Cultural Literacy: Opening the American Mind*, ed. Rick Simonson and Scott Walker (Graywolf Press, 1988), 3–12.

2. James Baldwin interview, *Mavis on Four*, February 12, 1987.

3. Baldwin, "A Talk to Teachers."

INDEX